Anyone Can...Arts

ANYONE CAN DRAW

By Peter Kraus

Anyone Can...Arts Publishing
www.anyonecanarts.com

ACKNOWLEDGEMENTS

**My many, many thanks to the following people
for their valued support and encouragement.**

Karen Higgins
Angie Harris

Anyone Can...Arts
ANYONE CAN DRAW

ISBN 978-1466463509

Published by Anyone Can...Arts
www.anyonecanarts.com

Printed in the U.S.A.

CONTENTS

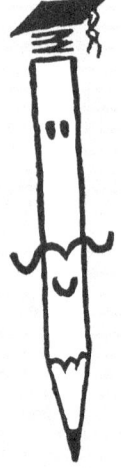

STUDENT PROGRESS

Prior to instruction,
beginners drew this still life.

LOOK AT THE
VAST IMPROVEMENT.

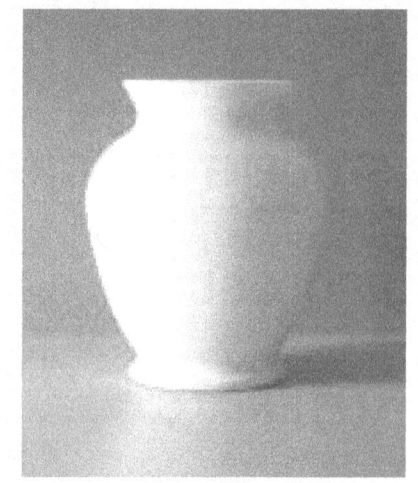

BEFORE INSTRUCTION

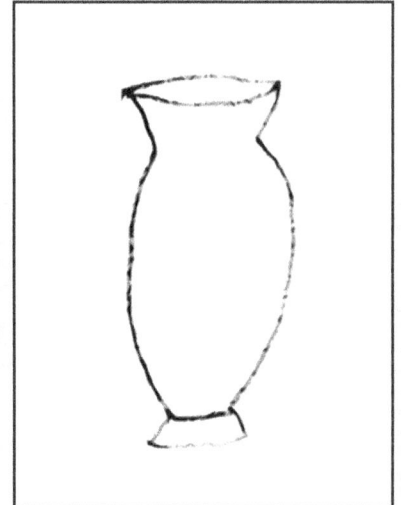

AFTER CHAPTER 1

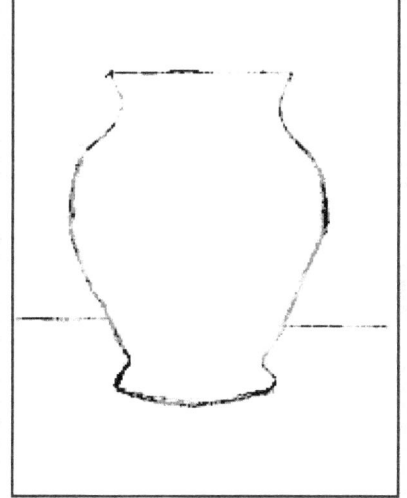

AFTER CHAPTER 2

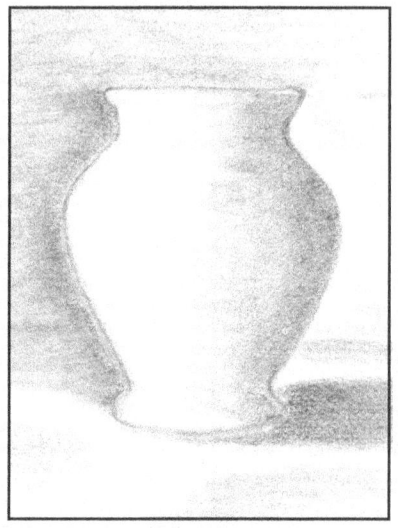

BEFORE INSTRUCTION

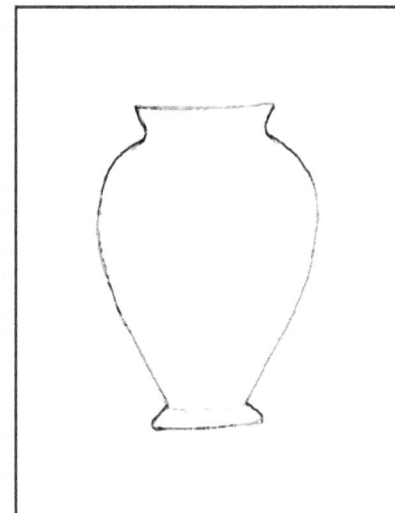

AFTER CHAPTER 1

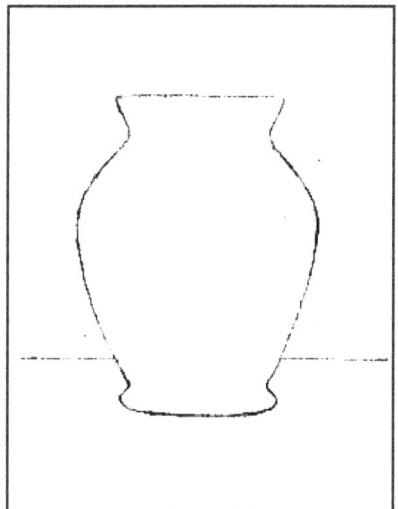

AFTER CHAPTER 2

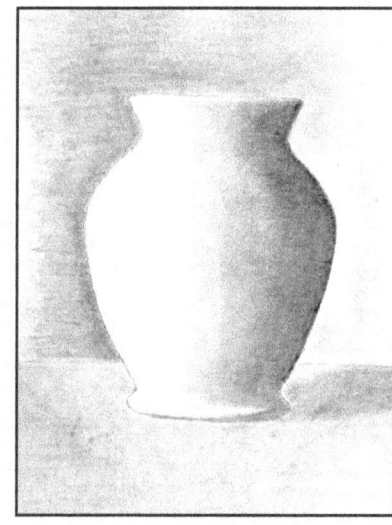

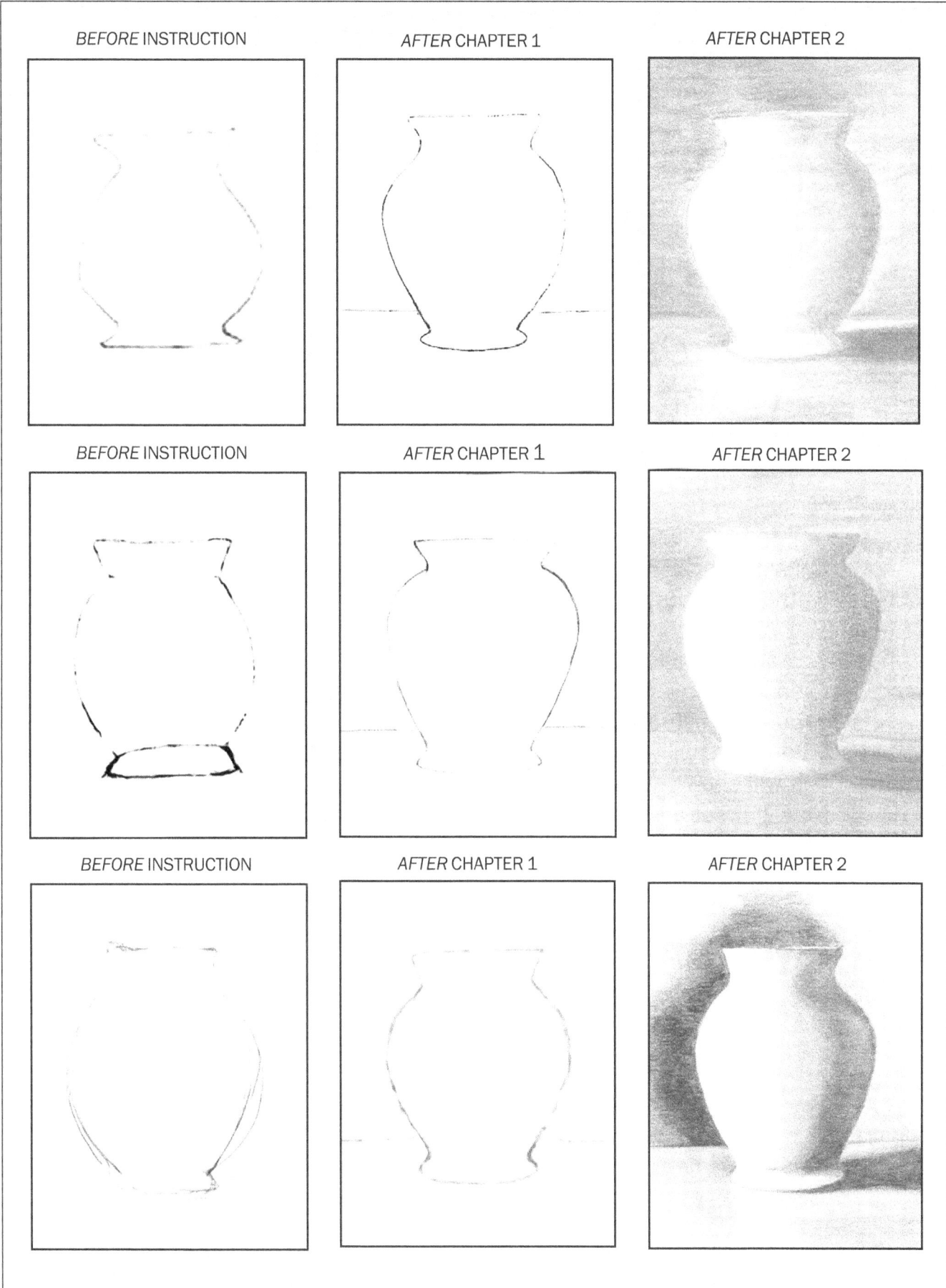

BEFORE INSTRUCTION	AFTER CHAPTER 1	AFTER CHAPTER 2
BEFORE INSTRUCTION	AFTER CHAPTER 1	AFTER CHAPTER 2
BEFORE INSTRUCTION	AFTER CHAPTER 1	AFTER CHAPTER 2

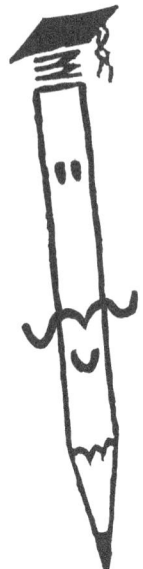

F.Y.I.
Drawing skill
can be learned.

Consider this: Did you always know how to tell time, or did someone teach you? Did you just pick up a book one day and read, or were you taught? Did you add, subtract, multiply and divide without help? Of course not. The same goes for drawing.

Even as you were being trained to form letters of the alphabet, guess what? You were actually *drawing*. Letters are also shapes. So you see, you already have the ability, but you need assistance to develop your proficiency. This book will show you how.

Now, get set to enjoy yourself and prove that indeed,

ANYONE CAN DRAW.

MATERIALS

Standard Size (8 1/2"x 11") **White Unlined Paper**

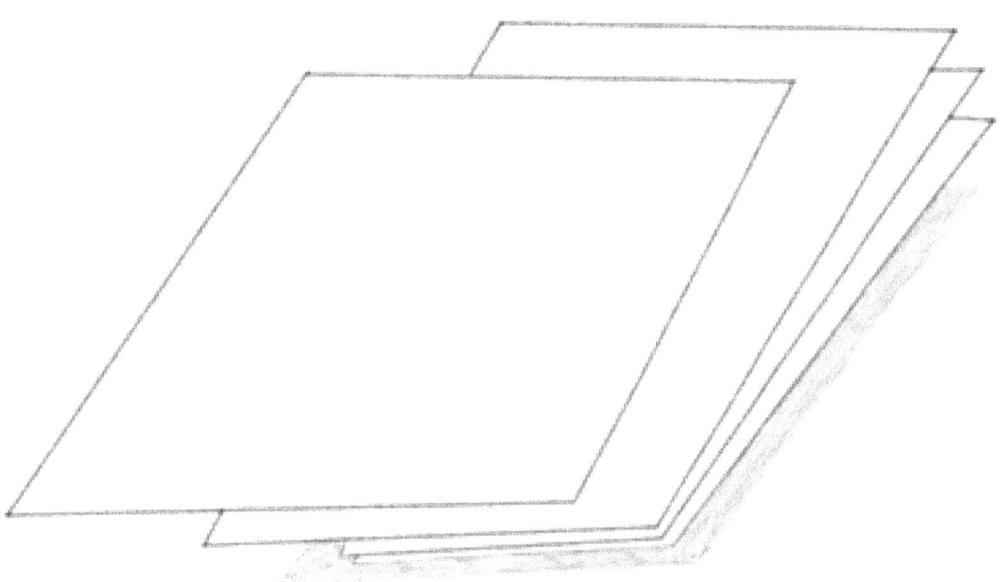

Standard #2 Pencil

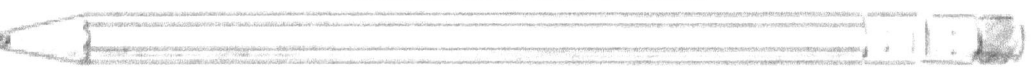

6B Pencil

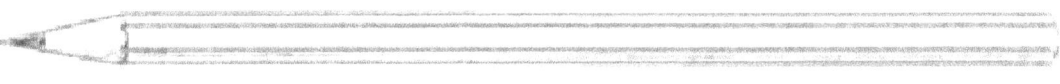

Blender (or Cotton Swab)

Putty Eraser

Pencil Sharpener

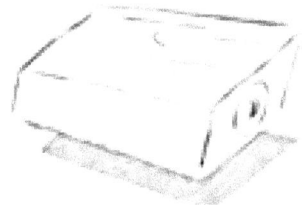

HOW TO USE THIS BOOK

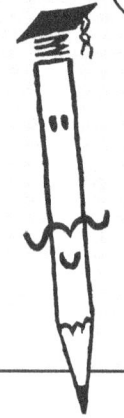

Here are some important things to keep in mind.

1. The subject matter in the chapters has been carefully chosen to convey fundamental principles and drawing techniques. While having fun replicating the pictures, step by step, you will be amazed by your quick improvement. And, to make things even easier, clearly written explanations, plus hundreds of tips, hints and illustrations show you what to look for, what to do, how to do it, and when to do each step from start to finish.

2. Rely on your perception. Your eyes and thinking cap will tell you when you are on target.

3. Since you are going to be working by visual estimation, *freehand* (without a ruler or mechanical devices) you should not expect your work to turn out as accurate, or as neat, as the printed drawing guides in the book. Copies of student examples are included so you can see how others have done.

Be sure to pay attention to the following symbols.

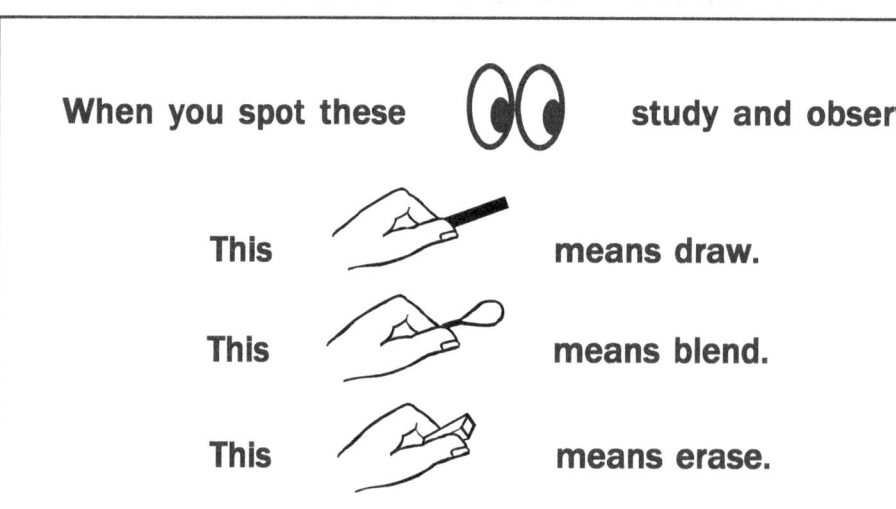

When you spot these ⦿⦿ study and observe.

This ✍ means draw.

This ☞ means blend.

This ✋ means erase.

USEFUL SUGGESTIONS

1. **Please, read and follow directions carefully**. Reading ahead before you draw can be helpful, but don't skim or skip around except where recommended.

2   **Avoid distractions such as talking on the phone, TV, etc.**
    Set aside an hour or two just for you, and focus on drawing *without interruption*.
    (Relaxing background music might be helpful.)

3. **Proceed at a comfortable pace, and let the lessons sink in.**

4. **Don't overlook the TIPS. They are very helpful and informative.**

5. **FORGET ABOUT TIME.** If you feel rushed, confused or fatigued, stop and regroup.
    Resume when refreshed.

6. **Ignore preconceived notions about how your drawing should look, how long it should take, or what others will think.** You miss the mark if you set your sights on the final outcome rather than on the steps it takes to get you there. Remember you are learning new techniques.

7. **Read the follow-up at the end of each chapter.** It summarizes what was covered and sheds further light on the skills learned.

8. **Stay open to, and explore all the possibilities for greater learning.** Certain methods may be more to your liking than others.   The quick convenient way is not necessarily the best.

9. **Review previous chapters or parts as often as you like.** Refer to the glossary and index in the back of the book for further clarifications.

Draw for pleasure.
The fun is in the doing.

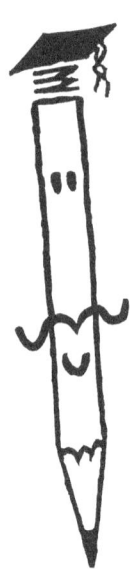

Each journey begins with a first step. Draw a likeness of this outlined figure and put it aside. Then, proceed with Chapter 1. Later you will have the opportunity to compare your results, before and after instruction.

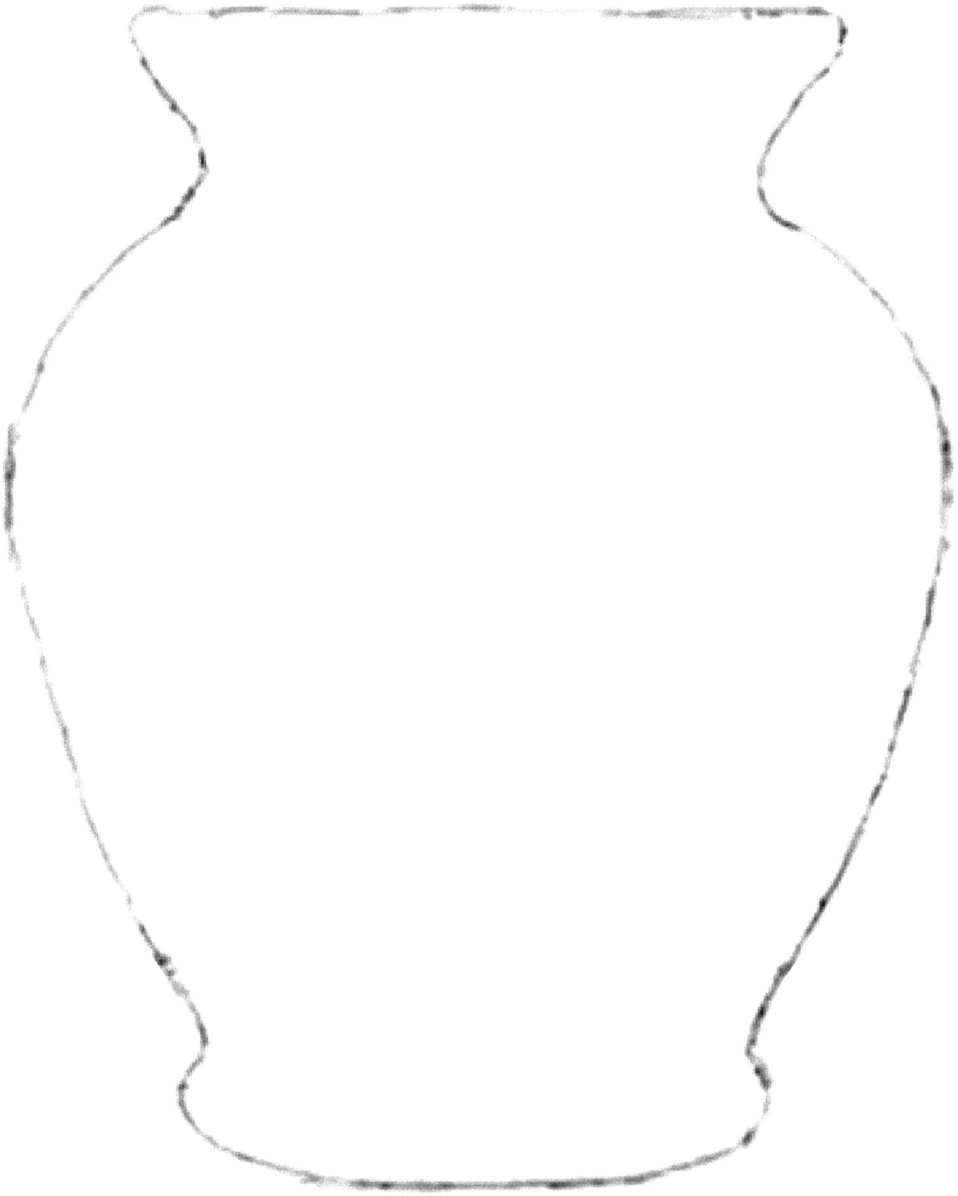

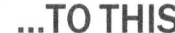

FROM THIS...

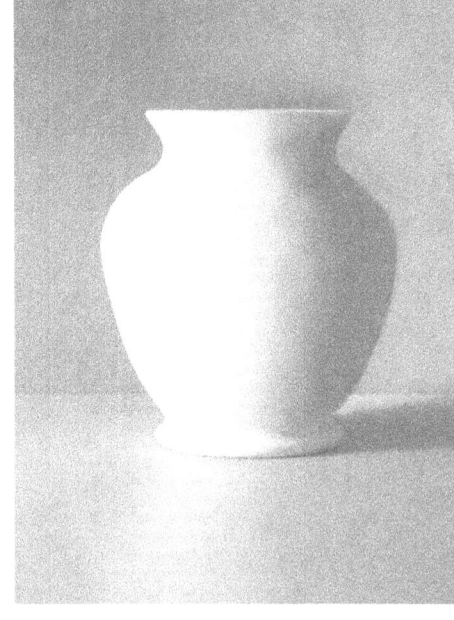

...TO THIS

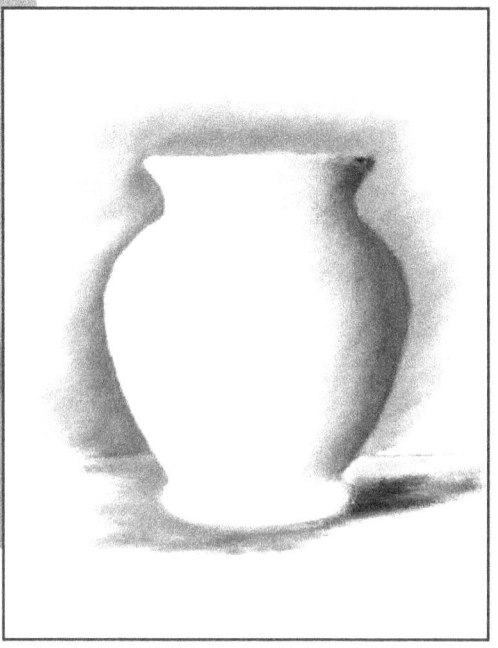

STARTS with SHAPING

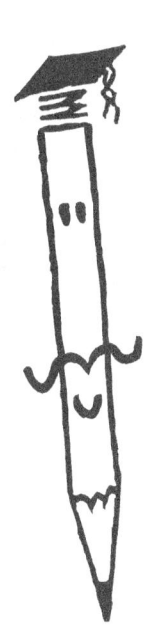

It's easy when you know the secret.

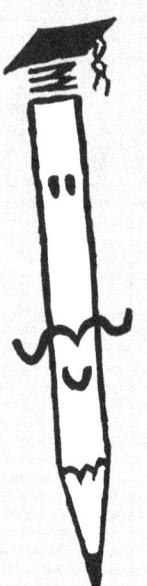

Before you grab your pencil,
become familiar with the figure.

But it's just a VASE,
you're probably thinking.

IS IT?

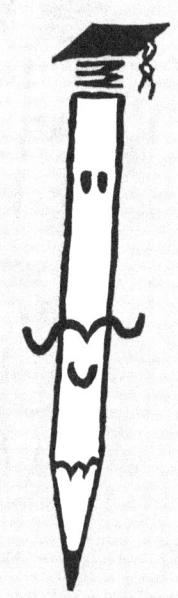

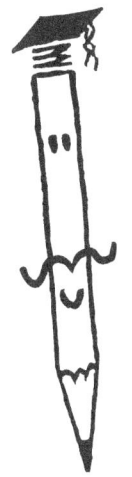

Pretend you have never seen this item.

Learn to read it like a road map.

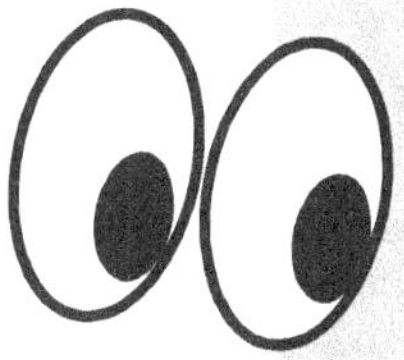

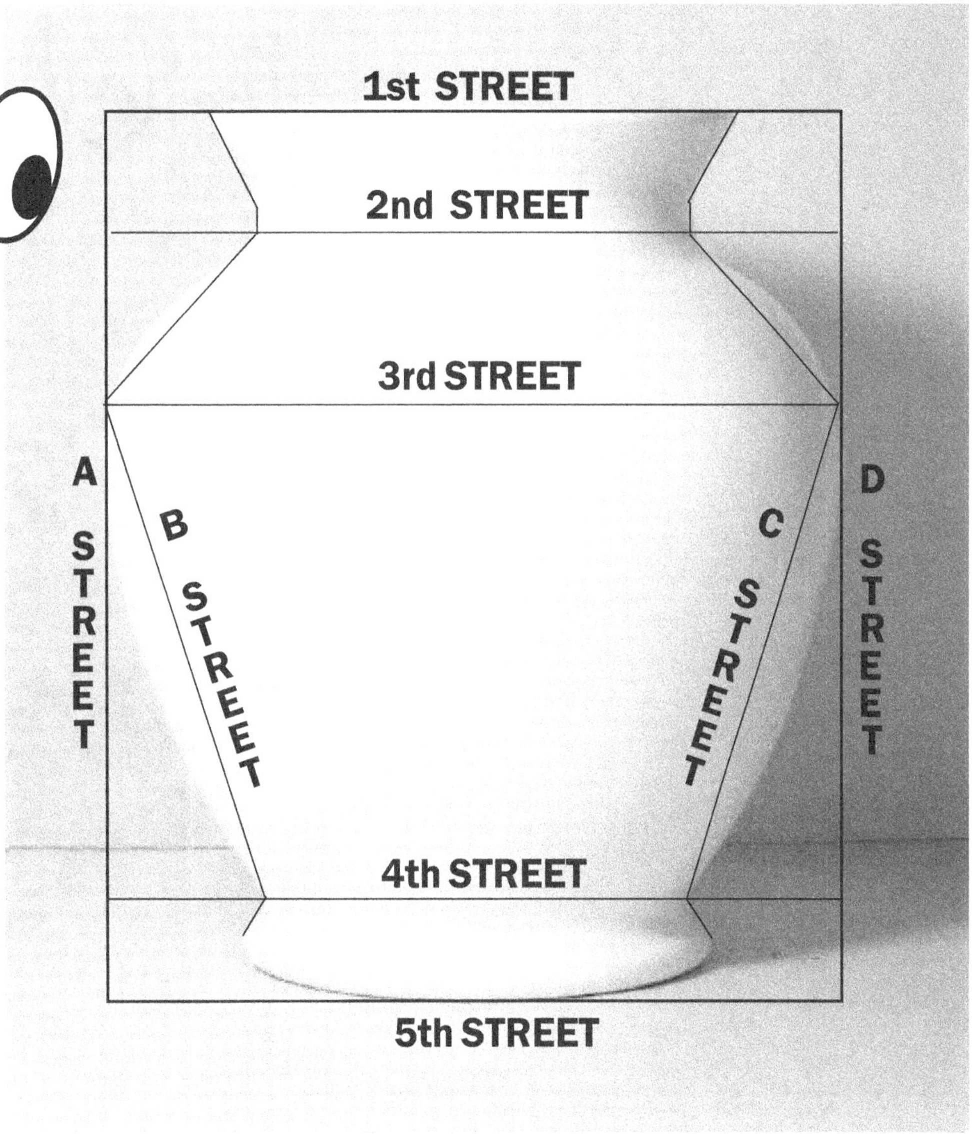

1st STREET

2nd STREET

3rd STREET

A STREET

B STREET

C STREET

D STREET

4th STREET

5th STREET

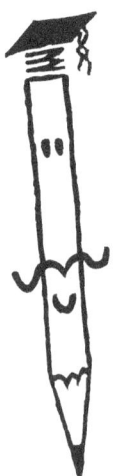

See FORM, not an object.
Dissect it with your eyes. Observe
that there are three main sections.
Neck-Body-Base

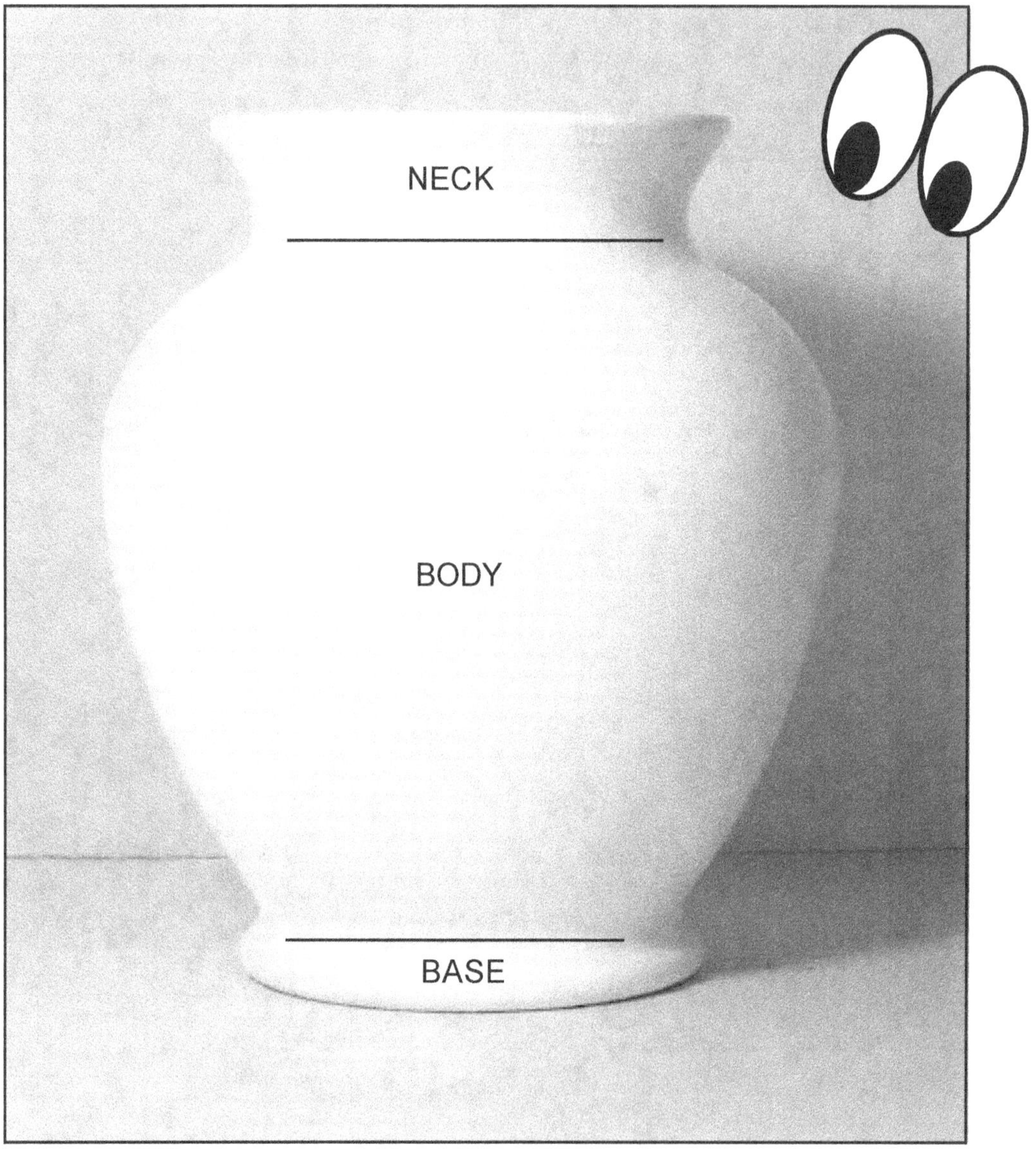

NECK

BODY

BASE

TIP Squinting (keeping your eyes partly open) helps you spot the basic shapes and divisions.

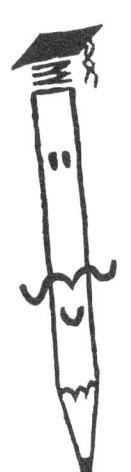

With respect to sub-proportion, the neck is about twice as tall as the base, is it not?

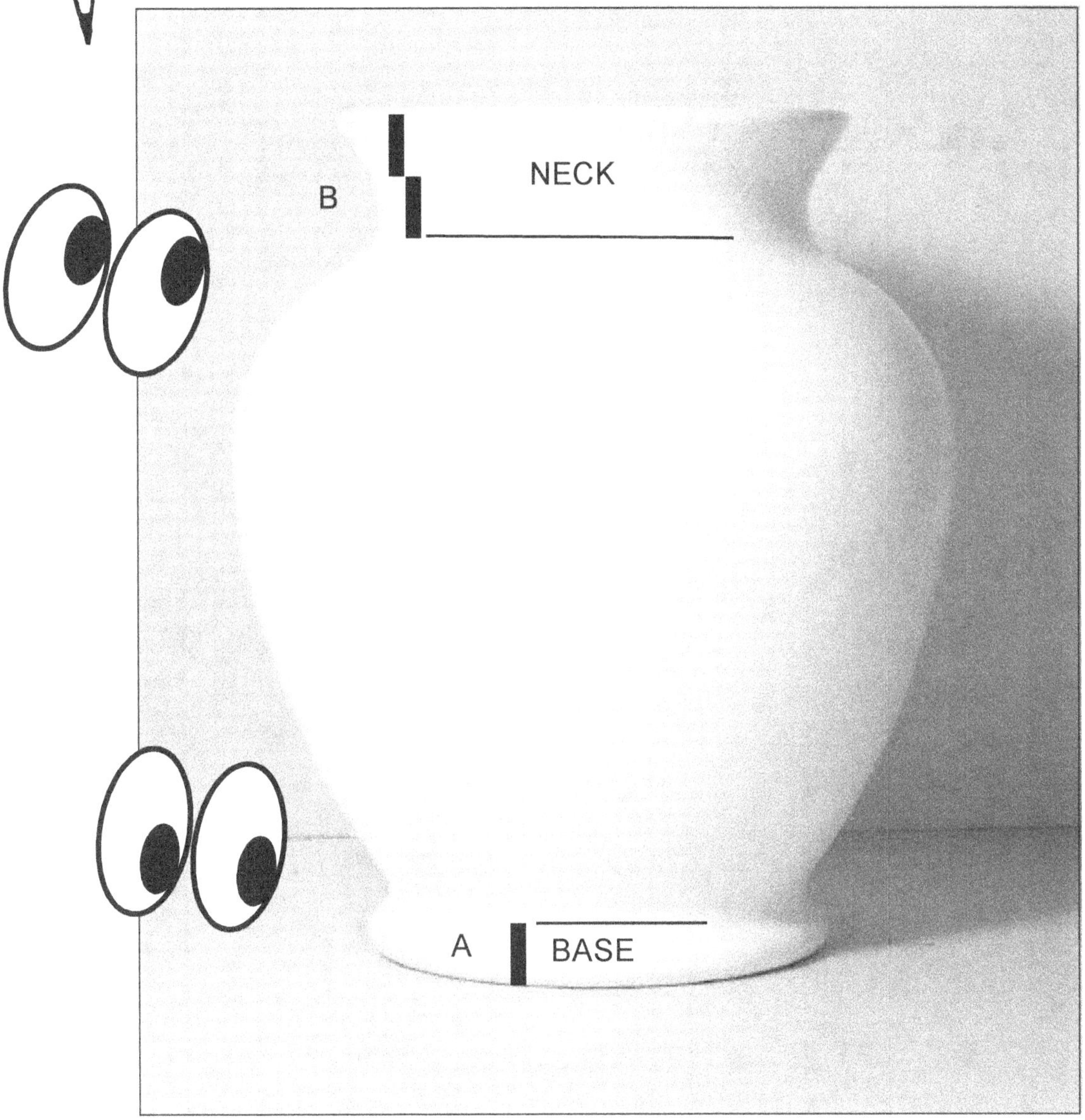

B   NECK

A   BASE

Proportion is a comparison of one size to another. *Overall proportion* is a comparison of a form's *entire* length to its entire width. *Sub-proportion* is a span comparison of one part of a form to another part of that form.

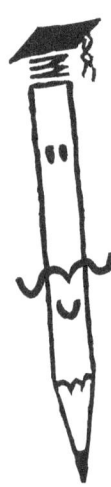

The INSIDE curves of the base and neck are vertically aligned. They are inset a little less than one quarter of the way from each side.

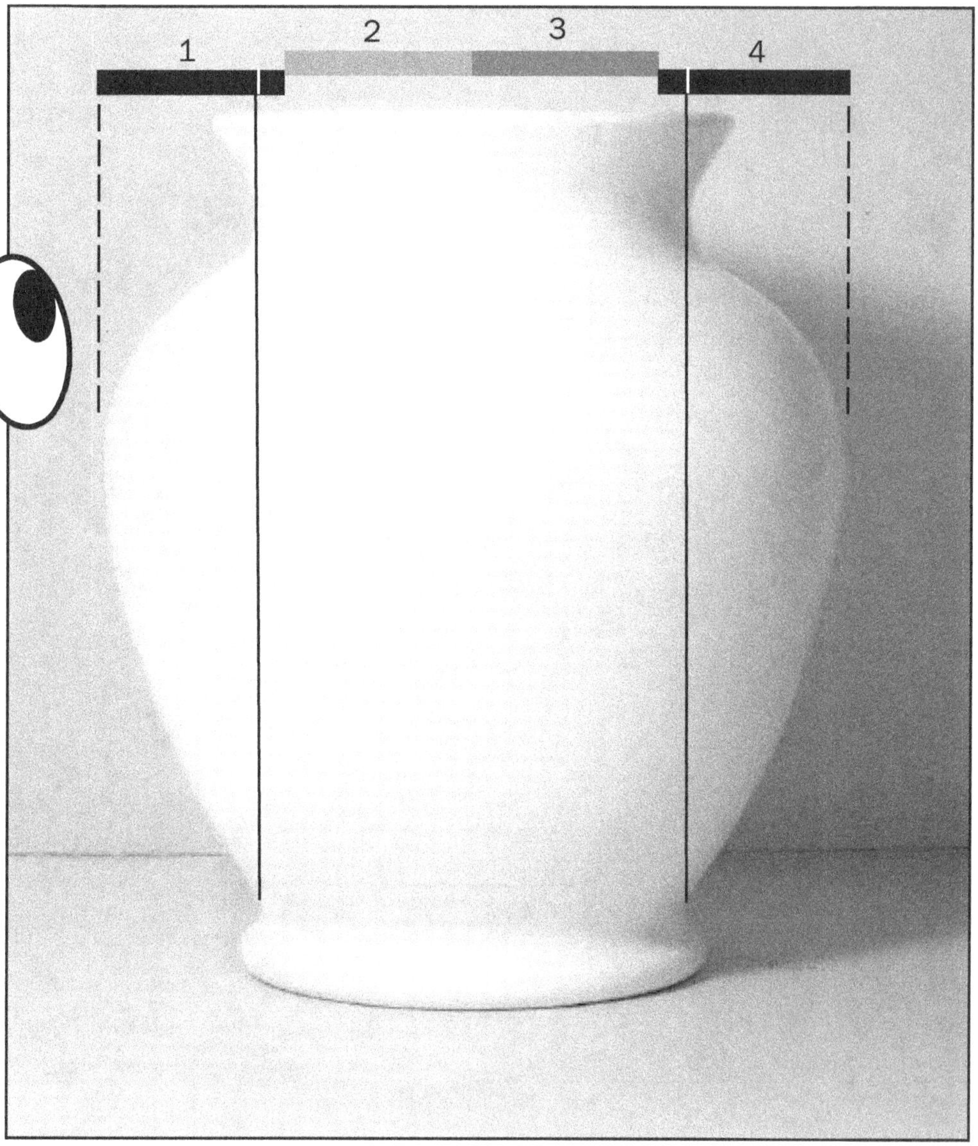

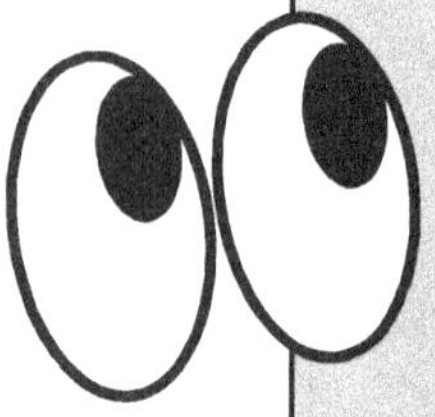

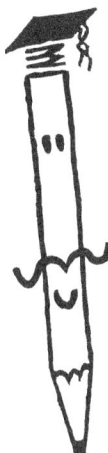

The OUTSIDE edges of the base
and neck are NOT aligned parallel,
are they? The span across the
top is slightly longer than the base.

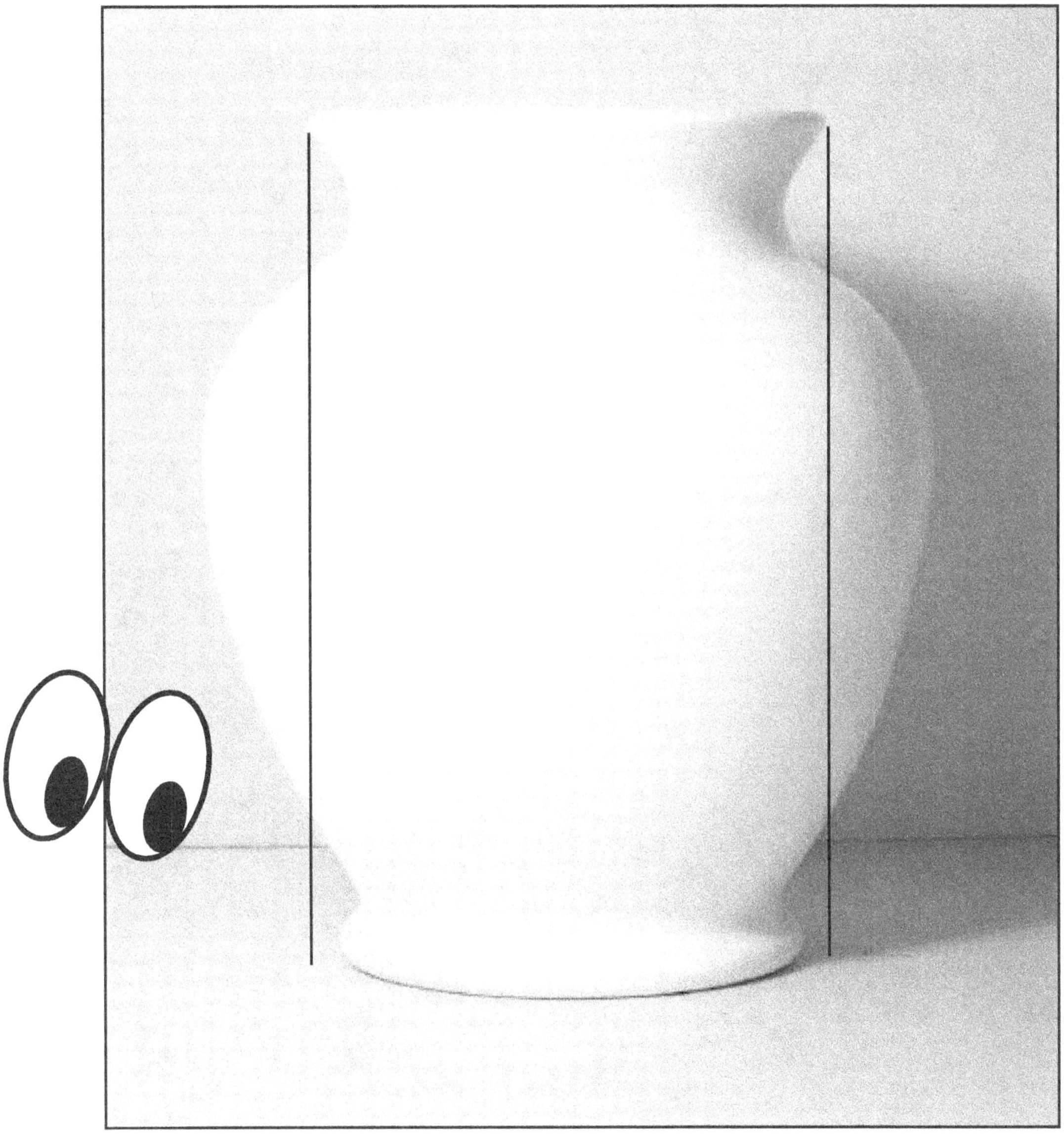

TIP The more you study the form you intend to replicate, the more useful things you find and the more easy drawing becomes.

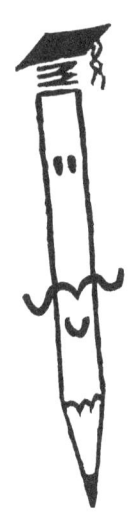

The NECK angles connect between two points. One point is on the neck-body division, inset about a quarter span from the sides. The other point is on the top, inset at <u>half</u> the quarter span

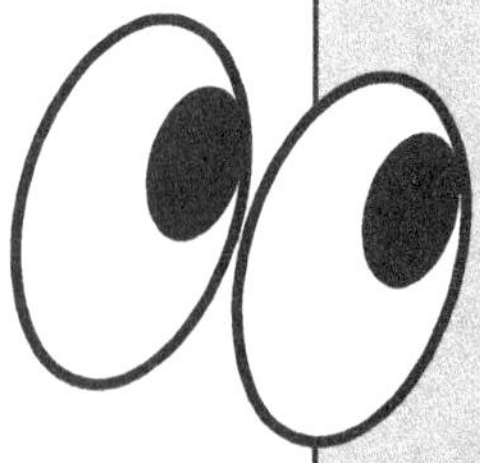

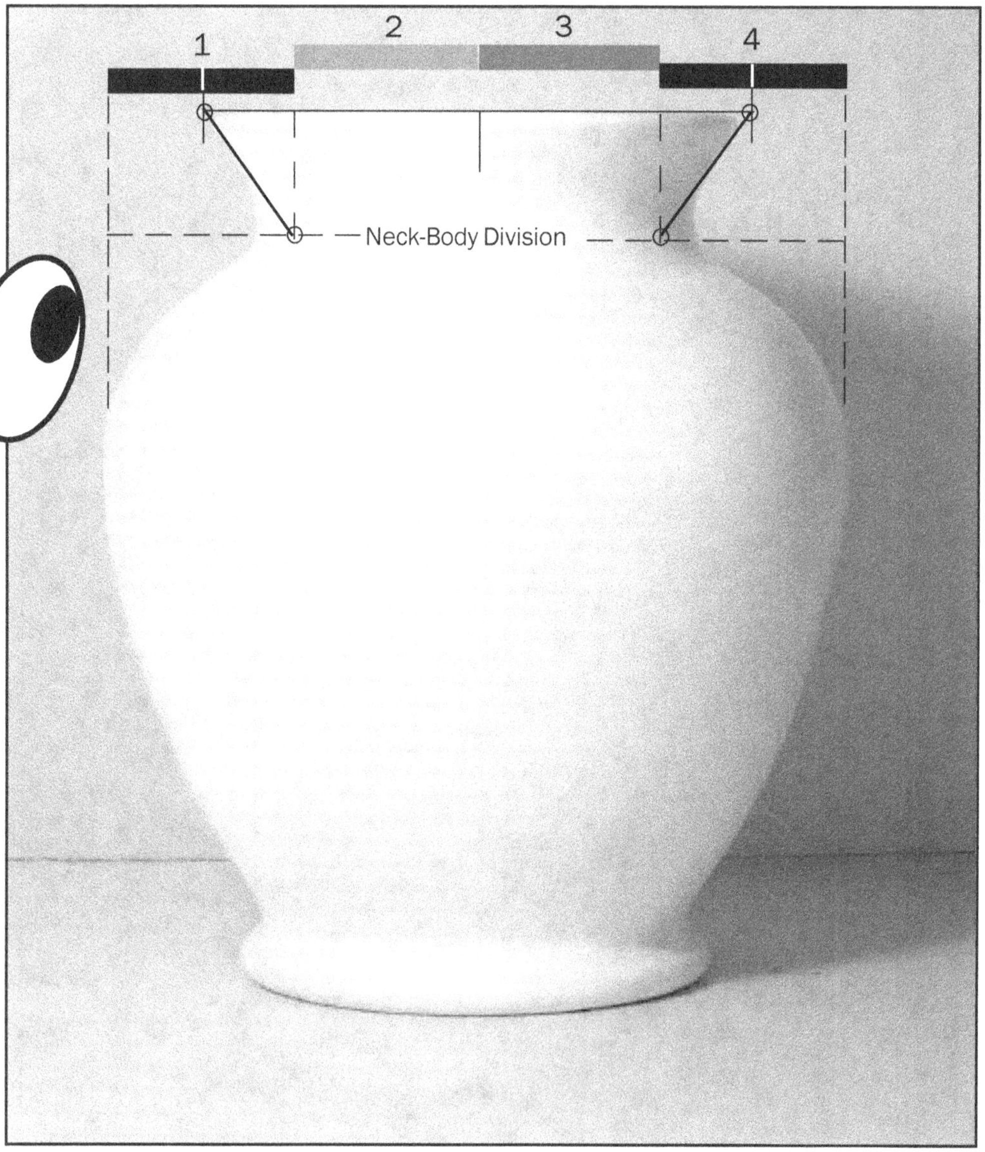

Neck-Body Division

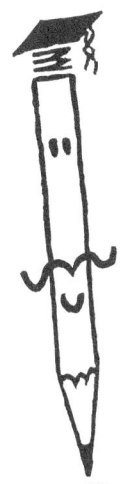

The UPPER BODY angles slant down from the bottom of the neck curves to a distance on the sides equal to a quarter of the body and base height combined.

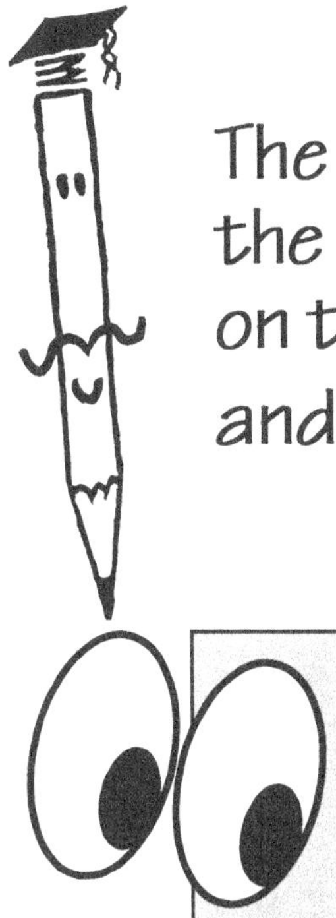

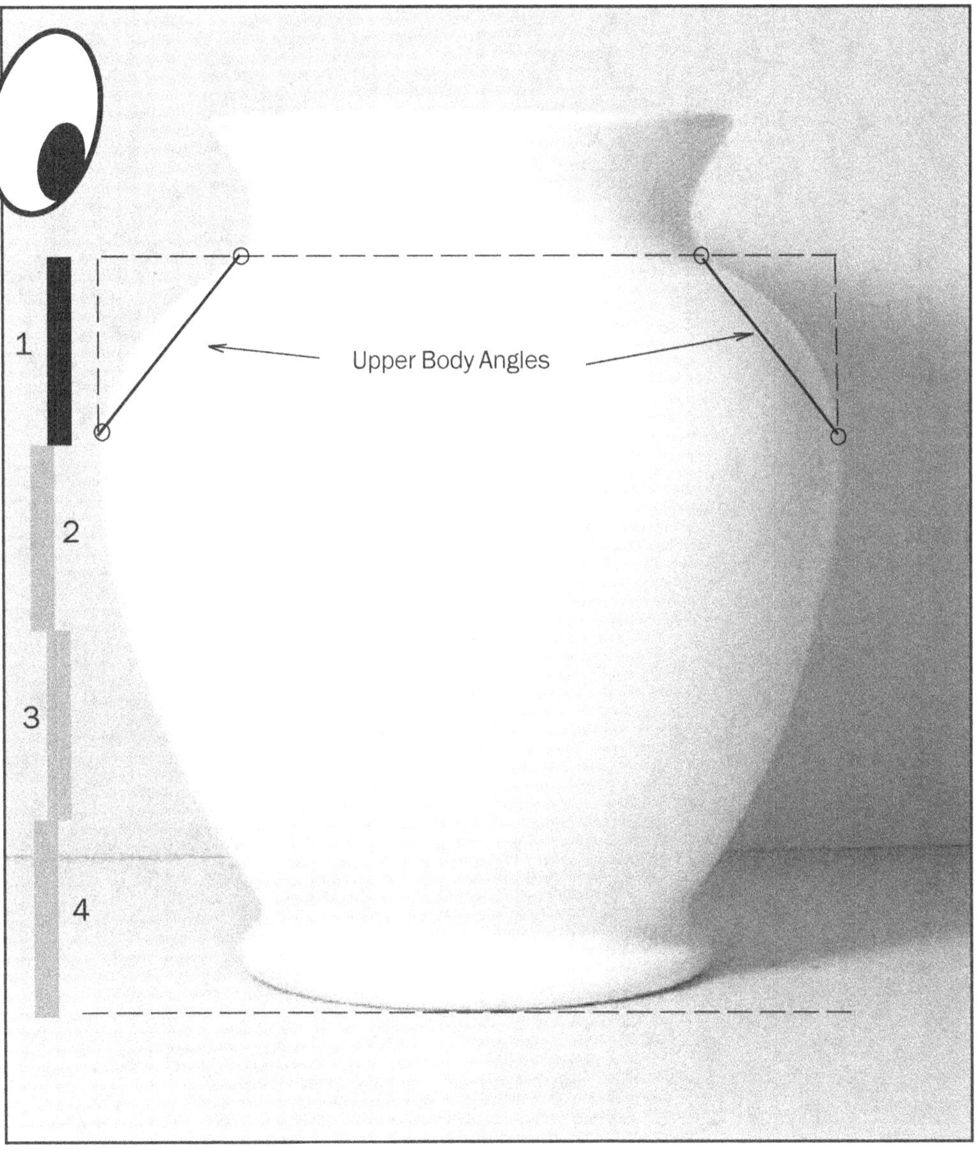

Upper Body Angles

1

2

3

4

TIP Hang in there. I know you want to draw, but you will do better if you study the figure first.

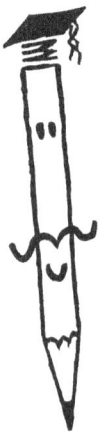

The body and base fit into a square. The NECK height is a little less than a fifth of the BASE and BODY height together.

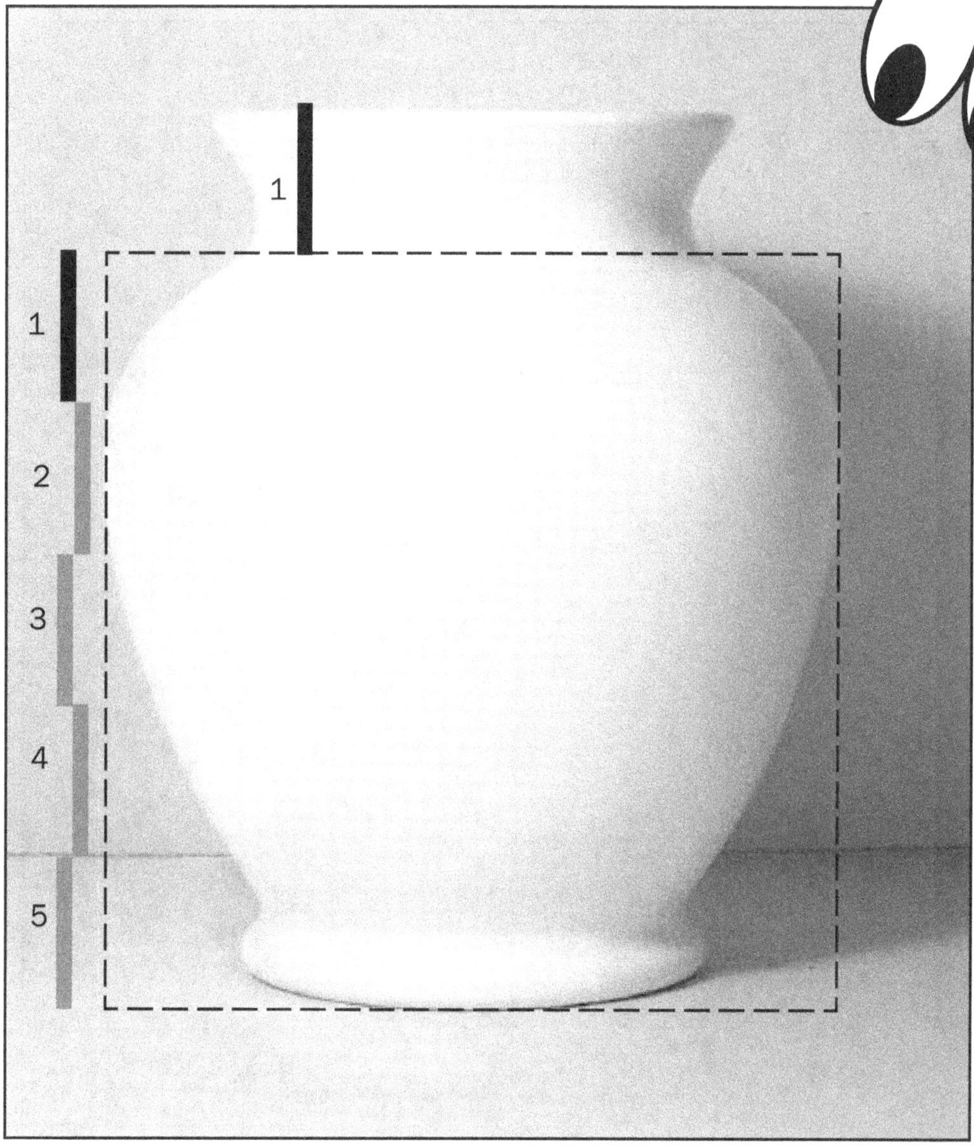

1

1

2

3

4

5

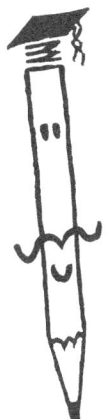

Having studied the figure, you've become better acquainted. Now you are prepared to draw it with confidence, accuracy and ease.

RECOMMENDATION: You will be shown three ways to form the figure's shape. The first method is the *Structural Approach*. It begins on this page with Step 1. Another way is the *Random Method*, found in Chapter 1A, page 47. *Doodling* is the third method. Turn to Chapter 1B, page 57. Try all three methods, one at a time and you will gain a wider range of valuable and enriching experiences, while discovering which method, or combination, works best for you.

STEP 1 Since the figure's combined body and base height are the same length as the entire horizontal span, in this case an easy way to start is with a square. It will serve as a preliminary guideline to help shape the figure and reduce the chance for tilting and distortion. Do not use a *ruler or straight edge*. On a fresh sheet of paper, FREEHAND draw your square, positioned evenly from side to side, but closer to the bottom of your paper. This leaves space for the figure's neck. In order to make certain the sides, top and bottom of your square are parallel to the edges of your paper and fairly equal in length, you can gauge with your pencil, as shown in diagram 1-1.

TIP Draw very LIGHTLY. Erasure and changes can be made more easily. First, try a few lines, then erase them to test your pressure. Next, PLAN AHEAD. Picture the figure in your mind as if it's already on your paper. This helps determine your square's size and location. Ultimately, you will be less likely to end up with a drawing which is in the wrong place, too small, or so large it may not fit.

1-1

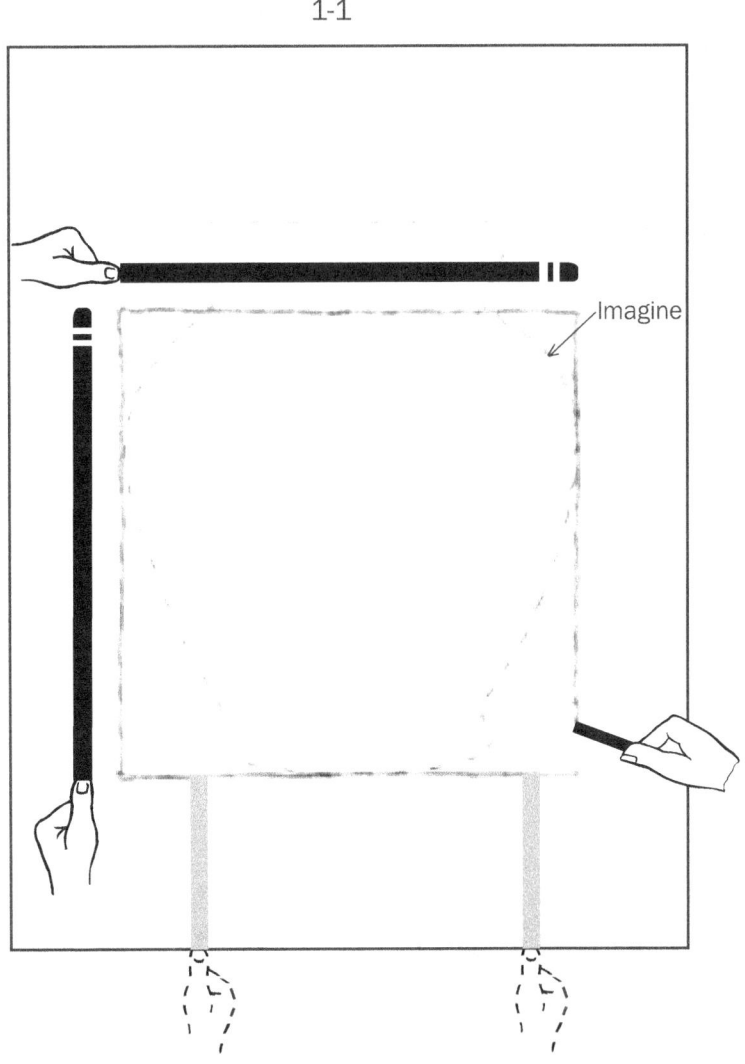

Imagine

STEP 2 Illustration 1-2 (here on the right) reminds us that while checking for proportion, we discovered the figure's neck height is slightly less than one fifth of the body's vertical span and base *combined.* Since *your square* represents that same combination, estimate a fifth of its height (1-3a). Place a dot above your square to indicate the distance (less a little (1-3b). Then lightly draw a continuous horizontal line or sketch line to serve as the *guideline* for your figure's top boundary (1-3c).

TIP Lightly divide your square's left side into five fairly equal sections with four dots. Use one section to determine the one fifth proportional span.

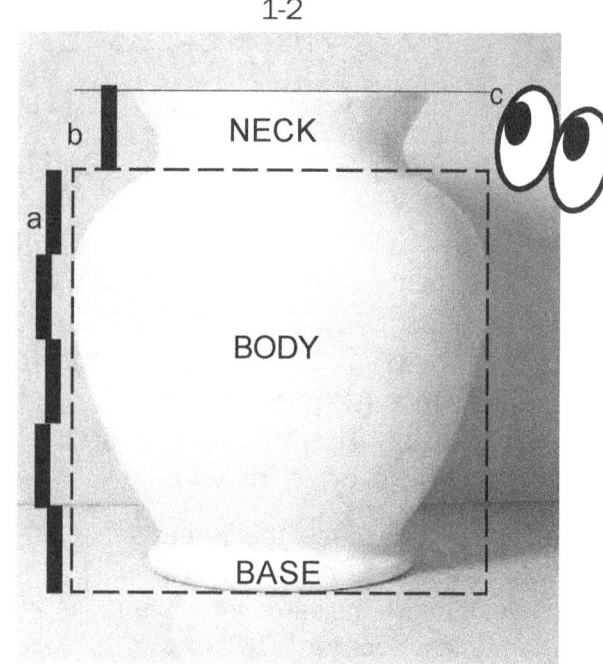

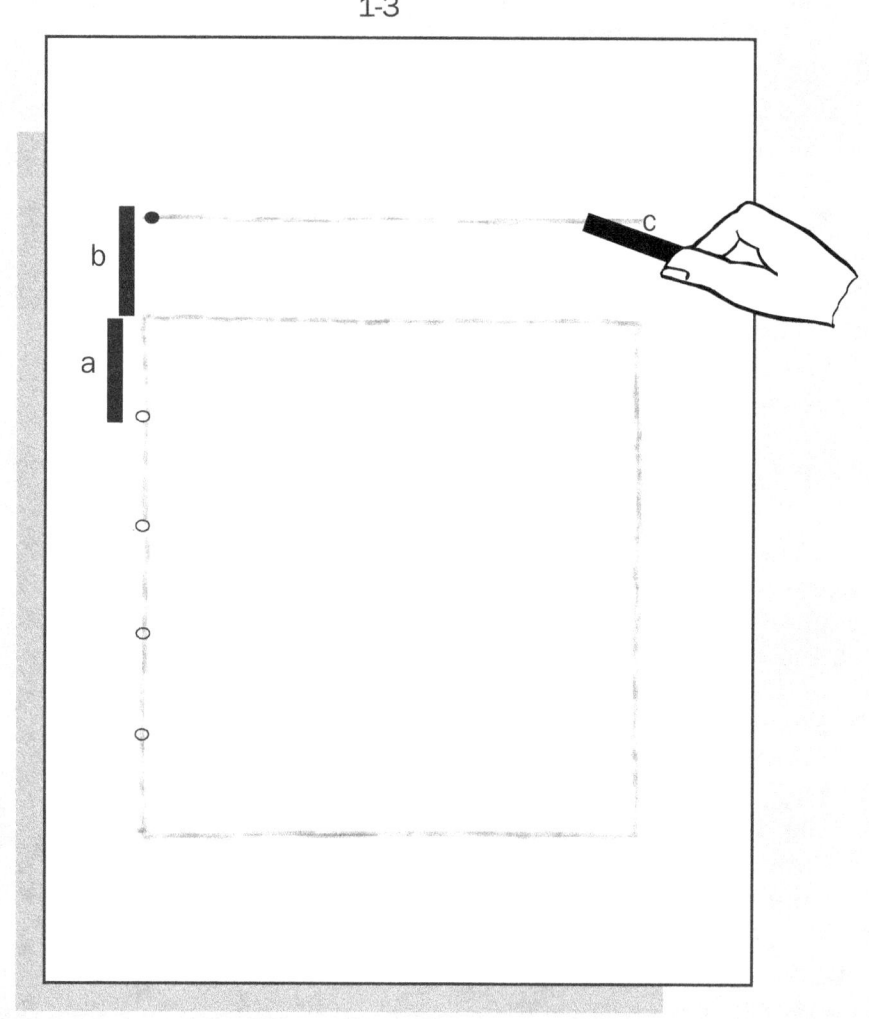

1-3

STEP 3   Diagram 1-4 reestablishes that the figure's base height (b) is about HALF the neck height (a). To find that proportion with respect to *your* drawing, take a visual estimate of *HALF your* figure's neck height (1-5a). This span is between the top of your square and the line you drew above it. Place a dot above the *bottom* of your square, on the left side to indicate the proportional half distance (1-5b). Then LIGHTLY draw a horizontal *guideline* from your dot to the right side of your square (1-5c). If you are a "lefty," work from the opposite end.

TIP   Draw lightly, by PULLING rather than pushing the pencil. Allow the point to barely touch the paper. Do not assume each line you draw is accurate. As your drawing develops, rely mainly on your vision & double check often.

1-4

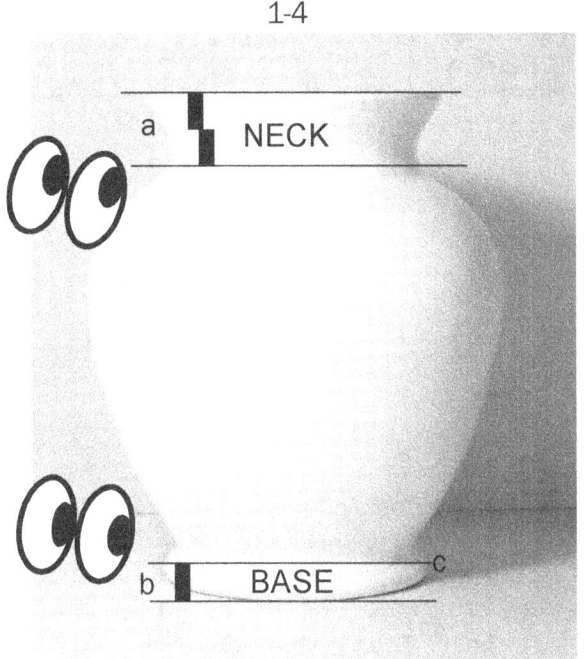

1-5

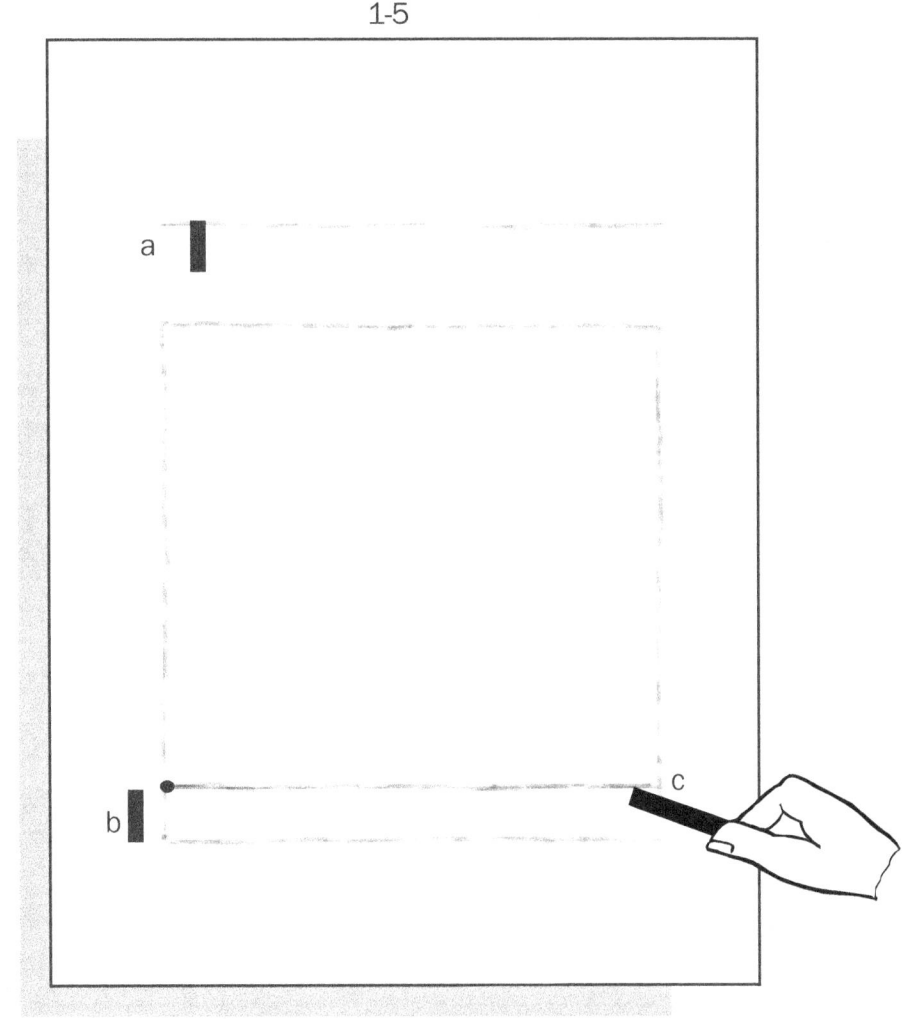

STEP 4 Illustration 1-6 shows the *inside* curvature of the base and neck are vertically aligned parallel. They indent from each end at slightly *less* than one quarter of the lateral distance across the body. Estimate the two spans proportionally on your top line. Then *lightly* draw the vertical alignments to serve as *guidelines* (1-7).

TIP Place a dot (a) in the center of your top line to create 2 halves. Judge by eye. Do not fold your paper to find the middle. Subdivide with two dots (b&c) to determine the quarter distances. Then locate reference points D & E.

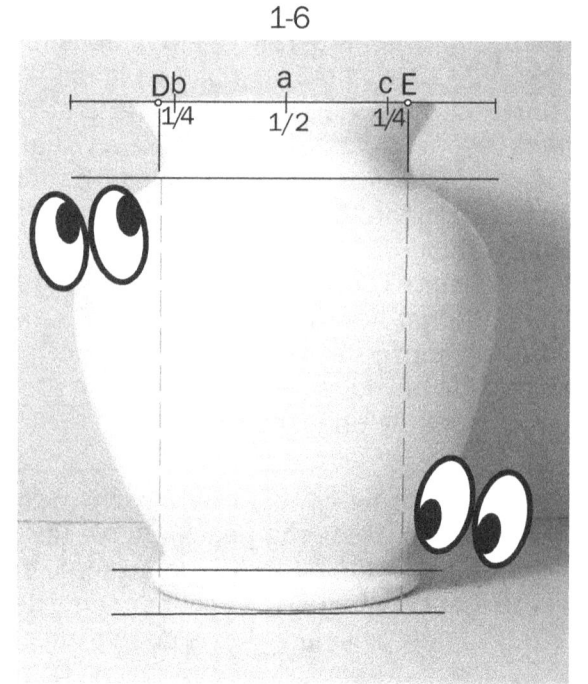

1-6

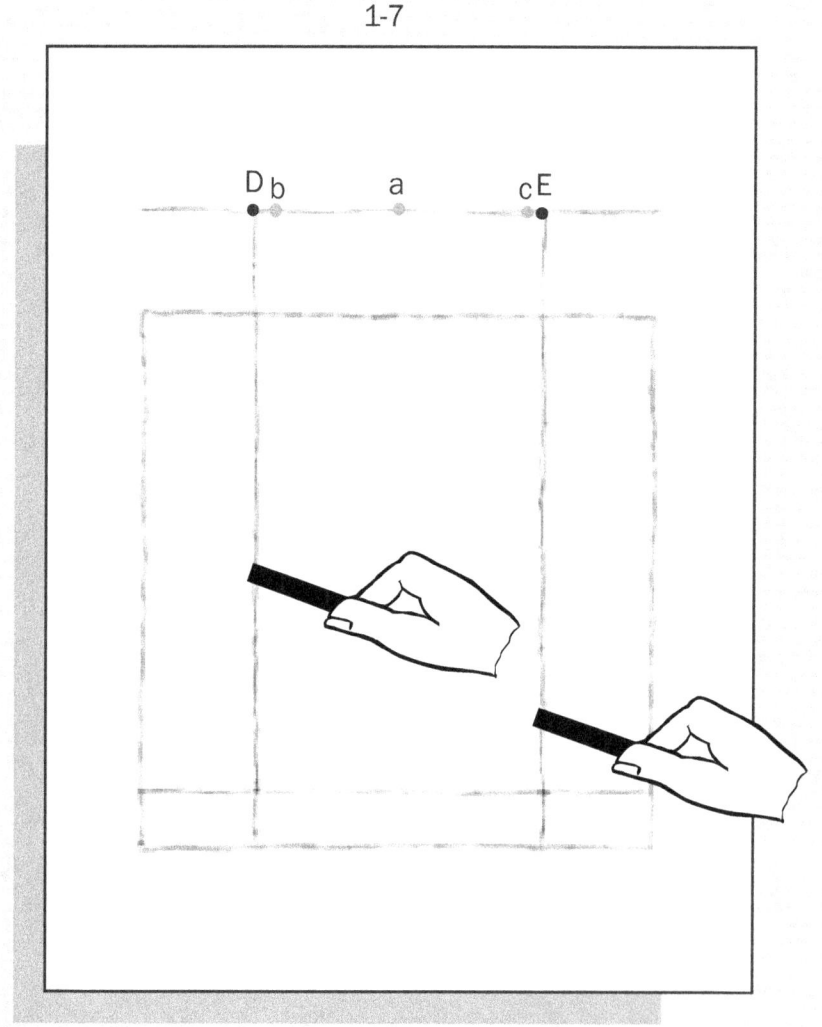

1-7

STEP 5 Diagram 1-8 indicates the neck angles are inset about a quarter of the way from each side of the body. They diverge in opposite directions on both ends, tilting *upward* to about the *midway* along the two quarter spans. Use these observations and *your* vertical lines from the previous step to help estimate the location. Then draw the *neck angles* proportionally, or place reference points first (1-9).

1-8

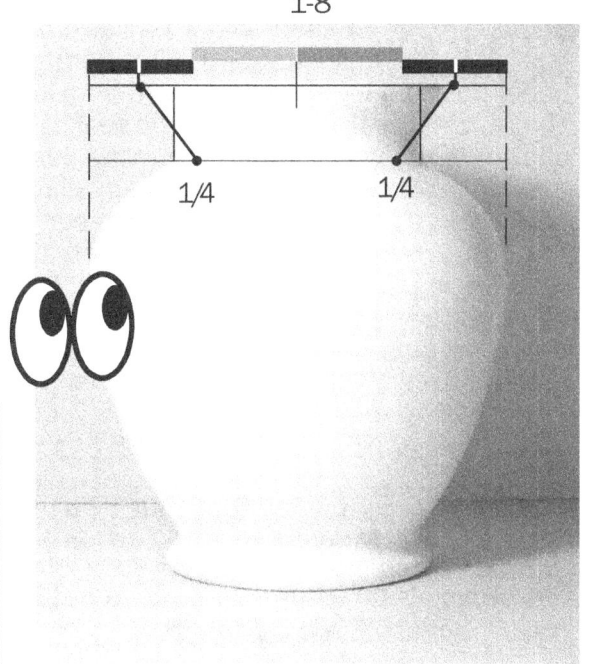

TIP For a *continuous line*, place your pencil on the paper surface. Do not lift until your line is finished. *Sketch lines* are achieved with short, overlapping strokes in one direction as well as back and forth. This enables you to adjust position and accuracy as you form your line.

1-9

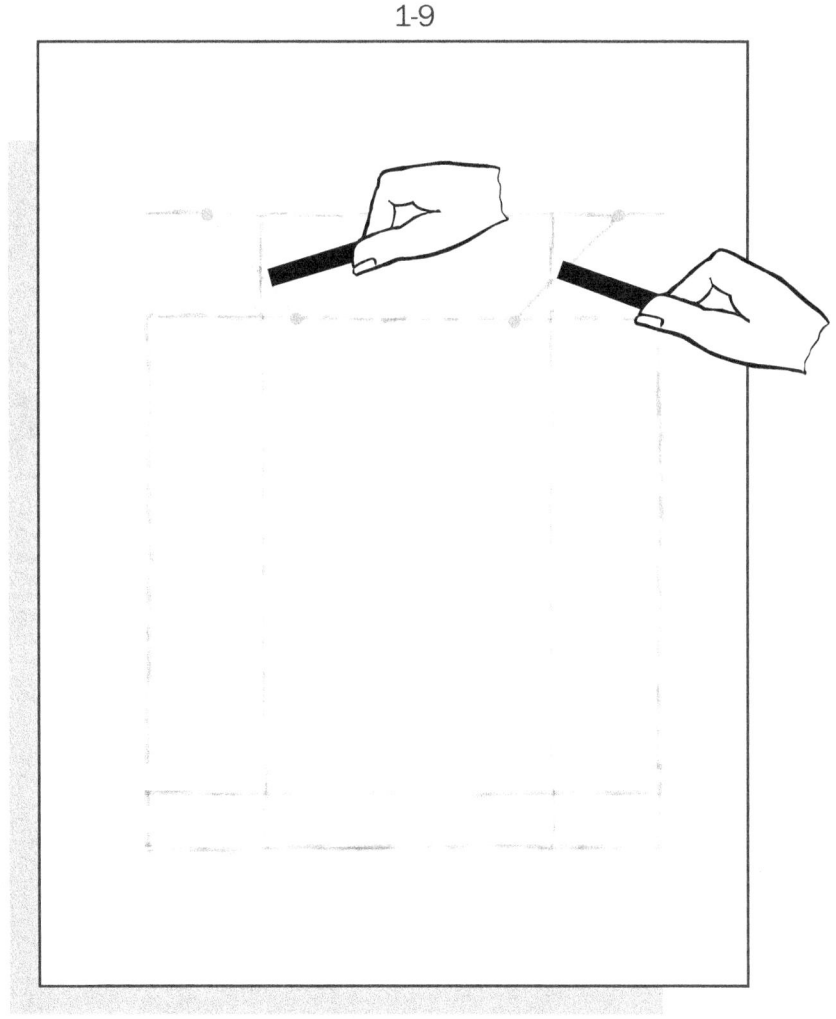

STEP 6 Based on our earlier observations, illustration 1-10 reitterates that the upper body angles slant downward from location (a). They end at the figure's edge. The span is about one quarter of the vertical distance to the bottom of the base (b). Your vertical alignment guidelines already locate where the neck and upper body curves join (a). For the *angle*, you need the proportional one quarter vertical distance from the top of *your* square, down (b). Estimate by eye, or place a dot on your square's left and right side. Bisect the upper halves with another pair of dots. Then lightly draw the two respective angles with your choice of sketch lines or continuous lines (1-11.)

TIP You may be tempted to use a ruler for measuring and forming straight lines. Such habits reduce your chance to improve visual estimation and do not help you learn how to draw *freehand*.

1-10

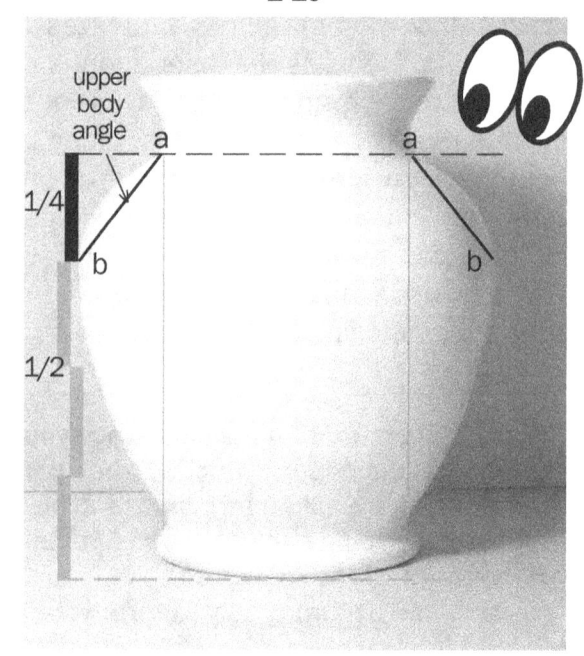

1-11

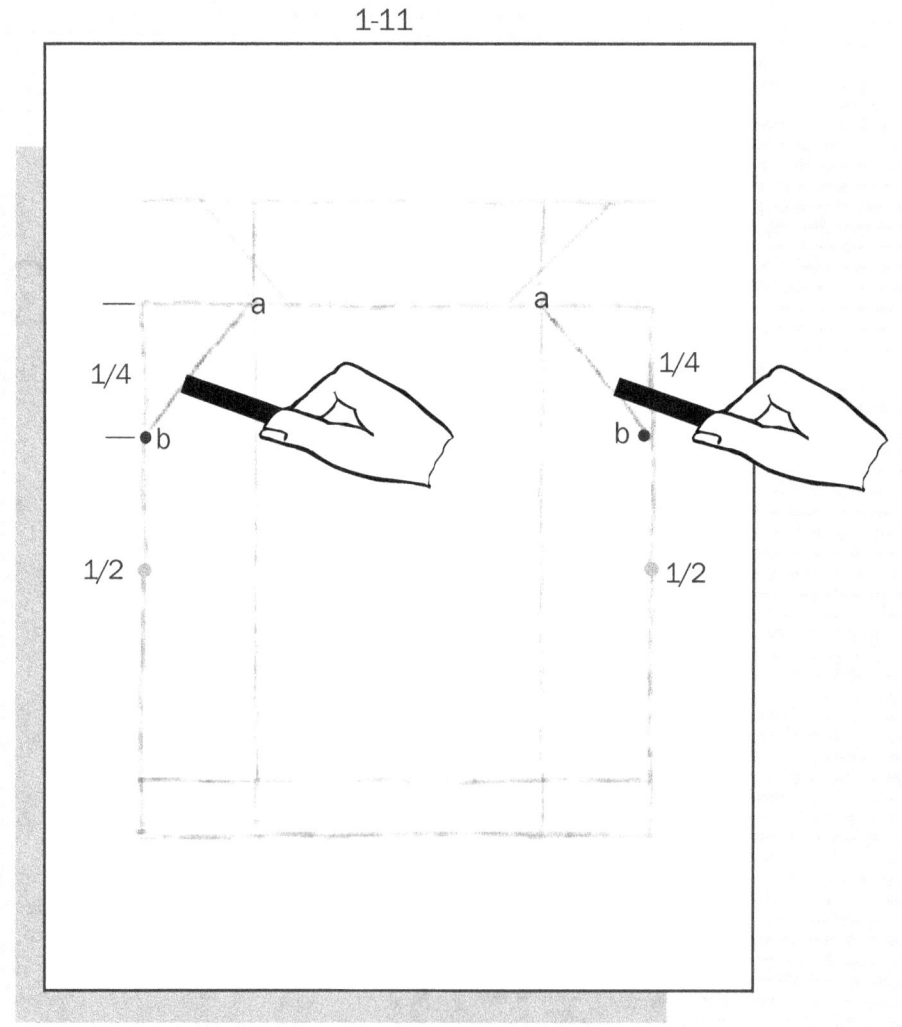

STEP 7   The *lower* body *angles* run from the *BOTTOM* of the *upper body angles*, (1-12b) to the *TOP* of the *base angles* (1-12c). You already drew your upper body angles. Now connect the two respective reference points between the bottom of your upper body angles (b) and the base alignments (c), as shown on diagram 1-13. You can opt for the continuous line or sketch line method.

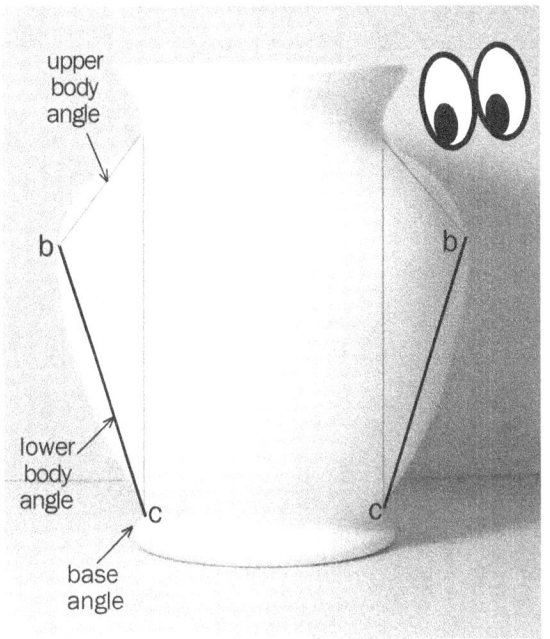

upper body angle

b   b

lower body angle

c   c

base angle

TIP   As more lines are added, things become increasingly apparent. Hold up your drawing at arm's length. Check to see the whole form with respect to the *parts*. Let your eyes be the final judge. Be ready to modify. Make verification and adjustment part of your drawing routine. But don't get carried away. Remember, accuracy means *approximately close*.

1-13

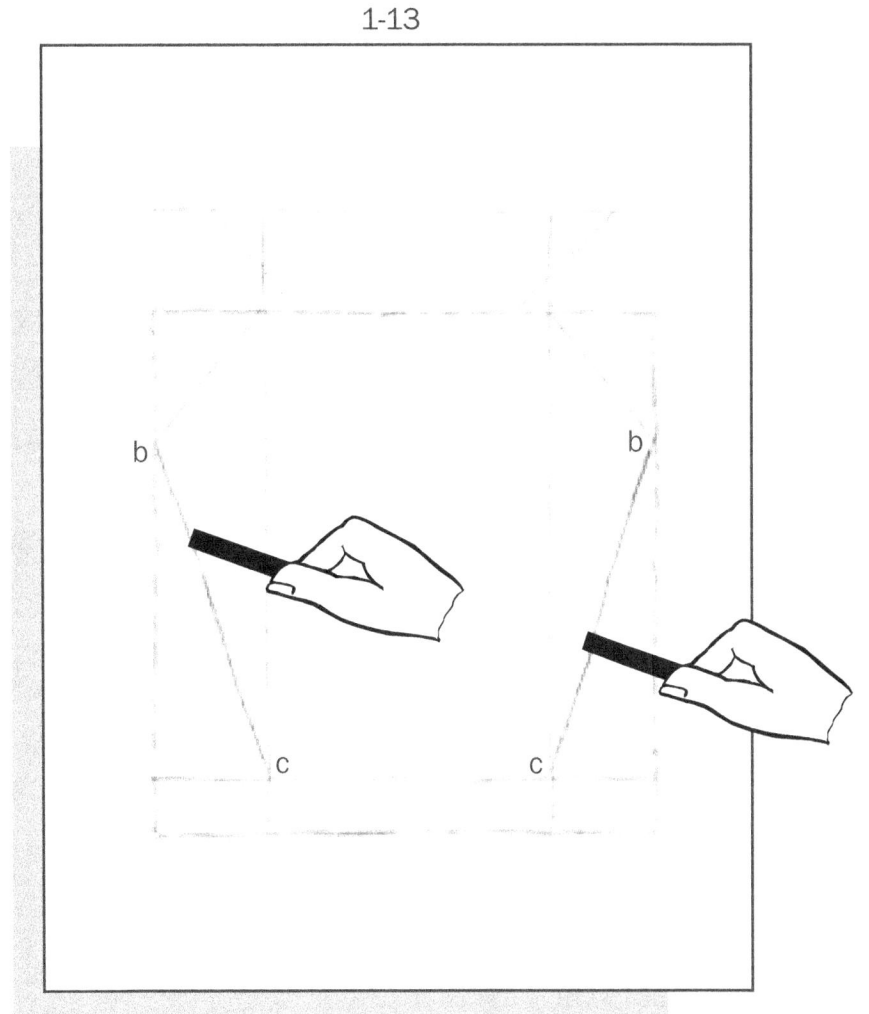

b   b

c   c

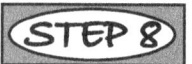

Several *guidelines* can be erased. The "X" marks portions to eliminate (1-14). If you accidentally delete any essential lines, carefully replenish.

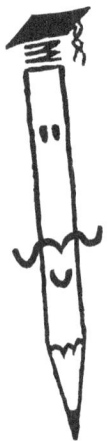

Aren't you glad you drew lightly? If you didn't, from here on, be sure you do.

1-14

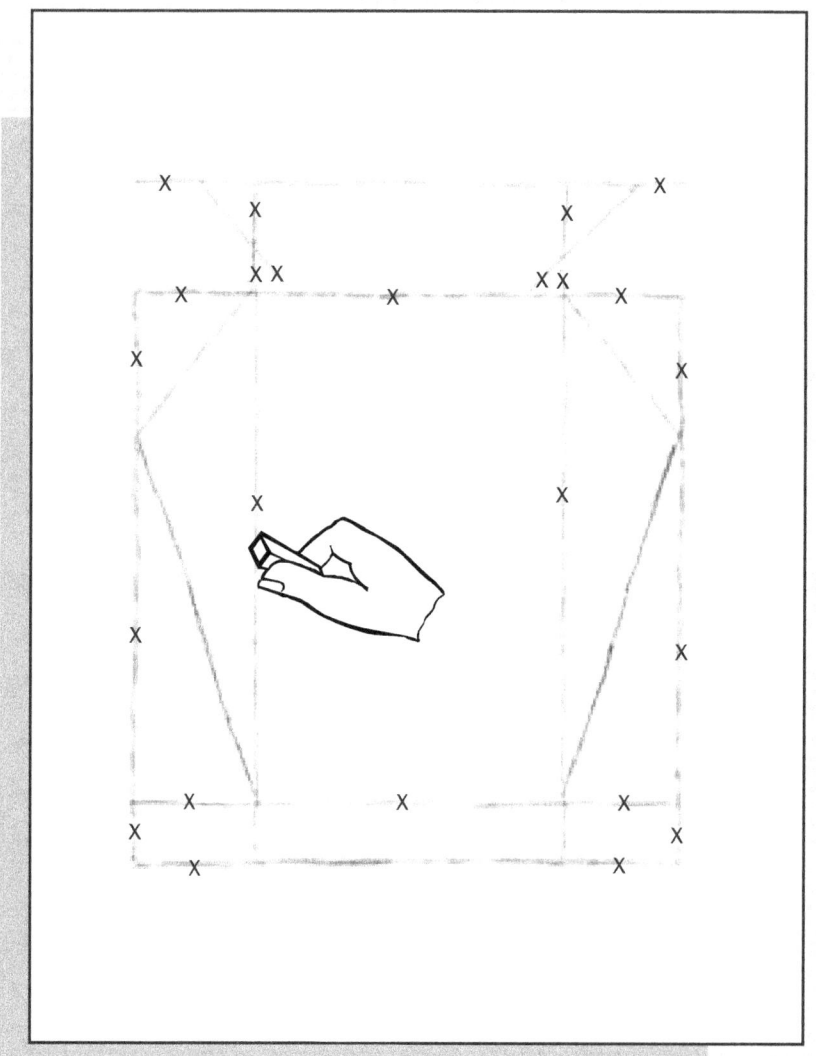

CAUSE FOR PAUSE

Please put your pencil down for a moment. Let's reflect on events thus far. You may be surprised by what I am about to share, but here goes, straight and to the point. The fact is, while you were busy working, you *divided* your attention. Switching back and forth from the book examples to your picture and vice versa, you actually split your concentration *three* ways; *(1) Looking, (2) Thinking, (3) Drawing.* Beyond that, *your eidetic imagery* (vivid details you saw) couldn't help but *fade* between alternating glances. How did this affect your results? *Good question.*

Before you jump to any conclusions, I'm not implying you goofed. On the contrary, visual fatigue often occurs when you have been drawing for a long time. Besides, forming line after line up close, you tend to focus on sections, not the whole figure. Also, remember you navigate primarily by *estimation. It seems only practical to take an occasional breather and initiate a progress review.*

An effective procedure I like to refer to as a *side-by-side comparison* works great. It's simple. Merely stop drawing. Get back far enough that both the model and your picture are simultaneously in view. Devote your energy just to observing and *you are bound to see more clearly. I can't emphasize this enough. Take full advantage.*

A word of caution, though. The instant you catch anything amiss, you are likely to call it a *flaw.* Generally, what follows is an irresistible urge to search for as many "flaws" as you can find, lump them together, then scramble to make the changes all at once. That way *errors* (as you would be inclined to label them) would completely disappear from sight as soon as possible. Is this rationale truly justified?

Bear in mind, you perform without a net, so to speak. Doing too much, too fast usually hinders. Consequently, a patient and positive approach is apt to be much better. Tell yourself there is no blame, fault, or mistakes, only room for *improvement.* Then handle each modification individually and objectively.

Easier said than done, you say? Yes, revision involves risk. You might inadvertently modify the wrong section. Maybe your upgrade reveals additional segments which need to be addressed. These are also part of the equation, including challenges if you *overdo.* For instance, you could uncover complexities your prevailing skill may not yet be able handle. What is the answer? Strive to stay balanced and satisfied. Revise with respect to your *present* ability.

Talking about the "present," currently your drawing is streamlined. *Streamline* is a term I use to describe form simplified with straight lines. Serving as a preliminary *foundation*, this basic method enables you to spot appropriate adjustments prior to the next phase: curves.

At this early stage, your work can already benefit from a status check. Turn the page and discover how.

Examine these two sets of figures. In the first set, the fundamental shape <u>wasn't</u> checked and adjusted. Notice the outcome after curves were added.

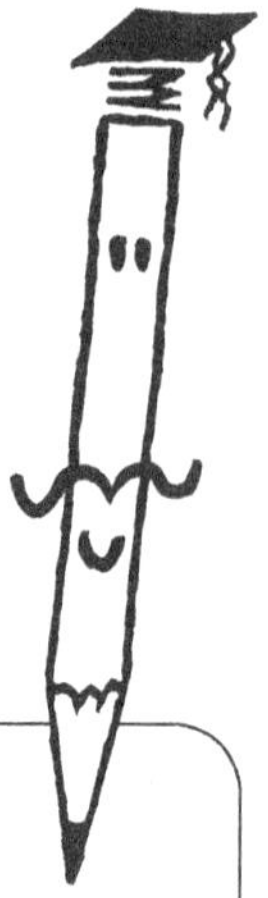

DEVELOPMENT FROM AN *INACCURATE* STREAMLINE

STREAMLINE   CURVE ADDITION   RESULT

DEVELOPMENT FROM AN *ACCURATE* STREAMLINE

STREAMLINE   CURVE ADDITION   RESULT

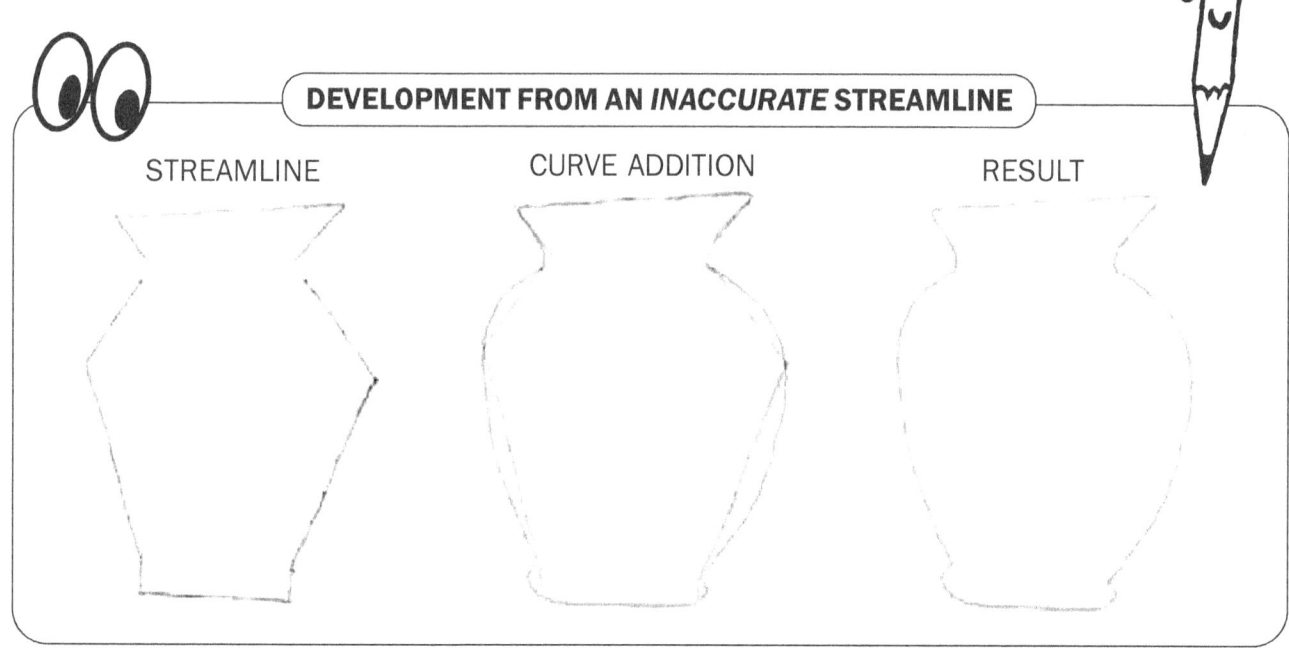

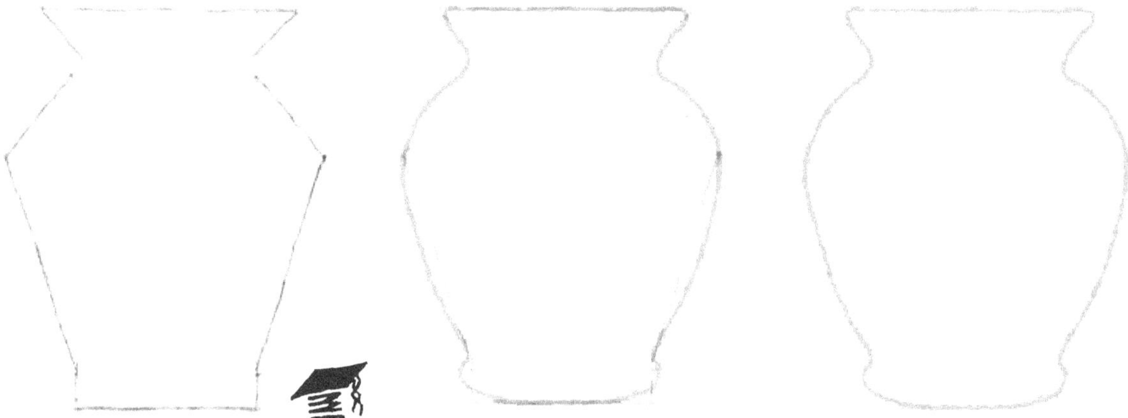

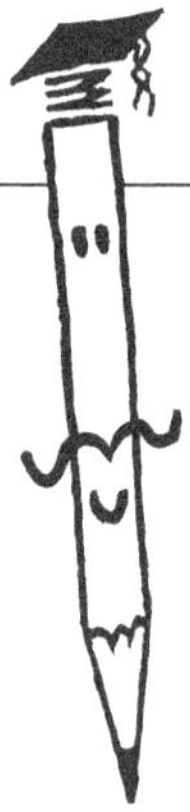

Get the hint?

Now is the best time to check *your* streamline. **DO IT. Prop up your picture side-by-side with this page and compare from at least four feet away.** Study sections in your drawing as they relate to one another and to the entire form, with respect to example 1-15. If something seems off, trust your eyes and your logic. The same principles used to draw can also be applied to determine accuracy and inaccuracy. Merely summon the TRUSTY 7 shaping components. In *no particular order*, they are: *reference points, alignments, proportion, angles, straight lines, curves, and negative space* (shapes displaced by form). Implement these in any order or combination and by process of elimination, find the dissimilarities as well as the reasons for them. Begin with the obvious things first. Sift for tilting, misalignment and parts that may appear too large or too small. Then focus on aspects such as angles that are too steep or too long. Execute one change at a time, step away and verify the effect immediately. For every required adjustment, be glad you found the discrepancy, so you can attend to it early. This saves much extra work later.

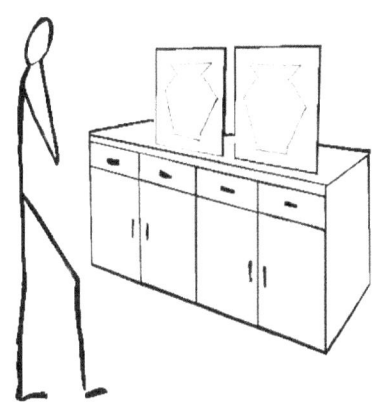

1-15

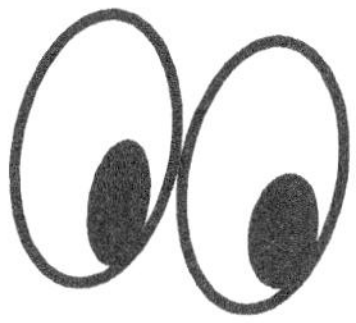

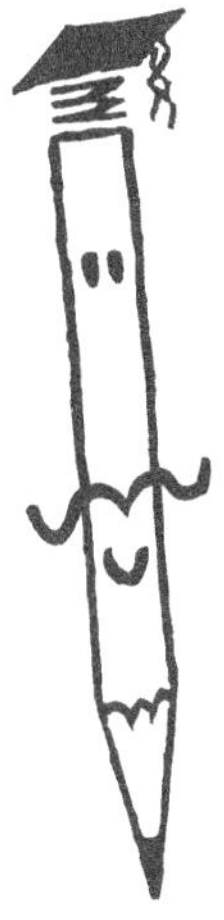

Make reasonable revisions, then move on.

ADD CURVES LIGHTLY

1-16

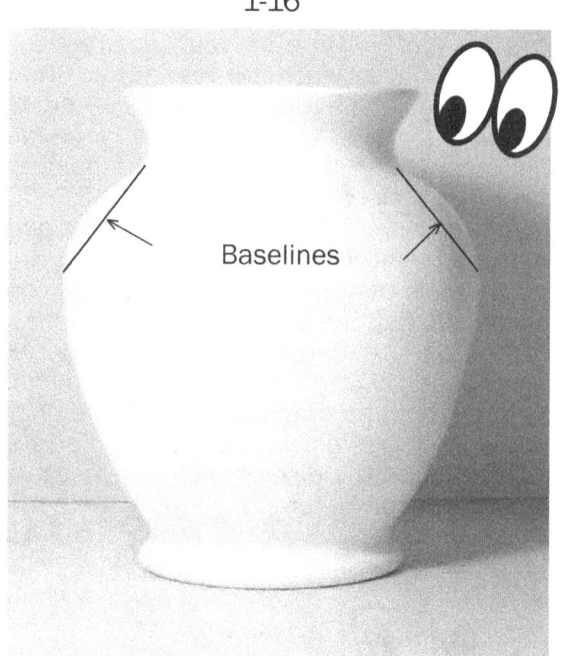

STEP 1 Refer to diagram 1-16 or turn to page 17 for a bigger view. Begin by drawing the two upper body curves, but manage them individually. In other words, when you copy one curve, do not assume the other is the same in the opposite direction, then form a mirror image. If your first curve proves to be inaccurate, your second curve will not be accurate either. It's wise to see every shape as integral (part of the whole). Handle each one *separately* (1-17). The straight lines in your figure's streamlined upper body angles double as baselines.

Baselines

TIP Baselines close in the curve like the string on a bow. This helps you see the amount of bend and the *shape* the curve creates.

1-17

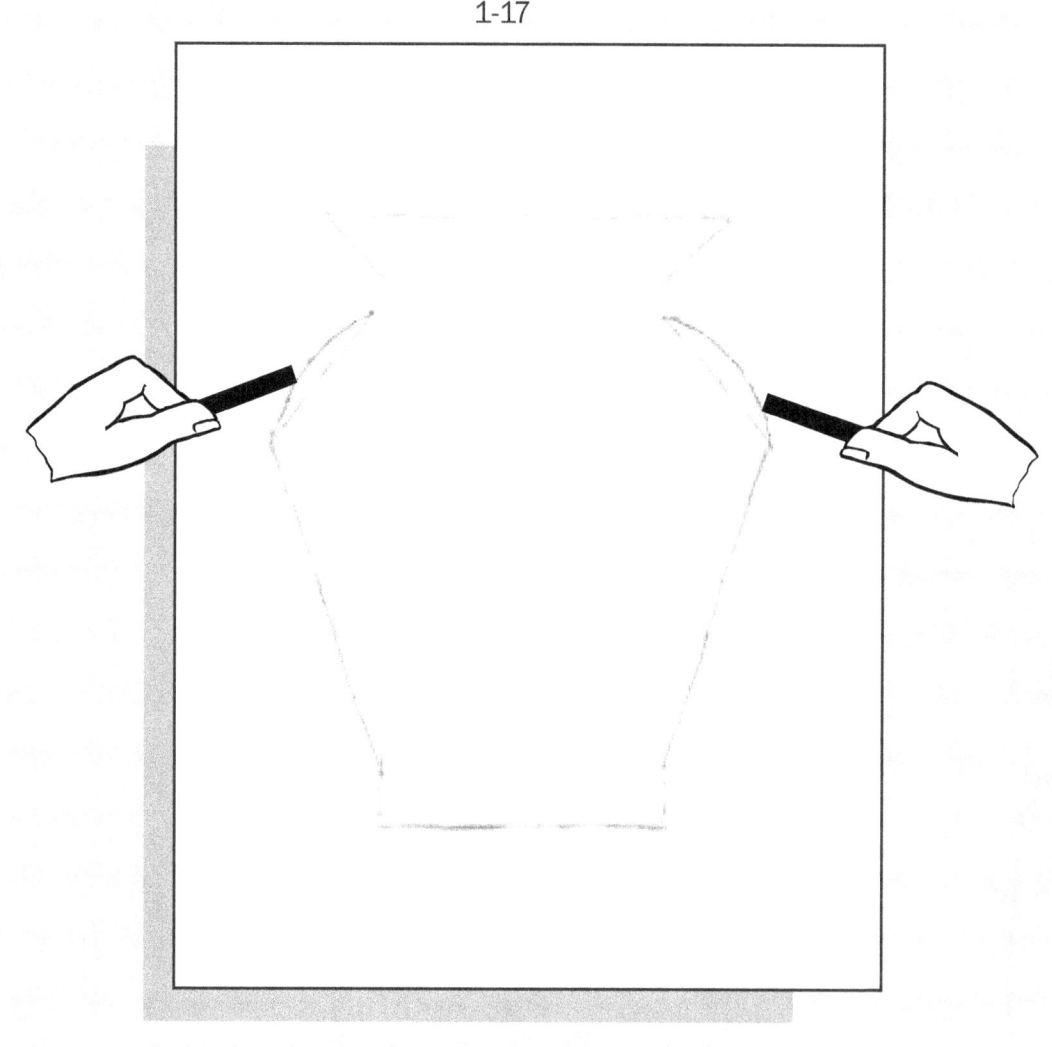

STEP 2 *Lightly* draw the two *lower body* curves *independently* with either sketch or continuous lines (1-19). Here in illustration 1-18, the baselines help you see the amount of curvature. You can also refer to the larger photo on page 11.

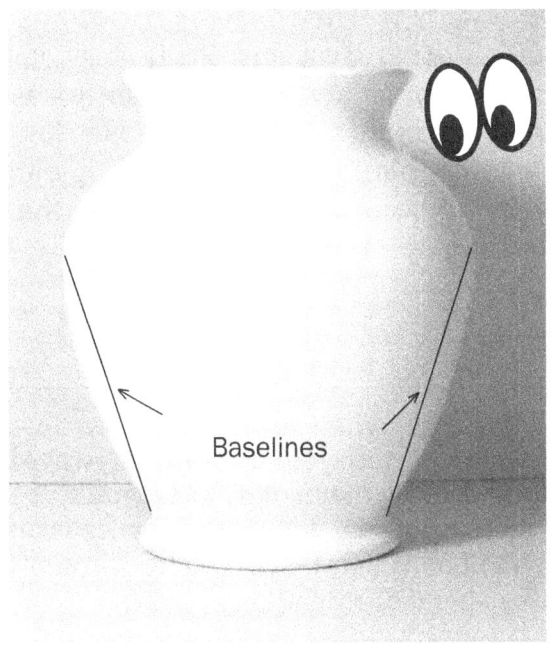

Baselines

TIP Don't just make *any* curve. Form the respective curve according to the figure. It doesn't have to be exact. Accuracy means fairly close. Find a balance between being too lax or too strict. Accepting less than what you are capable of achieving limits your potential. Overworking can be harmful.

1-19

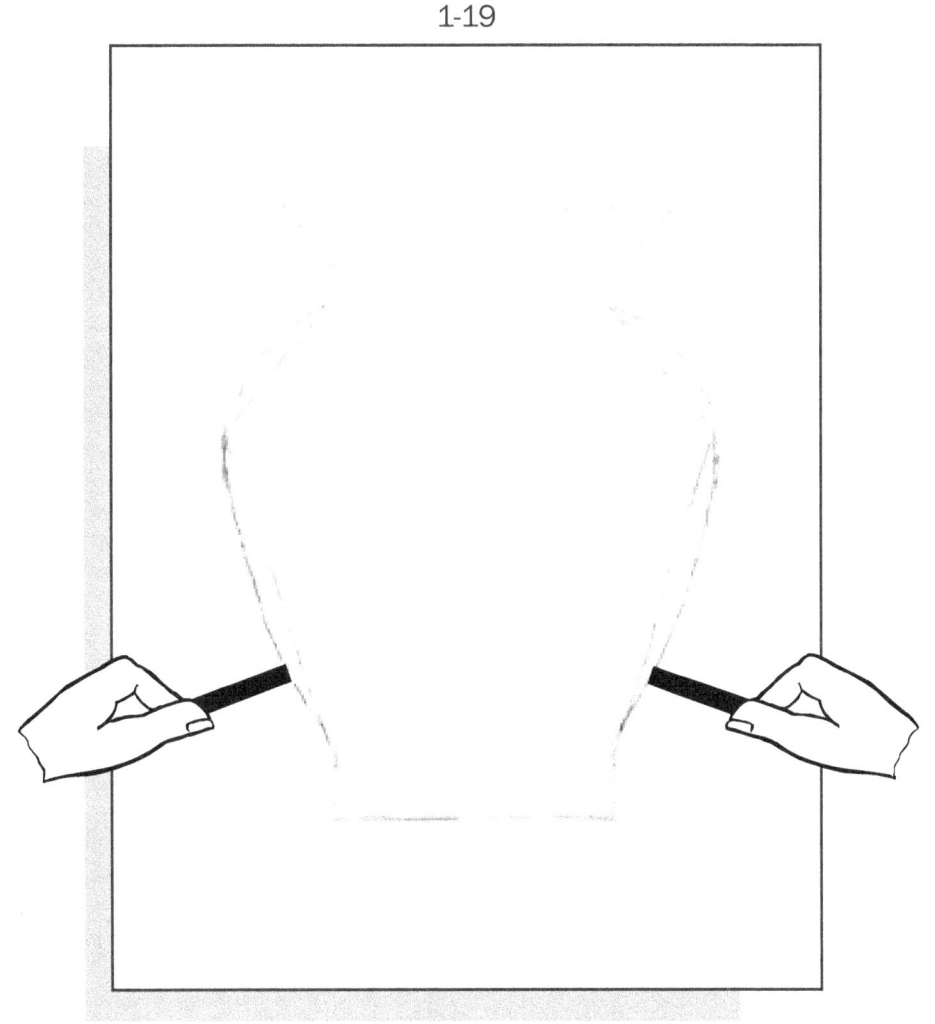

STEP 3 The vertical *baselines* shown in diagram 1-20 enable you to see the proportion, location and amount of bend in the figure's base curves. For a closer look, refer to the larger photo on page 17. Using either sketch or continuous lines, *lightly* draw the two *side* curves of the base (1-21).

TIP When forming your curves, *do not* turn your drawing *sideways* because the position may seem more comfortable for you to replicate an arc. Such practices can form a habit and likely hinder you from improving your eye-hand coordination.

1-20

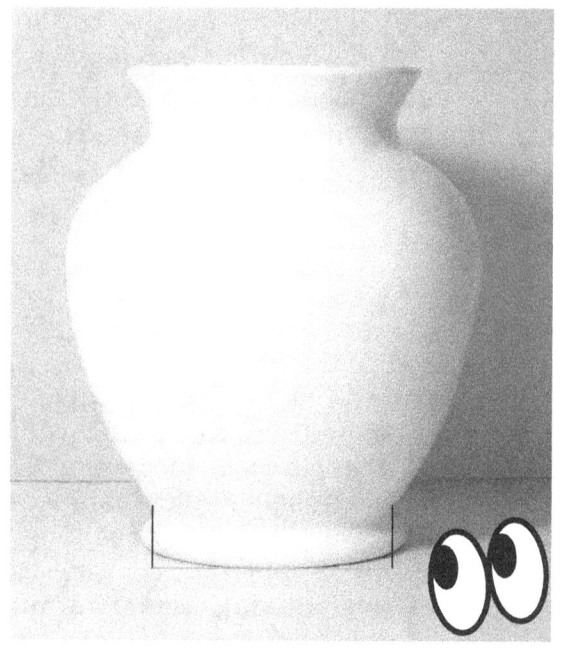

1-21

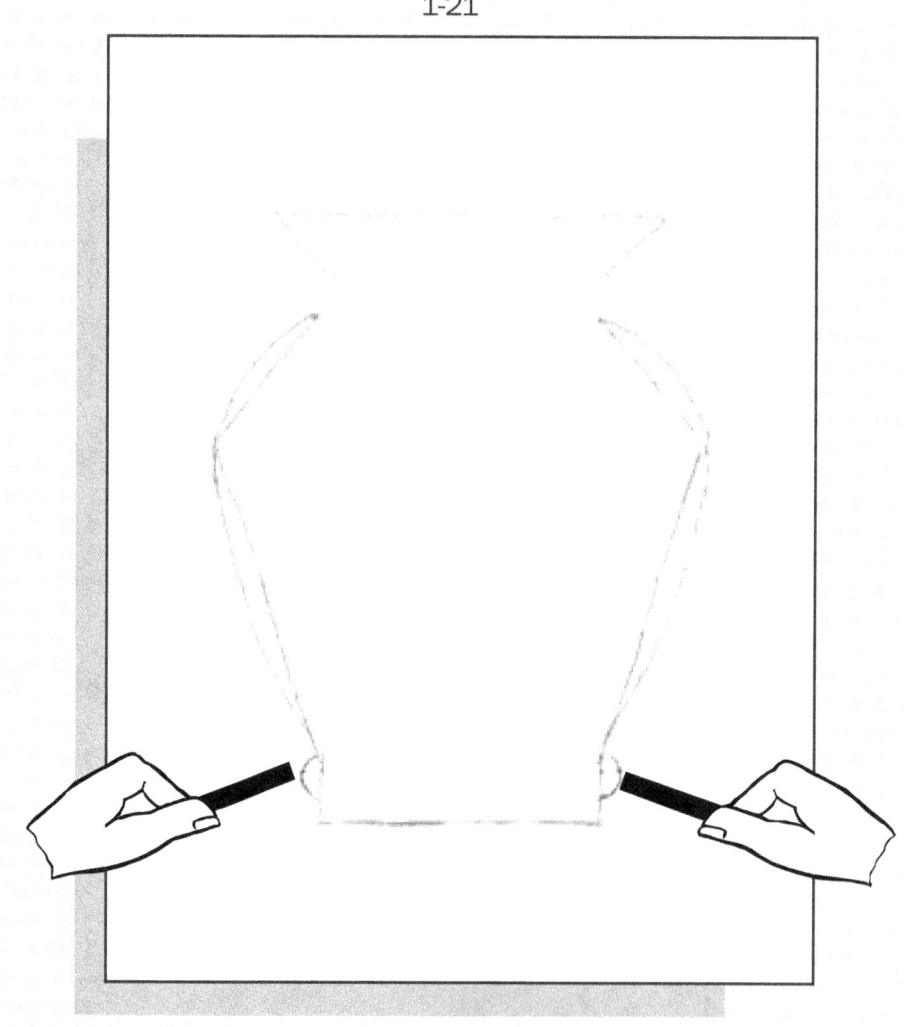

STEP 4 In diagram 1-22, the straight horizontal *guideline* along the bottom of the base helps to establish the curve's size, location and flex. For an up close view, refer to the larger photo on page 17. *Lightly* draw the bottom base curve proportionally on your figure with either the sketch or continuous line method (1-23).

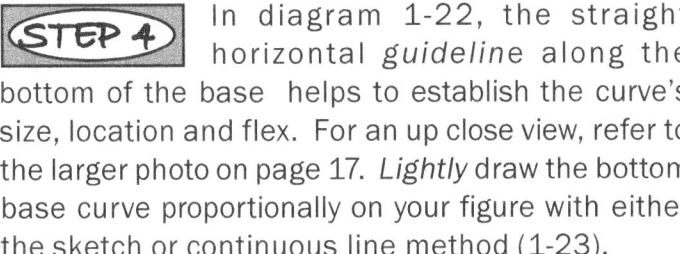

TIP Look at a curve in the photo and trace the bend in the air with your pencil until you feel it. Then draw the arc. You can draw a curve by forming one half, then the other half.

1-23

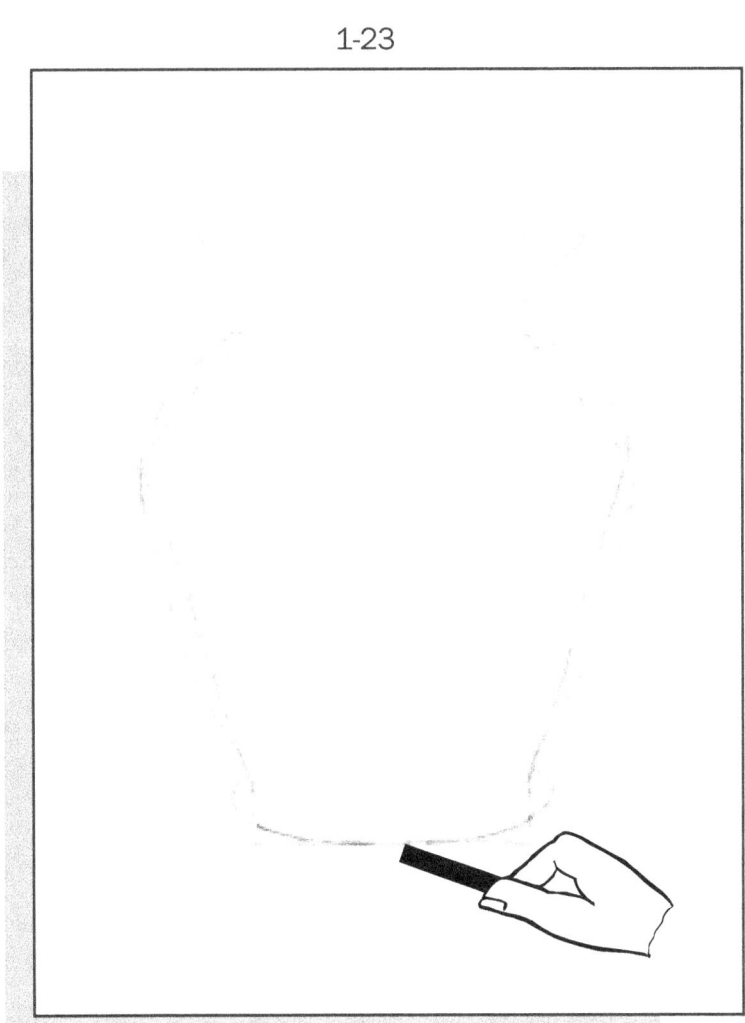

STEP 5 More *guidelines* can be erased. These include a small part of the two corners on top. "X" marks which guidelines to eliminate (1-24). If you removed too much, simply redraw. Example 1-25 indicates how your figure should basically appear.

TIP Drawing line by line and piece by piece, you tend to notice segments. Stop occasionally to observe the *whole*. Considering the many stages your drawing underwent, it may have changed more than you might think. Using illustration 1-25 for comparison, examine one part at time, as it relates to your total figure. Make any adjustments also *one by one including a double check for accuracy.*

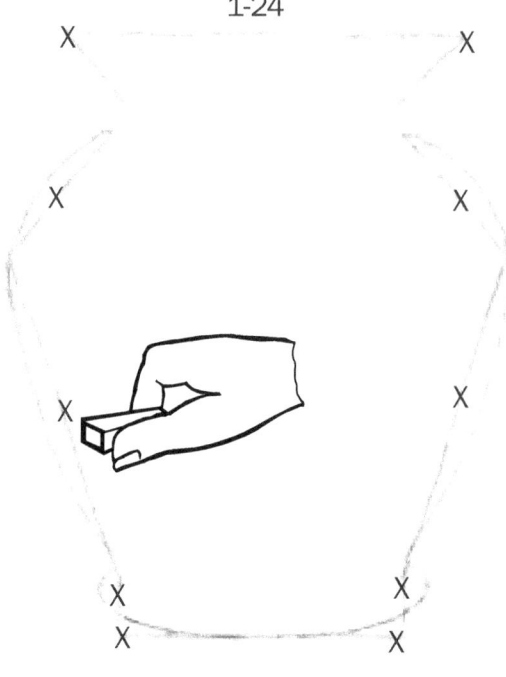

1-24

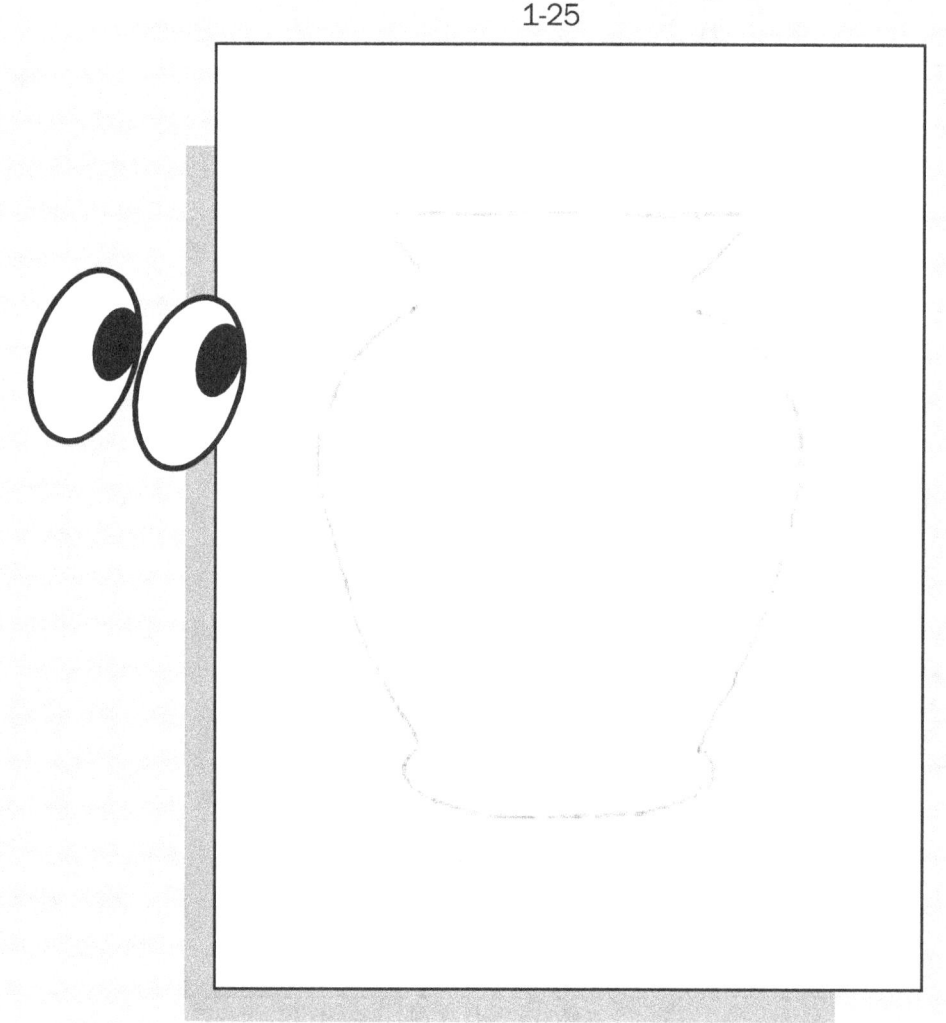

1-25

STEP 6 Diagram 1-26 shows how you can pretend a pair of vertical lines enclose the concave neck curves. I've enhanced these areas, called *negative space,* for visibility. They enable you to assess the background *shapes* created by the curves. Whether visualized, or actually enclosed with *guidelines*, this helps estimate *curve* size and amount of bend. Use the procedure to form your figure's neck curves. Also include a couple of small arcs to round the two top curves (1-27). *Then check your results.*

TIP During reworking, don't get carried away by trying to be too precise, or your drawing may get out of hand. In illustration 1-27, we see the neck curve on our right is a little wider, made apparent by comparing negative space. Such a small detail can be adjusted later. Besides, accuracy means *fairly close*, not an exact match.

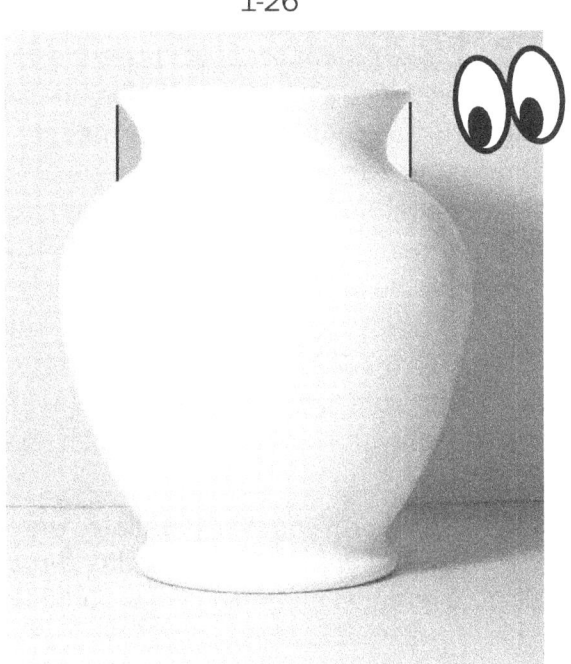

1-27

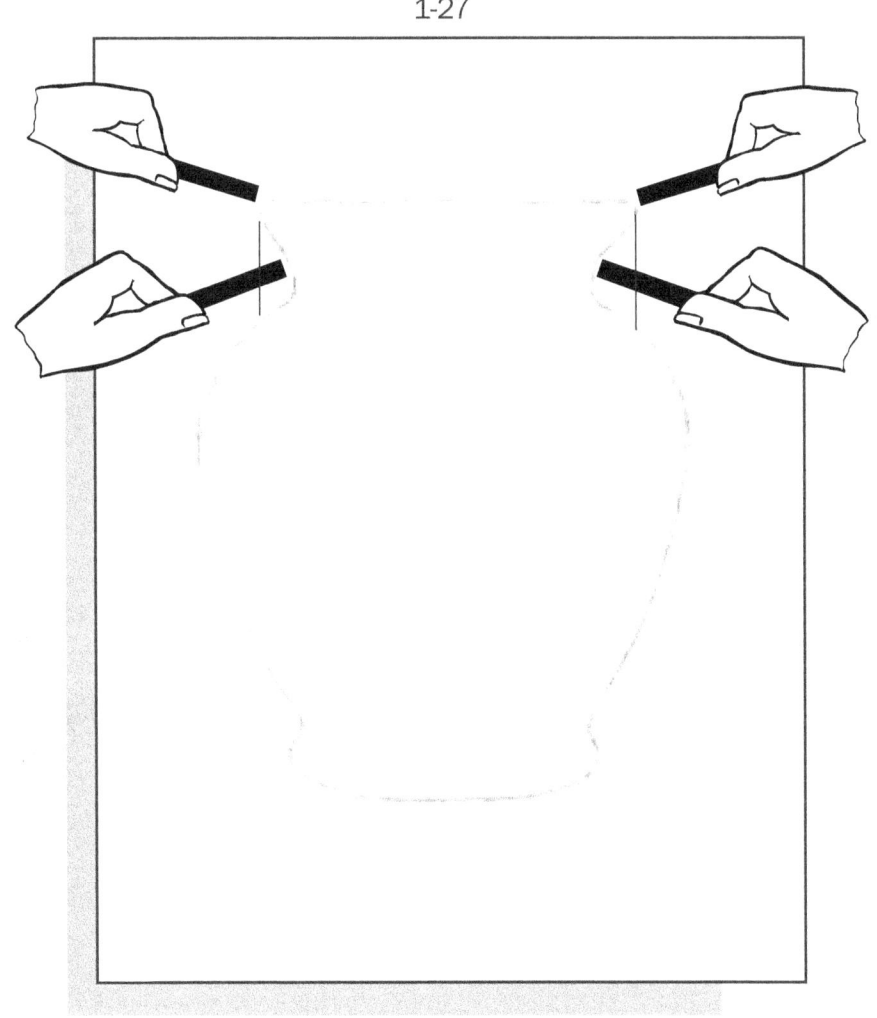

STEP 7 Imagine you have X-ray vision, enabling you to see the table edge *behind* your figure (1-28). Since the distance from there to the figure's base represents a *third* dimension (depth) but your paper is a TWO dimensional surface, convert the expanse to a *vertical* measure (b). Coincidentally the span appears to be about the same as the height of the *neck* (a). With the aid of this observation and illustration 1-29, estimate the proportional location of *your* figure's table edge (a/b). Then *LIGHTLY* draw a continuous or sketch line (c).

> **TIP** Form your line parallel to the bottom of your paper. Drawing *through* the figure ensures alignment from both ends.

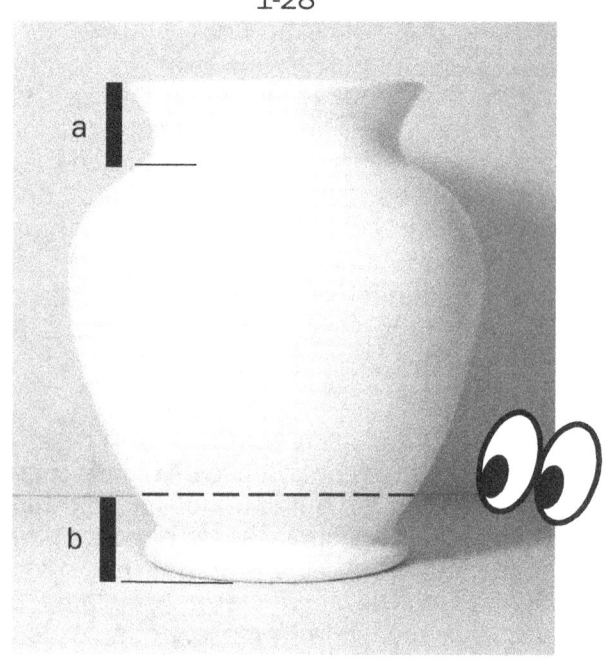

1-28

1-29

-36-

STEP 8 Carefully erase the unwanted portion of your horizontal line *inside* the figure (1-30). Replenish if you accidentally erase too much. Figure 1-31 shows how your picture should appear. The next several pages explain and illustrate ways to review your work for accuracy.

TIP Resist impatience. Enjoy every step of your drawing odyssey. The journey is as rewarding as the destination. You and your drawing deserve the time needed to assure success. Checking and adjusting is part ot the routine.

1-30

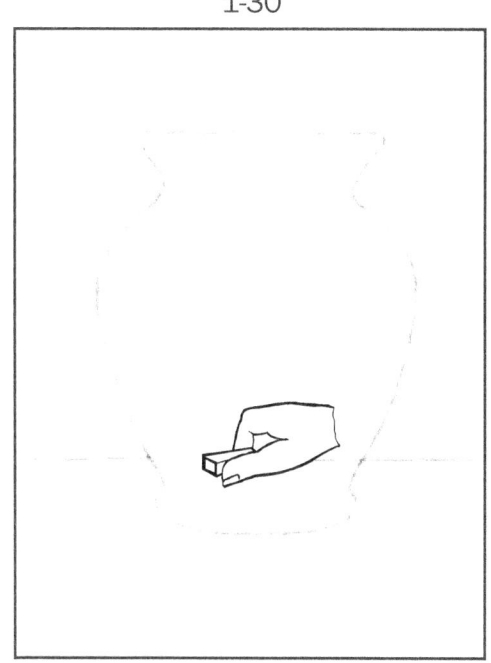

1-31

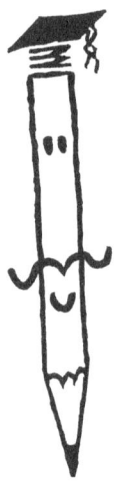

You saw what a progress check did for your streamline. Curves also need evaluation.

Model

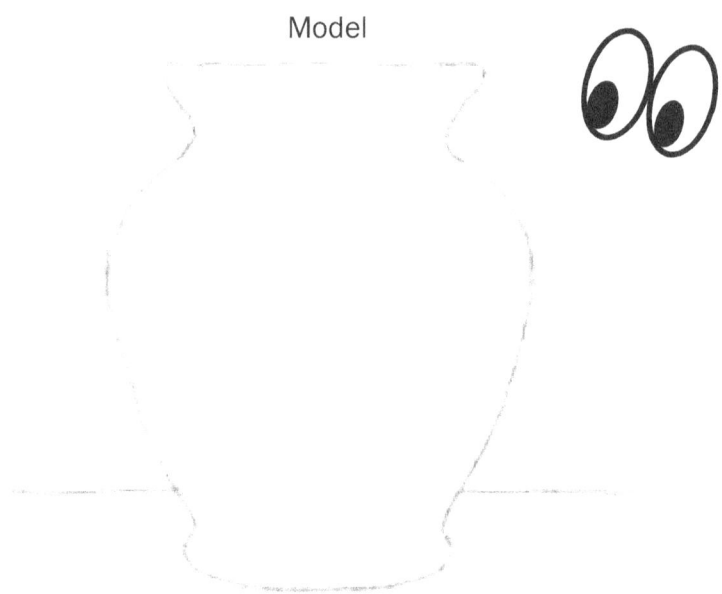

Let's study the following pair of student drawings, *before* and *after* revision. In example 1-32, an alignment survey reveals helpful clues. Apparently, the neck is too short laterally and the left arc needs to align with the respective base arc. After moving the neck arc to the left, the adjustment solved the misalignment as well as the short neck, simultaneously, (1-33).

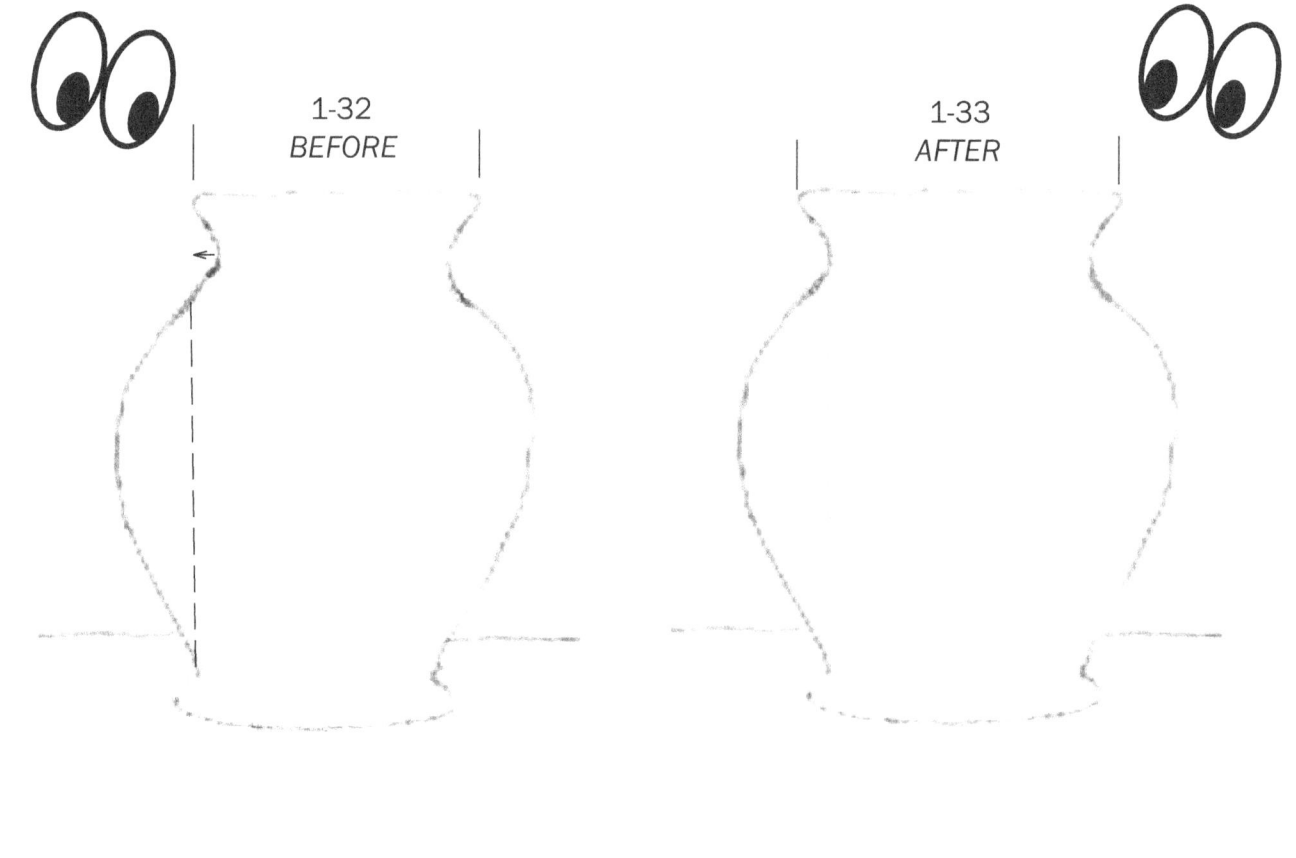

1-32
BEFORE

1-33
AFTER

Here's another great method.

NEGATIVE SPACE-The Amazing Phenomenon

Model 1-34

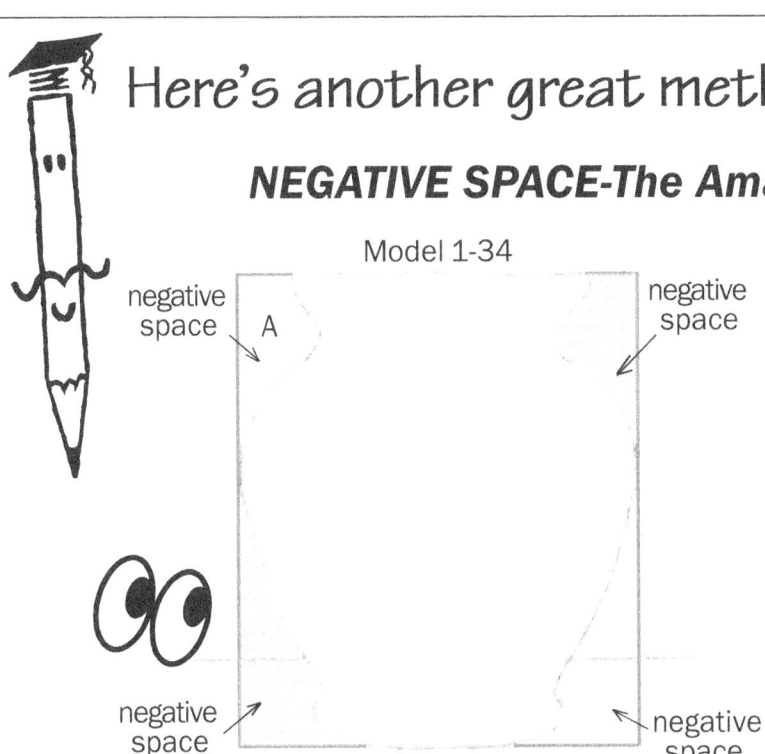

negative space A

negative space

negative space

negative space

Earlier, on page 34, you learned that by visualizing, or using actual guidelines in the *neck curves*, the process helped you draw the right amount of bend. Now let's make believe a rectangle tightly surrounds the *entire* model (1-34). This procedure is another means by which to see opposite shapes displaced by form. I filled a couple of them with gray to improve the visibility. Although commonly known as *negative space*, I prefer the term *reverse* space because the word "negative" suggests something bad. Whether called negative or reverse space, the principle truly comes in handy.

Based on model 1-34, in drawing 1-35 the left upper body curve droops quite a bit. The telltale sign is evident by the *negative space* comparison. After adjustment, (1-36) the curve is less angular and more closely resembles the model. Compare negative space A *before,* to negative space B *after.* The change is subtle, yet significant. The question is, was the *curve* altered, or the *negative space*? It could have been *either way.* When *negative space* changes, so does *positive shape*, and vice versa. Positive and negative shapes are inexorably linked. They affect each other. In the art world, they are *equally* important. At the very least, they offer the option to *draw directly, indirectly and interchangeably.* By working with both negative and positive forms, the combination just about doubles your chances for accuracy.

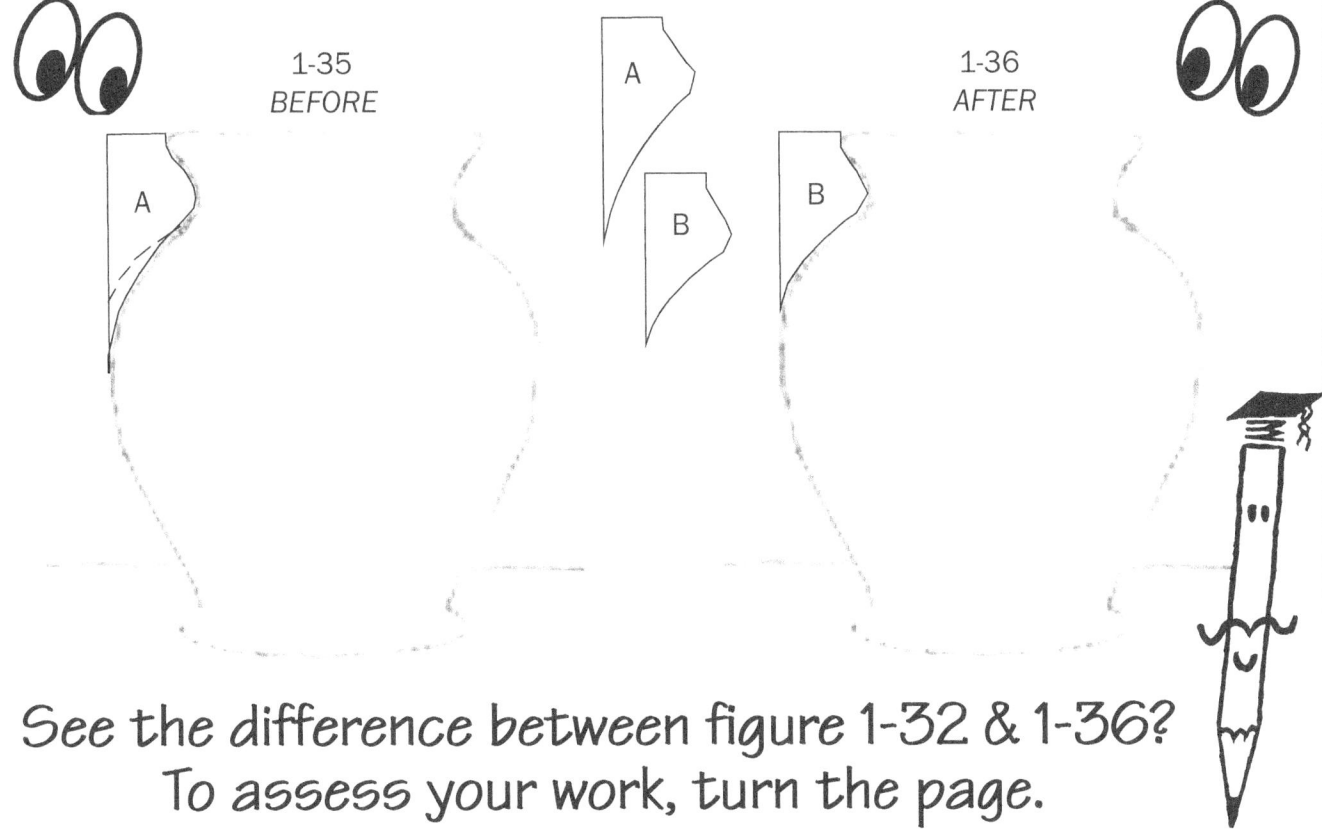

1-35
BEFORE

A

A

B

1-36
AFTER

B

See the difference between figure 1-32 & 1-36?
To assess your work, turn the page.

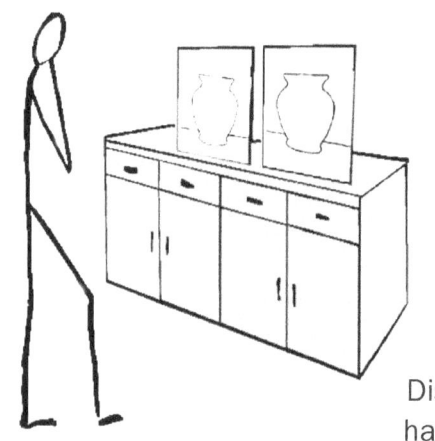

A THOROUGH ONCE OVER
SIDE-BY-SIDE FROM A DISTANCE
IS WELL WORTH THE EFFORT
AFTER EVERY MAJOR PHASE

Distortion may have occurred while drawing your curves and could have gone unnoticed. Having checked your straight lines earlier for accuracy, now verify your arcs to determine how they contribute to your figure's development. *Take your time. The clues are in front of you, but you must look slowly, carefully and methodically.*

Observe from far enough to see both your drawing and the model together. Start your critique by searching for the most prominent disparities. Your figure may be bigger or smaller. That is as it should be, providing things are in *proportion*. Assuming they are, survey for other factors such as alignments and possible tilting. Next, scan for curvature irregularities, like too much bulging on one side, or the other. Ignore the impulse to tally everything, so all the changes can be performed quickly together. Instead, attend to them *individually and <u>confirm</u> the result.* As you do this, be mindful you are *not* searching for "mistakes." *You are seeking to improve what you have done.*

Use the shapes your figure displaces, called *negative space,* as helpful references. You just might detect one upper body curve in your figure has more bend than the other. You may like it better. That doesn't mean it's the one you should guide by. Base your decision on the model in order to make your judgment and your change objectively. Continue by repeating the cycle. Back up and double check the outcome to ensure that you altered wisely. For a new perspective (or *fresh view*), you can also turn both your drawing and your model *sideways.* Should you find your revision made things worse, and restoration becomes necessary, don't get discouraged or blame yourself. Implement what I call *painless experimentation.* Simply trace your figure and test possibilities on the tracing. *Reworking is part of drawing process and part of learning.*

Granted, your latest version could still turn out undesirable and perhaps appear worse than before; so what? At least you tried, having grown wiser from the experience. Often, more can be gained from lack of success than the other way round. Be that as it may, choosing to be content with less than your capability, for fear you might spoil what you have, cheats your potential. On the flip side, working out of control in a frantic attempt to excel way beyond your capacity usually proves futile. The same advice applies for continuing to modify, even after your revisions do not make much difference. Underworking or overworking tend to cause more harm than good.

Freehand drawing is not meant to be an exacting process. Precision is apt to appear stiff. With regard to the figure, symmetry is not the goal, so don't demand perfection. Both sides do not have to match like mirror images. Close is good enough. Aside from that, even if you see further refinement is needed, sometimes your hand may not be able to deliver. If so, leave well enough alone. Unreasonable expectations set you up for disappointment. Your observational skills tend to improve faster than your manual dexterity. Consequently, your eye-hand coordination is perpetually in a state of flux. Alter only to the extent you feel capable, *now.* Sure you could do better tomorrow, next month, next year, but be content with what you did today. When your figure's shape looks fairly accurate to you, *based on your current proficiency,* that's a sensible place to proceed to the next level. You have already accomplished much and you will continue to advance.

STEP 9 Prop up your drawing beside this one, compare from a minimum of four feet. **Don't hesitate. Get back from your table and do a careful side-by-side analysis.** Follow the recommendations, principles and methods you learned on the previous pages (38-40) and your efforts will be rewarded.

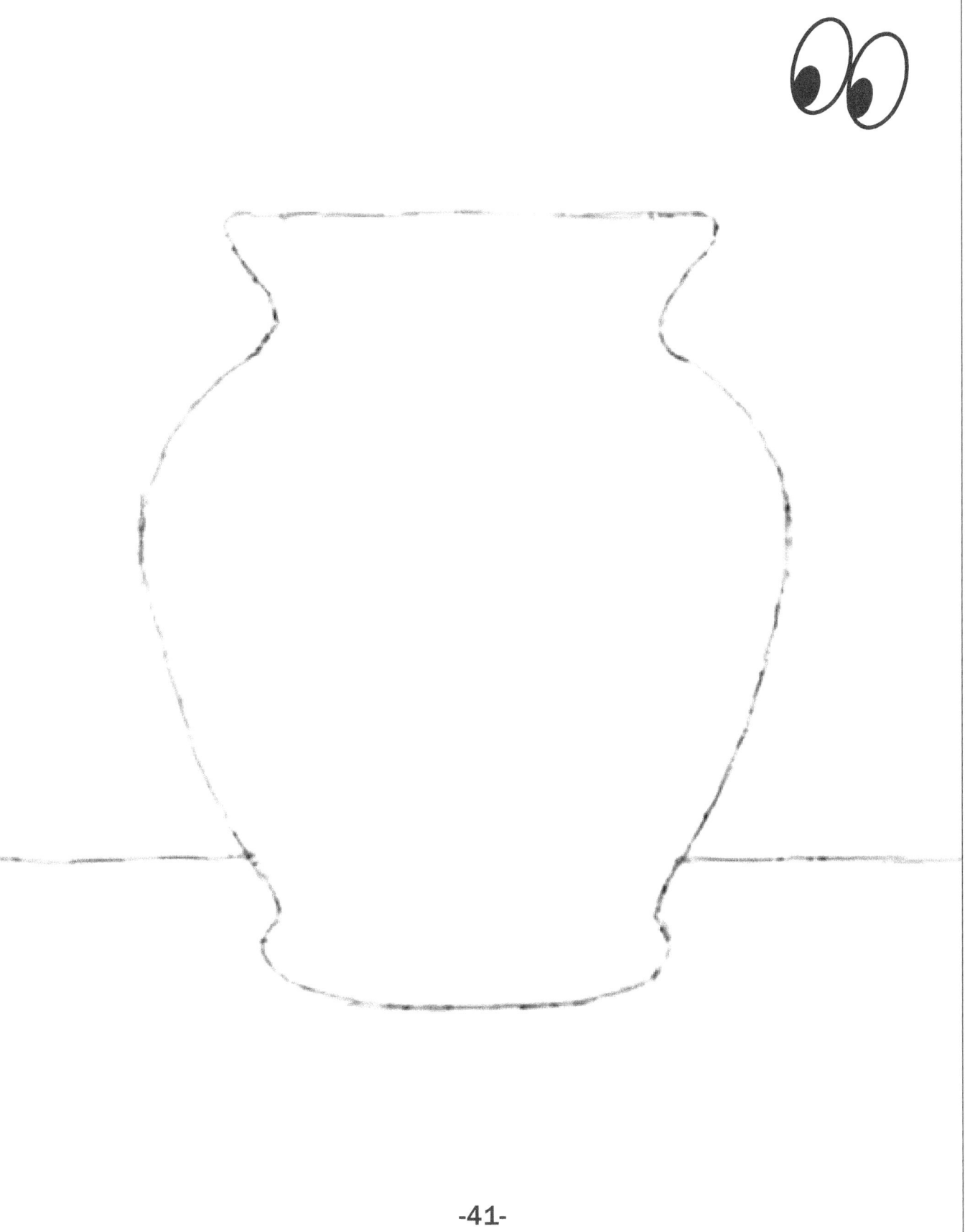

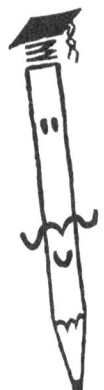

With all the working and reworking, you may find your paper is messy. Possibly your figure ended up in an undesirable position. Simply transfer it to a new sheet.

TRANSFER METHOD

DIRECTIONS: Affix your drawing *backwards* to a window with adhesive tape. *Be sure the side you drew FACES THE GLASS.* During daylight, you will be able to see a reverse image. As shown in illustration 1-37, tone the backside of your figure's boundaries and table line, preferably using the *side* of the point of a 6B (soft lead) pencil. Next, tape a fresh sheet of paper on a board or table. Place your drawing (*now face up*) in the desired location on top of your *new* paper. Fasten it with two strips of adhesive tape along the upper portion. Then re-trace your drawing with dash lines. A colored pencil or a colored pen is recommended. This will enable you to see which lines have been traced and which ones are still needed. The pressure transfers the graphite from the back side of your original to the fresh paper (1-38) Occasionally, lift your upper sheet and verify your progress to determine how much pressure is too much, and how much is just right (1-39). When you have finished, carefully remove your tape strips. Your duplicate drawing will resemble illustration 1-40. Although my marks are dark to make them prominent, yours should be barely visible. If you like, your can *lightly* connect your dots to form a faint outline.

1-37

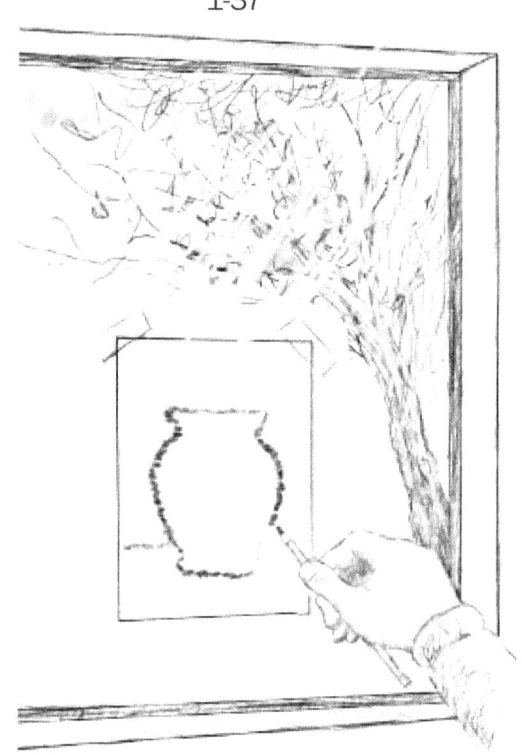

TIP If you have run out of daylight and you happen to have a glass door between one room and another, you can attach your drawing to the glass door. Then turn the light on in the room facing you.

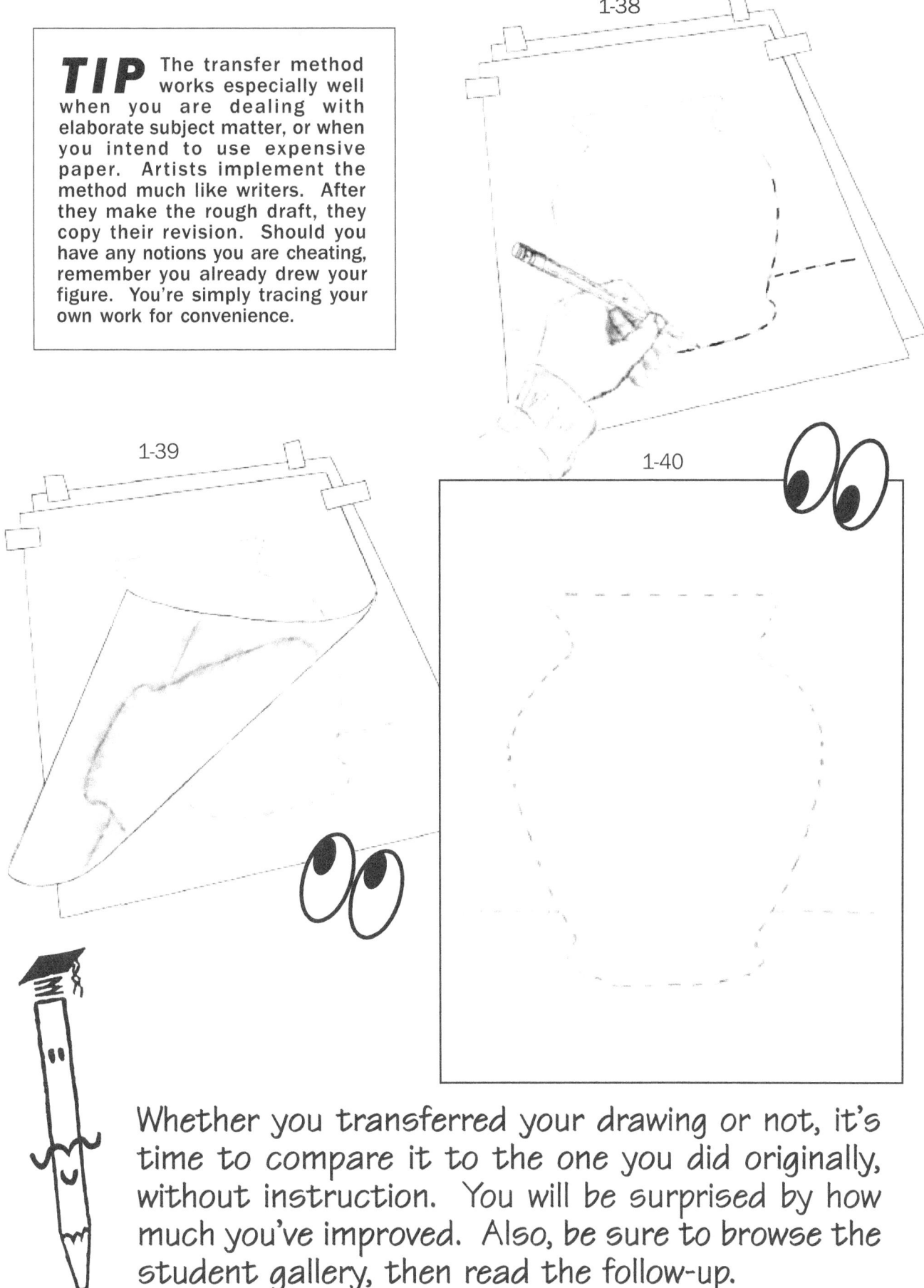

1-38

1-39

1-40

Whether you transferred your drawing or not, it's time to compare it to the one you did originally, without instruction. You will be surprised by how much you've improved. Also, be sure to browse the student gallery, then read the follow-up.

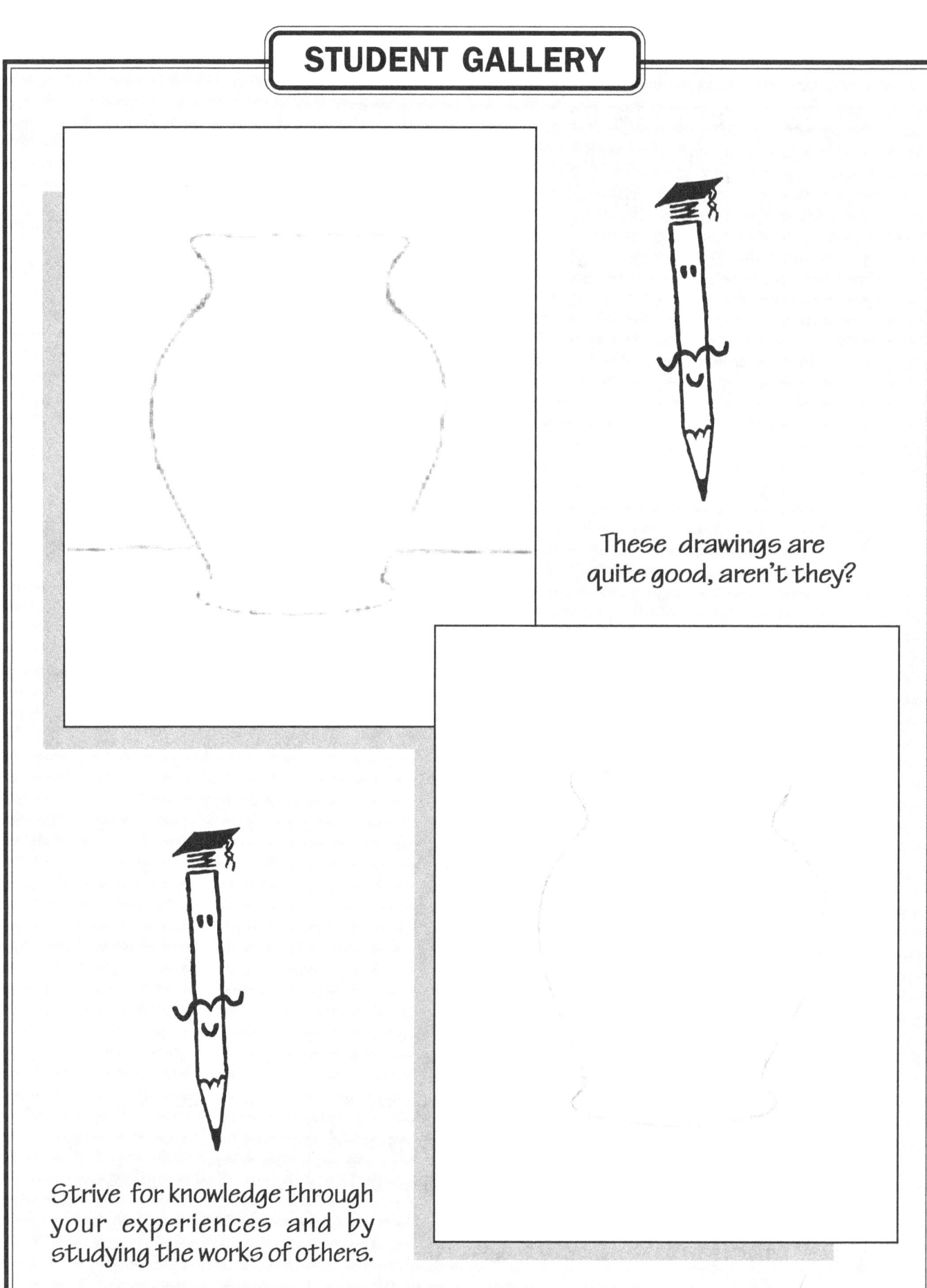

These drawings are quite good, aren't they?

Strive for knowledge through your experiences and by studying the works of others.

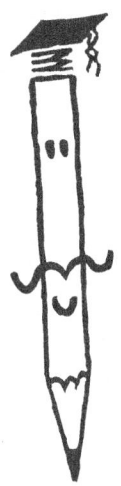

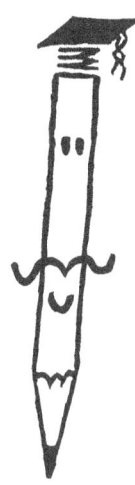

The true measure of your achievement is not how well you think you did. It's what you learned that counts.

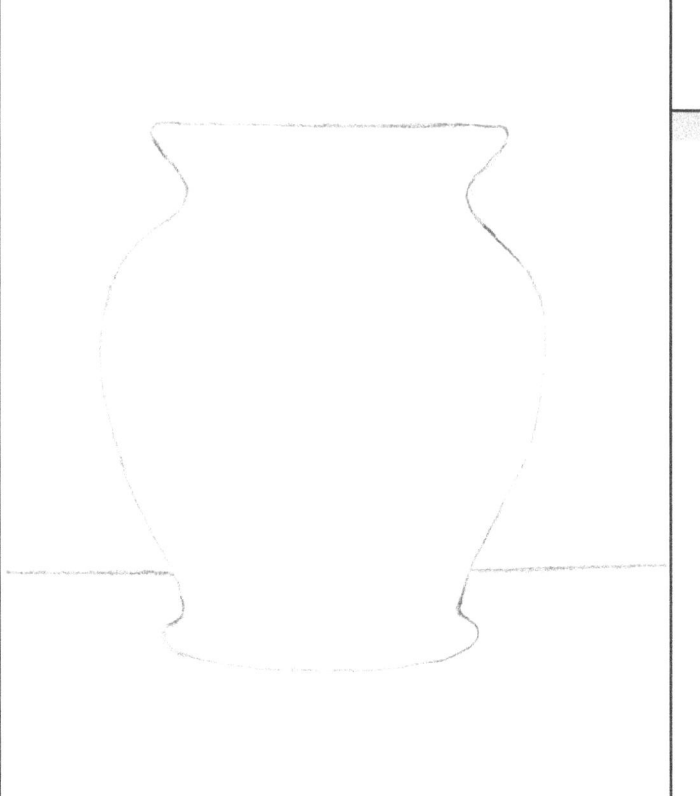

Isn't it great that each version is unique? I'm sure yours is, too. Take pride in your accomplishment.

Chapter 1
FOLLOW-UP

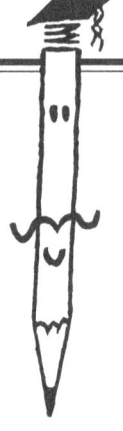

You've learned a lot, haven't you? Let's recap.

1. Drawing is a process which can be organized into manageable steps and stages.

2. Becoming familiar with your subject BEFORE you begin to draw is very helpful.

3. Shapes can be taken apart with your eyes.

4. Squinting (partly closing your eyes) helps to see basic shapes more easily.

5. Much of what you are searching for is right in front of you but you have to take the time to look.

6. When drawing on flat surfaces, it is important to see shapes in two dimensional terms: *horizontal and vertical.*

7. At the start, it's sensible to *plan ahead* by taking placement and size into consideration. Otherwise, you might run out of room or end up with a drawing that is smaller than you may have wanted.

8. Drawing lightly is practical because you can erase guidelines and make adjustments more easily.

9. Streamlining with guidelines is a worthwhile means by which to "map out" (or chart) a course for shape.

10. Reference points, alignments, straight lines, curves, angles, proportions and negative spaces are the *Trusty 7* handy ways by which to assess and draw the structural aspects of shape.

11. Whether the model you are working from is real or a picture, pausing to stand back and conduct side-by-side comparisons is not only a smart practice during the drawing stages, but afterward as well.

All told, this is quite a tally indeed.
And now that you're off to a marvelous start, always remember:

Successful drawing doesn't stem from able HANDS alone.
It also comes from skillful THINKING and OBSERVING.
Hone all three of your abilities.

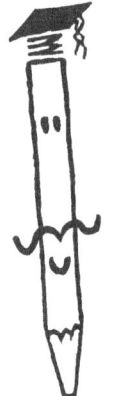

Now, take a break. Another day, resume by turning to Chapter 2. Or explore other exciting ways you can draw the figure by continuing to Chapter 1 A, then 1B.

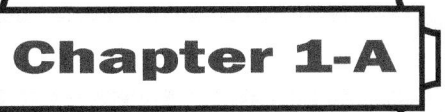

Chapter 1-A

FROM THIS...

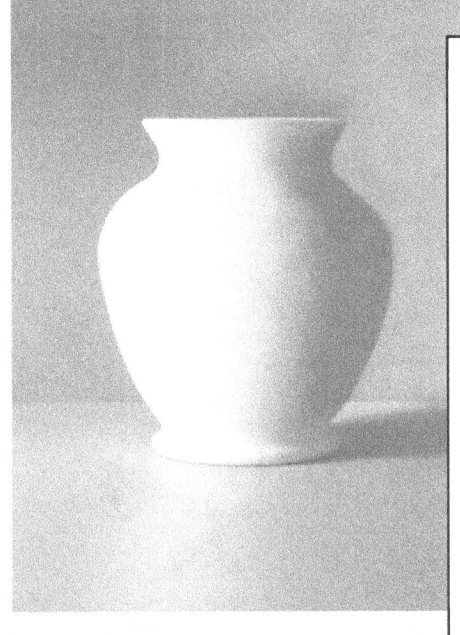

...TO THIS

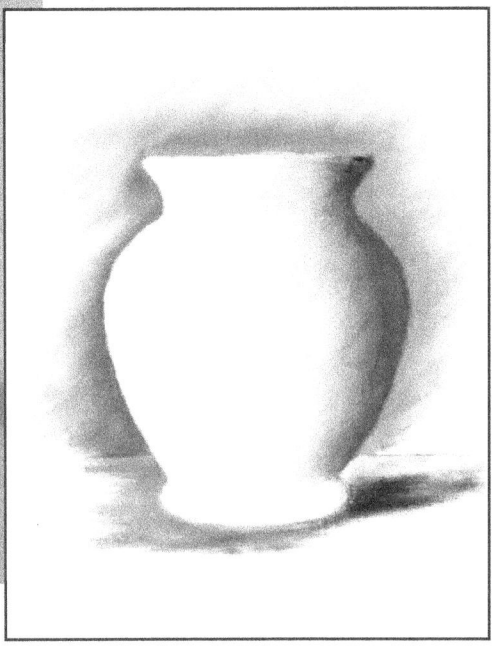

BEGINS with RANDOM SHAPING

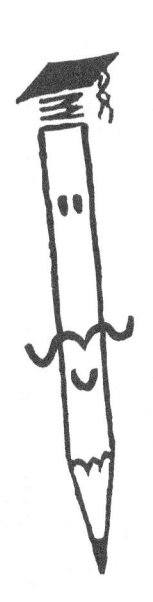

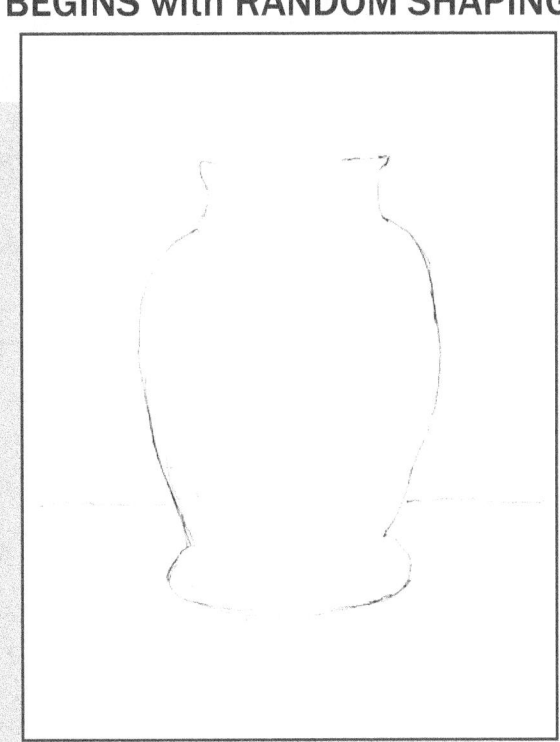

A snap, when you understand the process.

How is random shaping achieved? Imagination sees the forms made with lines. Eye-hand coordination kicks in to produce a likeness.

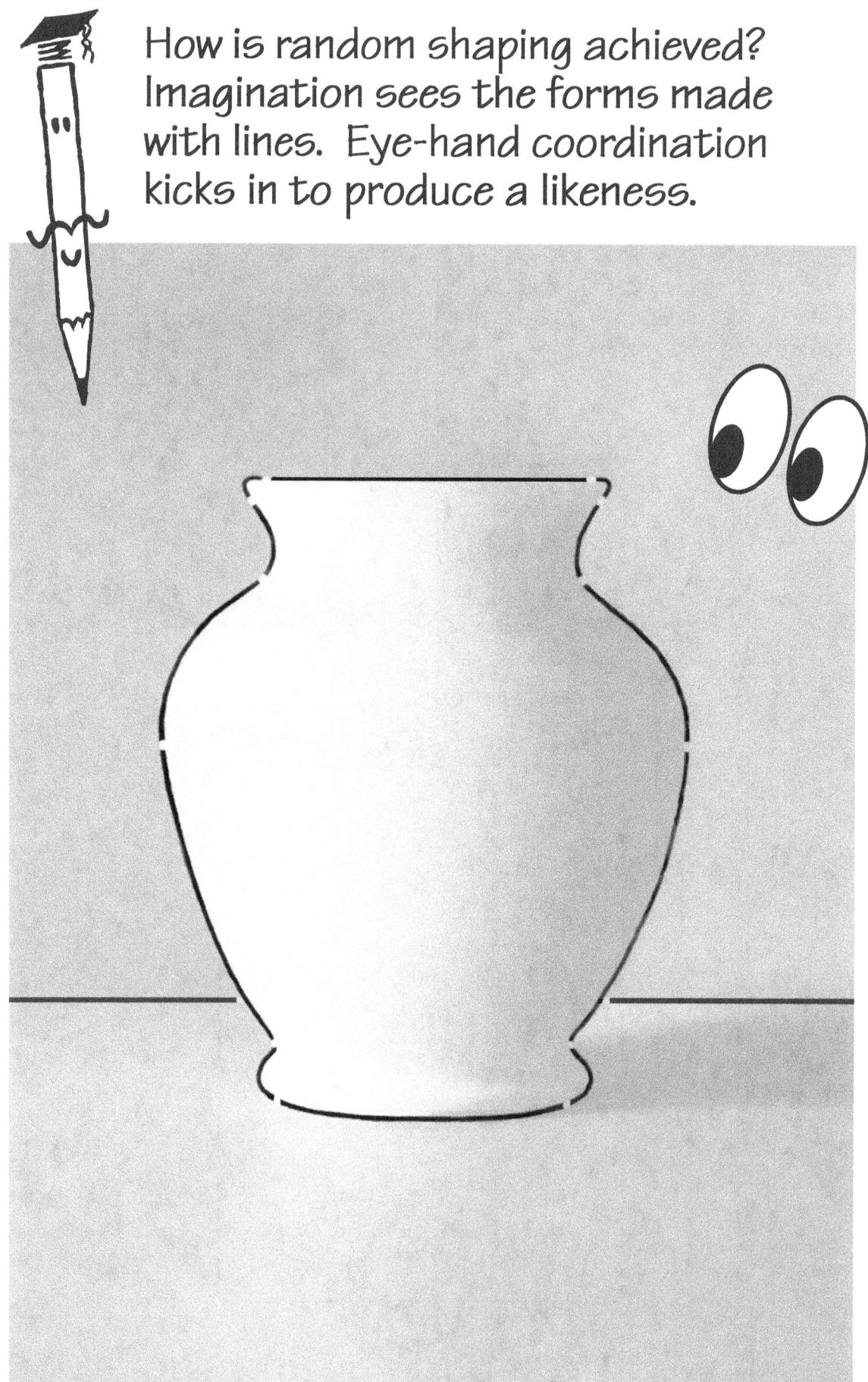

Here's a typical example of random shaping by a beginner.

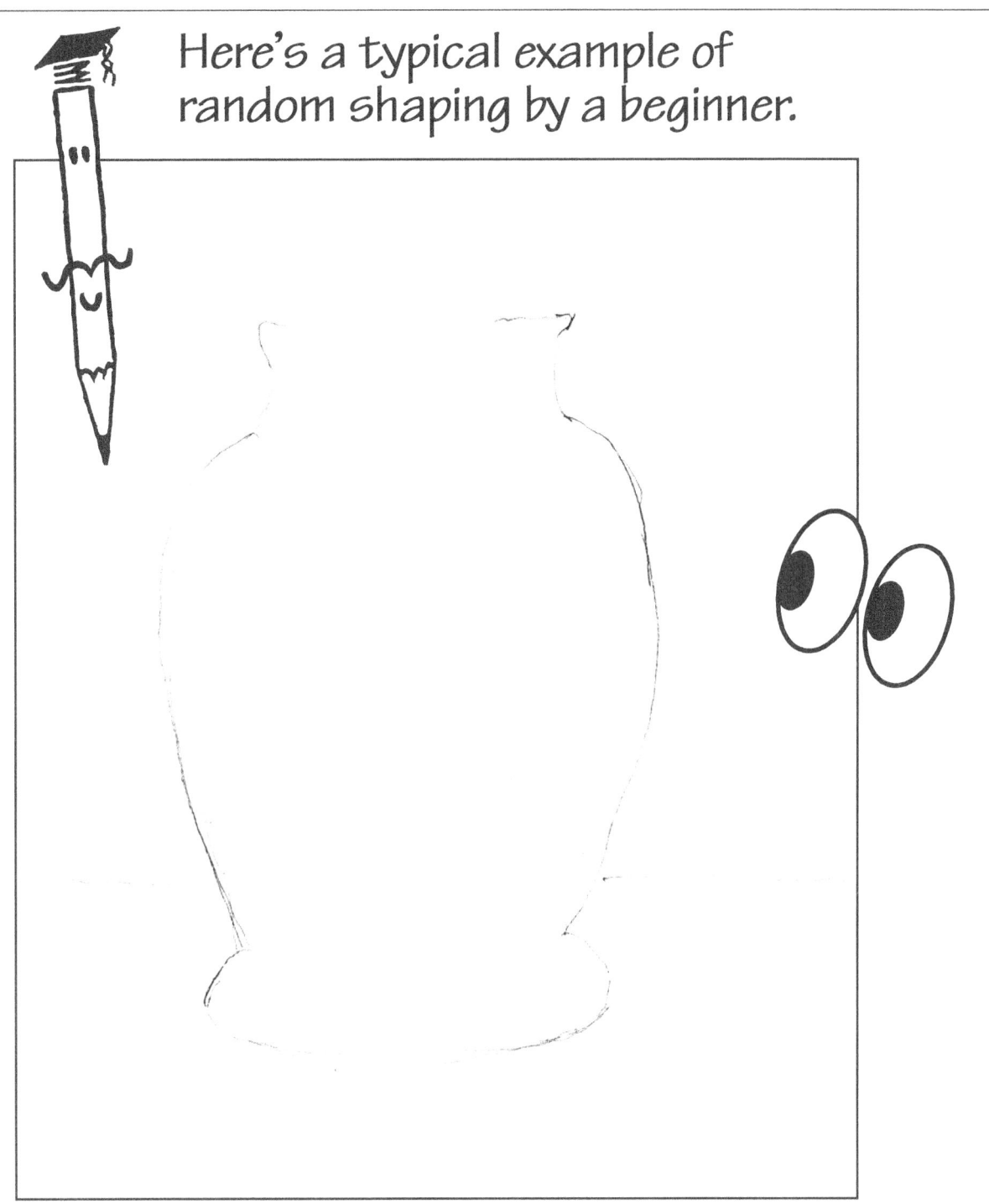

Random shaping comes with a multitude of delights. Unlike the structural method, this technique is faster, more liberating and full of fabulous surprises. While the individual lines are being formed, you only have a slight notion how your picture will eventually turn out. Working feverishly, you glance back and forth between your drawing and your model, doing your best to copy what you see. With growing anticipation, you check results for accuracy, modify if necessary, and move to another area. Piece by piece, sections start to fit together until finally, the moment arrives. You survey the whole picture to discover some features exceeded expectation. Others didn't fare as well. What do you do? Start over? Throw your hands up in disgust? No. You work with what you've got. Beginners think they are done when all the lines are formed. That *CAN* be the end, unless you desire *more*. Random drawing offers freedom, speed, as well as adventure into the unknown, not to mention a nice bonus: a promising foundation on which to build, including the one above. Read on to find out how.

A side-by-side comparison and a bit of tweaking can accomplish amazing feats.

Compared to the model, the form similarity in drawing 1-41 is not very close, is it? To remedy the situation, the same *structural components* used for drawing and verification can be put to work for revision. I call these the TRUSTY 7. In *no particular order*, they are: *reference points, alignments, proportion, straight lines, curves, angles, and negative space.* Administered in any sequence, individually or in combination, they expose virtually everything about shape. For instance, with regard to *proportion*, figure 1-41 is apparently too tall or too thin (whichever way you prefer to see it). Reducing the height, or extending the distance across, improves the body's *overall proportion* (see page 13). Next, sub-proportion shown in illustration 1-42 indicates the base needs to be smaller. After adjustment, what may *not* have been apparent becomes evident. The left inside neck curve should be *aligned* with the respective inside base curve, (1-43). When that's moved, the neck *curves* reveal they also require change (1-44). Are you catching on? By process of elimination, using various factors of the Trusty 7, slowly but surely, a marvelous transformation can take place (1-45).

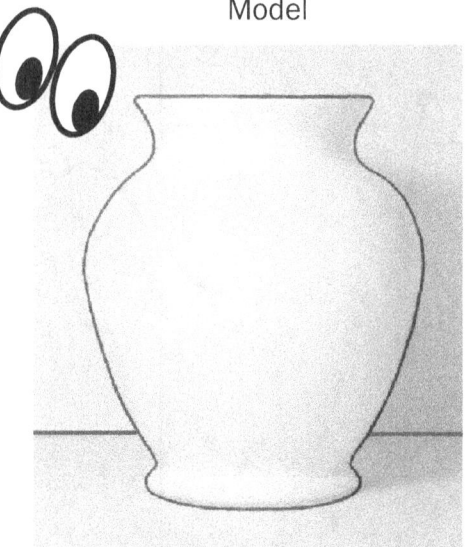

Model

1-41 Body scale too tall or too narrow

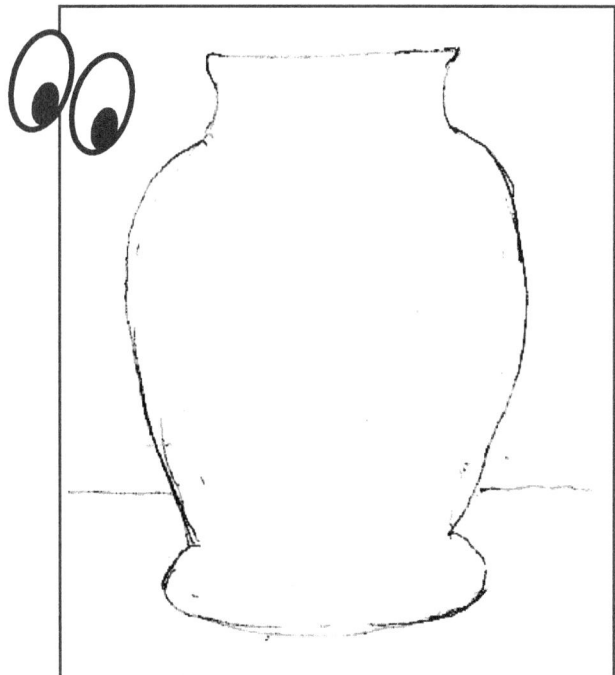

1-42 Body scale adjusted-Base is too big

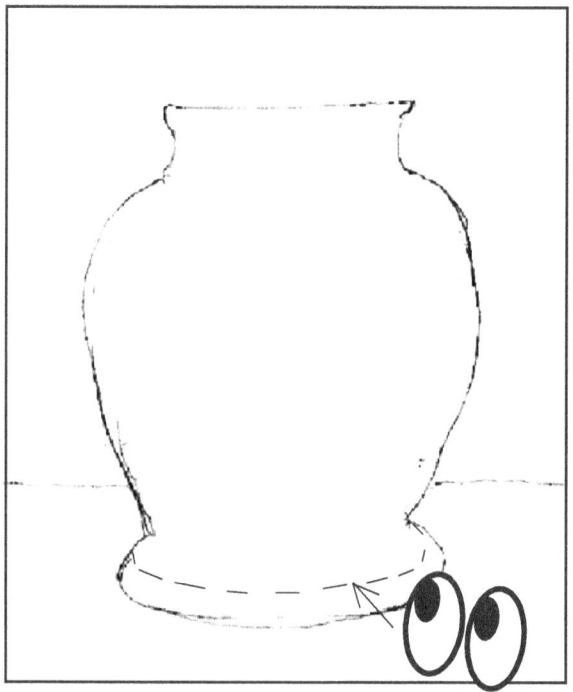

1-43 Base adjusted-Left side neck curve must align with left side base curve

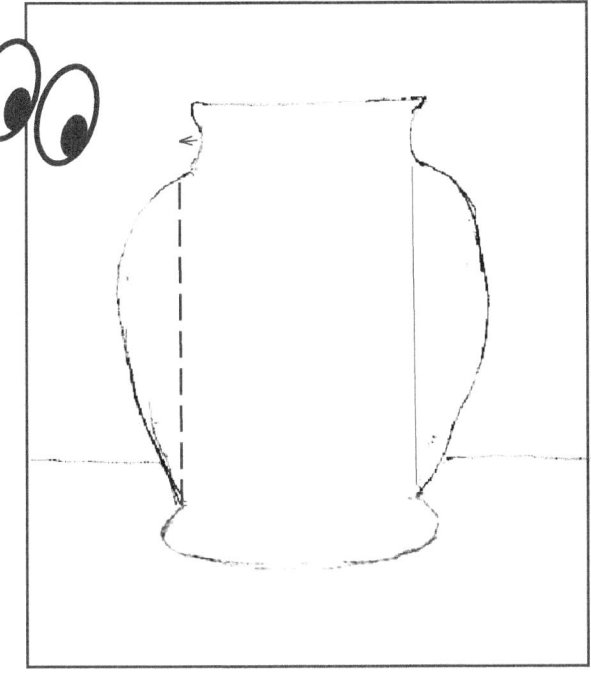

1-44 Alignment adjusted
Neck curves need alteration

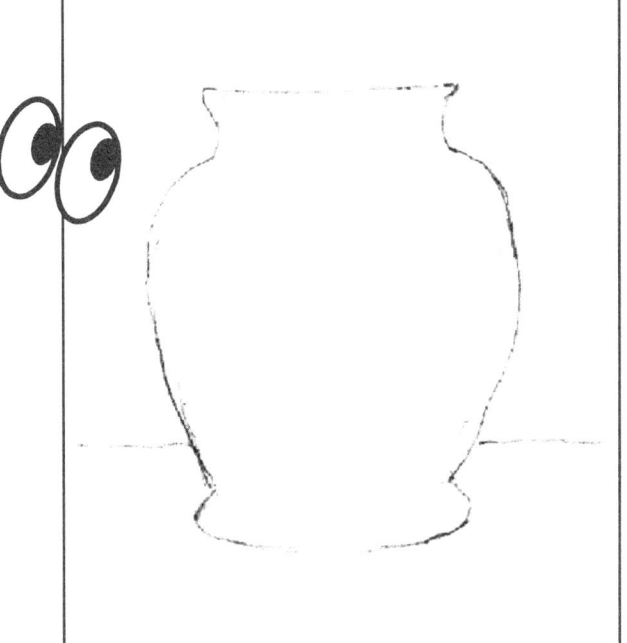

1-45 Neck curves modified

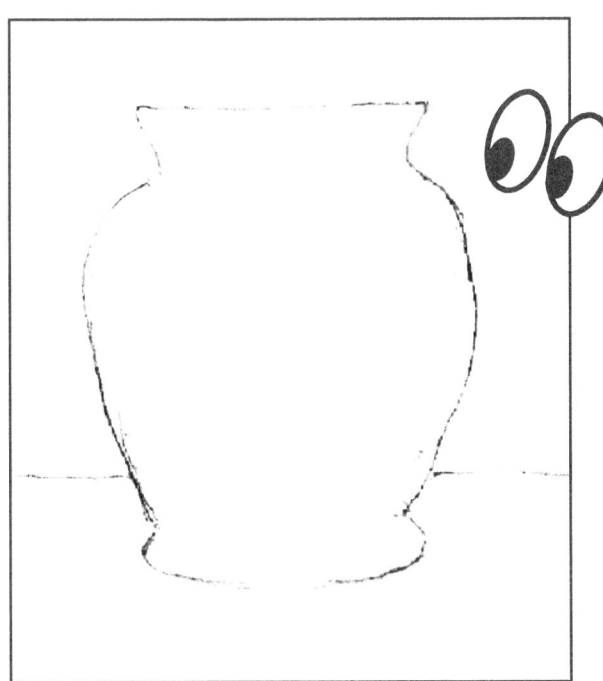

Let's look at example 1-41 (before adjustment) and example 1-45 (after adjustment) with respect to the model. As you can tell, the form *with* modification is a closer match. More fine tuning can be done of course, but all in all, the side-by-side comparison/revision method is proving to be quite effective, isn't it? The procedure functions best when each progressive change is handled and verified *individually*. One thing usually leads to another, occasionally revealing a different area should really have been altered. No big deal. Working and reworking is all part of the routine. It's a game of hide and seek. The areas requiring adjustment hide from you. Your task is to find them.

TIP Negative space is a terrific way to check accuracy. See how it works on pages 35 & 39.

Let's survey another random
drawing example on the next page.

Impressive, what a little revision can produce.

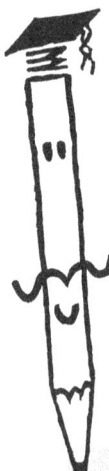

As the illustration 1-46 shows, compared to the model, the inside *neck* curves are not aligned with the inside *base* curves. Since the figure's base is fairly proportional, the *neck* curves are the logical choice to move. After doing precisely that (1-47), the *right side body curve* reveals it requires modification as well (1-48). Compare *revised* figure 1-49 to figure 1-50 *before* revision. Although some areas still remain unattended, the general shape already more closely resembles the model, wouldn't you agree?

Model

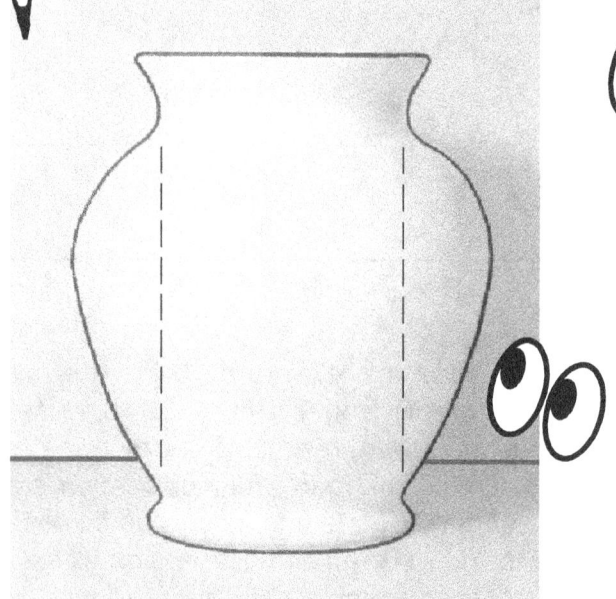

1-46 Inside neck curves need to align with base curves

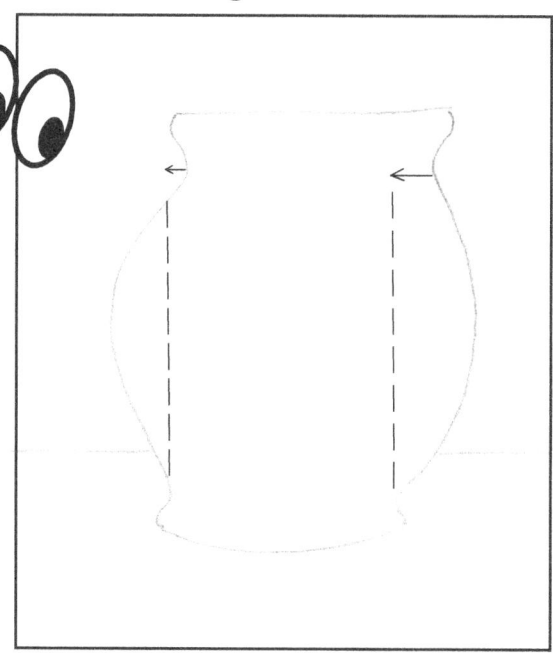

1-47 Neck curves moved

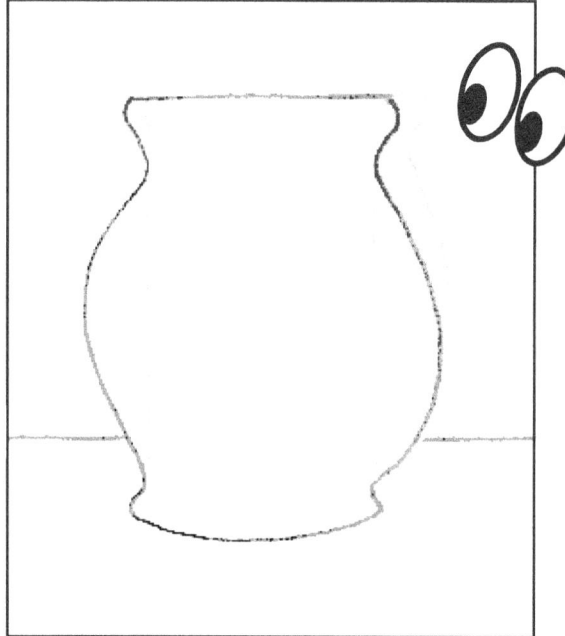

1-48 Right side body curve needs adjusting

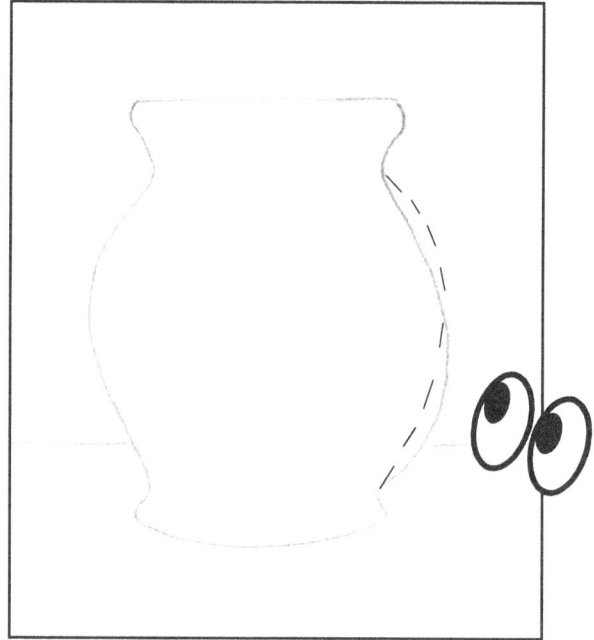

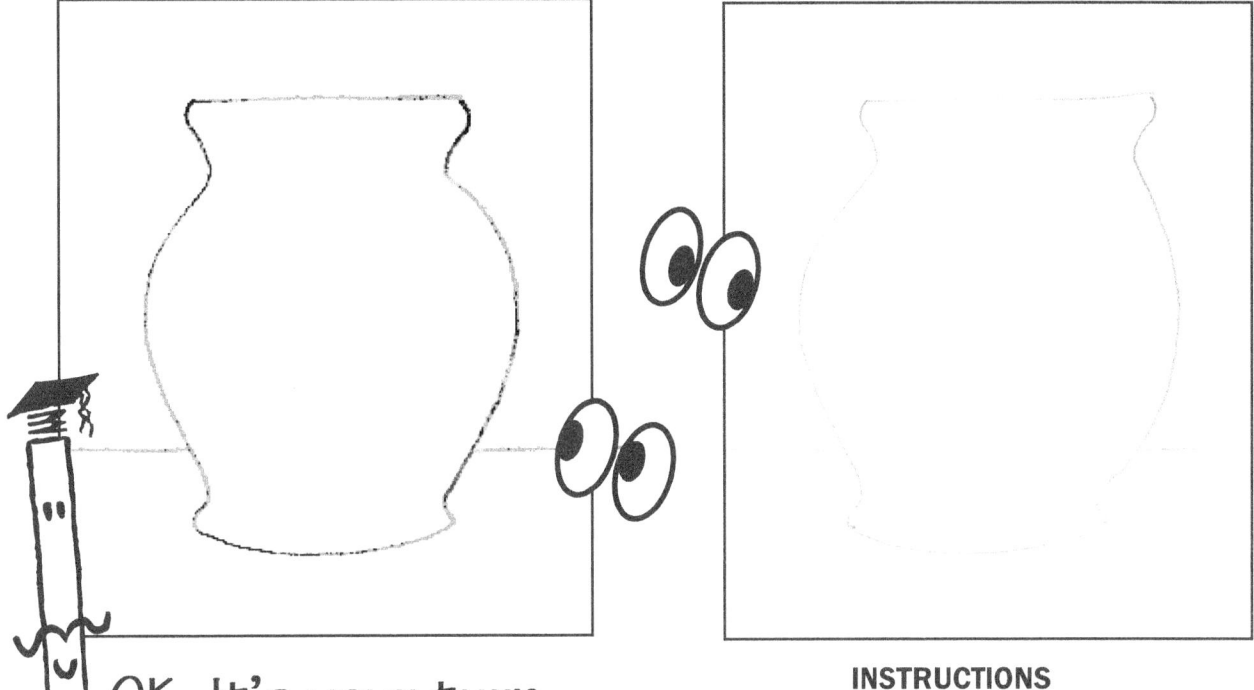

OK. It's your turn. Get ready to draw... ...randomly.

INSTRUCTIONS

Plan ahead. Using the large outline of the model on page 48 for reference, imagine your figure is already on your paper. This helps choose size and placement. Having made your decision, begin your picture anywhere. For instance, start with the top of the figure, then draw the two side curves. Long curves, like the two lower body curves and the bottom base curve, can be formed with *two halves* each. Perhaps you would rather draw an upper body curve first, and advance clockwise, or counter clock wise. You could even initiate with the lines representing the back of the table. With the random approach, the options are wide open, but work *lightly*. Erasing and revisions are more manageable. Apply the continuous or sketch line method or combine them. For the *continuous line*, place your pencil on the paper. Do not lift until a line is finished. If you prefer *sketch lines*, make them with short, overlapping strokes in one direction, as well as back and forth. Choose whatever sequence and techniques work best for you. The important thing is to keep the TRUSTY 7 components in mind as you draw the figure, line by line.

Refinement Stage: Once you have the figure formed, give your work a thorough evaluation. Refer to the large model on page 48. As you make your side-by-side comparison, be sure to take advantage of the recommendations on page 27 and page 40. Pay special attention to the adjustment tips. If you feel uncertain about a possible change, trace your drawing. Then test the revision on the tracing. While we're on the subject of changes, you might eventually find erasing and altering causes messiness, and/or your figure could wind up on your paper in an undesirable position. Easily solved; you can transfer your drawing to a fresh sheet. The directions are on page 42. Of course you may choose to skip the transfer step, but it's nice to have it available when needed.

After creating your figure, compare it to the one you did originally, without instruction. You will be amazed by your improvement. Be sure to also browse the student gallery, (next pages.) Then read the follow-up.

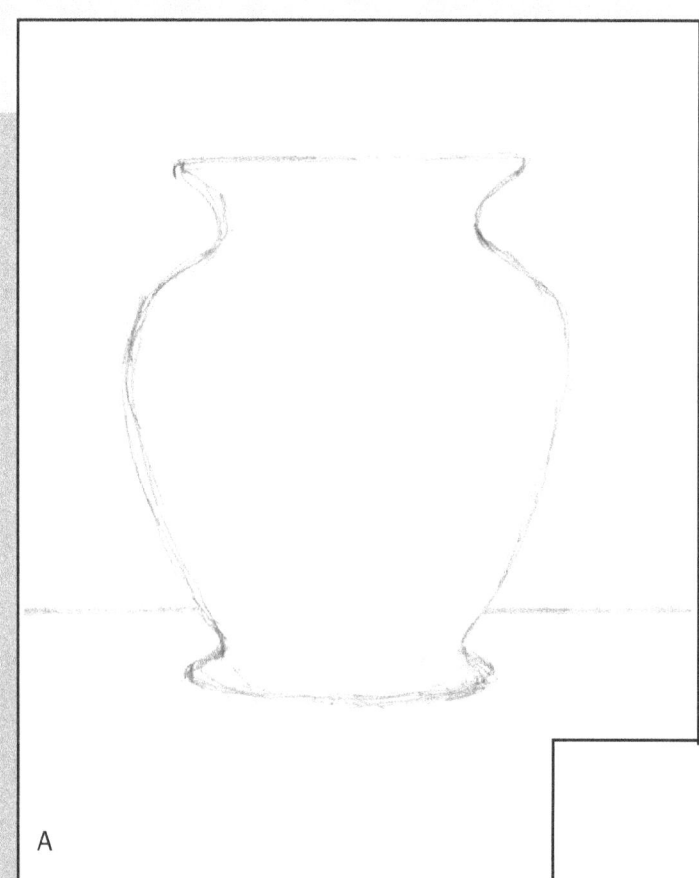

A

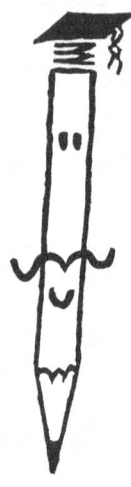

Strive for knowledge through your experiences and by studying the works of others.

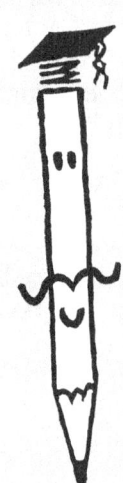

These drawings are quite good, aren't they? Notice the sketch line method in example (A) and (D) compared to the continuous line method in (B) & (C).

B

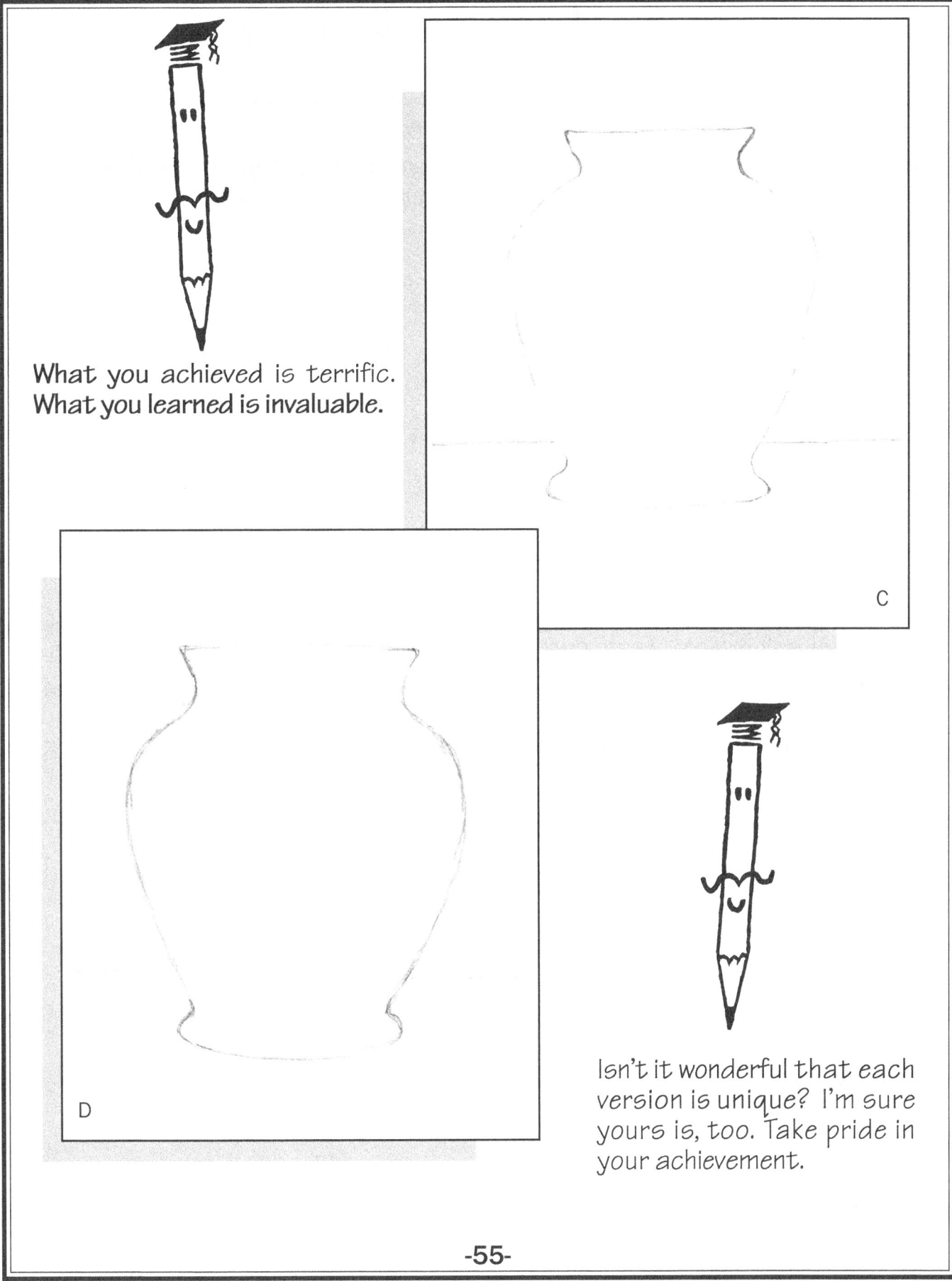

What you achieved is terrific. What you learned is invaluable.

C

D

Isn't it wonderful that each version is unique? I'm sure yours is, too. Take pride in your achievement.

Chapter 1-A
FOLLOW-UP

I bet, you were surprised to see how effectively a random drawing can be utilized as a foundation. The key is knowing what to look for by initiating the TRUSTY 7 shaping components. In no particular order, they are:

* REFERENCE POINTS
* ALIGNMENTS
* PROPORTION
* STRAIGHT LINES
* CURVES
* ANGLES
* NEGATIVE SPACE

A word of caution is warranted here. Because the Trusty 7 can help replicate shapes with or without guidelines, this doesn't justify abandoning the *structural approach* in favor of the random method. Both procedures have their merits. Like tools at your beck and call, they can be used interchangeably. You see, there isn't just one way to draw, there are many. Each has specific functions and advantages. At this stage of your advancement, it's not only OK to experiment, it's *encouraged*!

Drawing shouldn't be confining or restrictive. In fact, the next chapter introduces techniques offering even more flexibility.

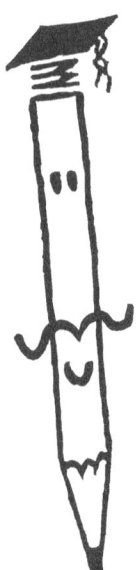

Yes, you could skip Chapter 1B and go directly to Chapter 2, but you would miss out on a valuable drawing experience.

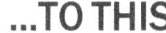

FROM THIS...

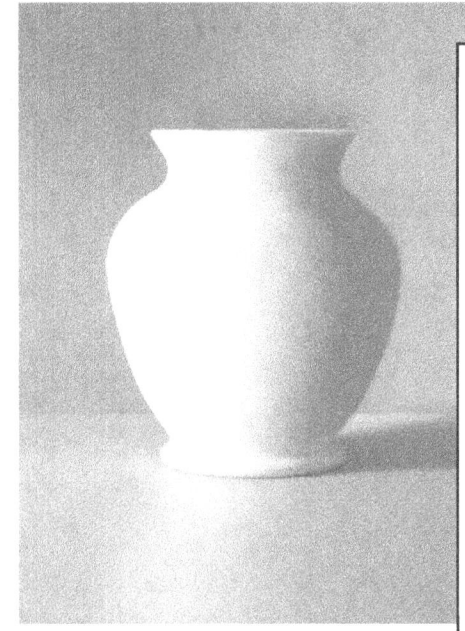

...TO THIS

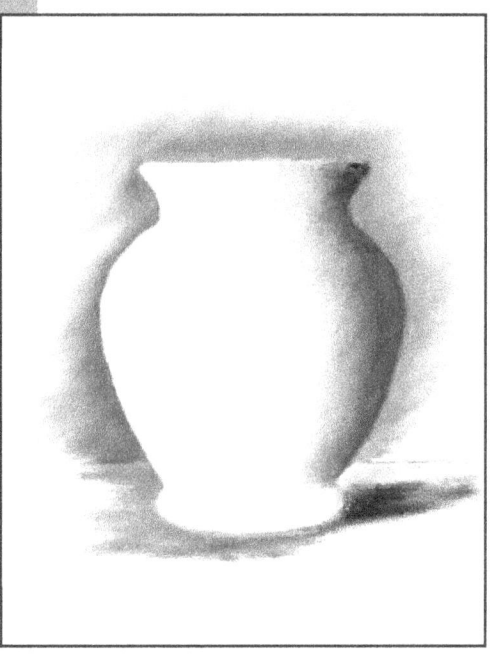

STARTS with a SQUIGGLE

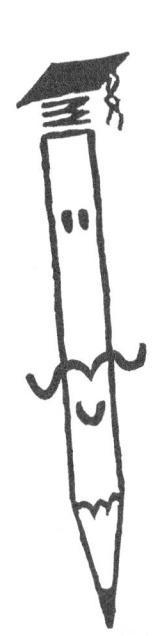

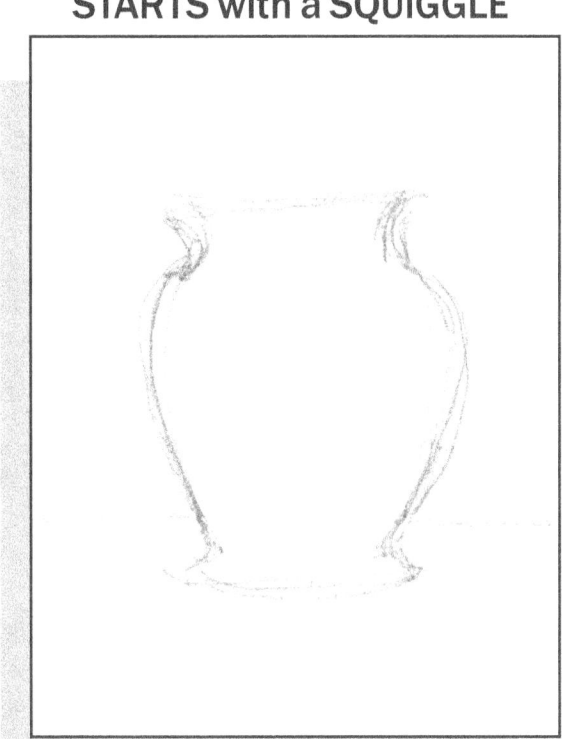

It's simple. Just let yourself go.

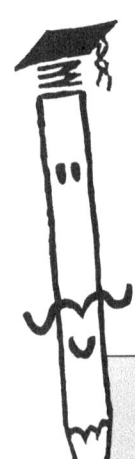

How is a squiggle drawing accomplished?
Eyes scan the model. Instinct takes over.
The hand responds, directing the pencil
and a likeness appears, SPONTANEOUSLY.

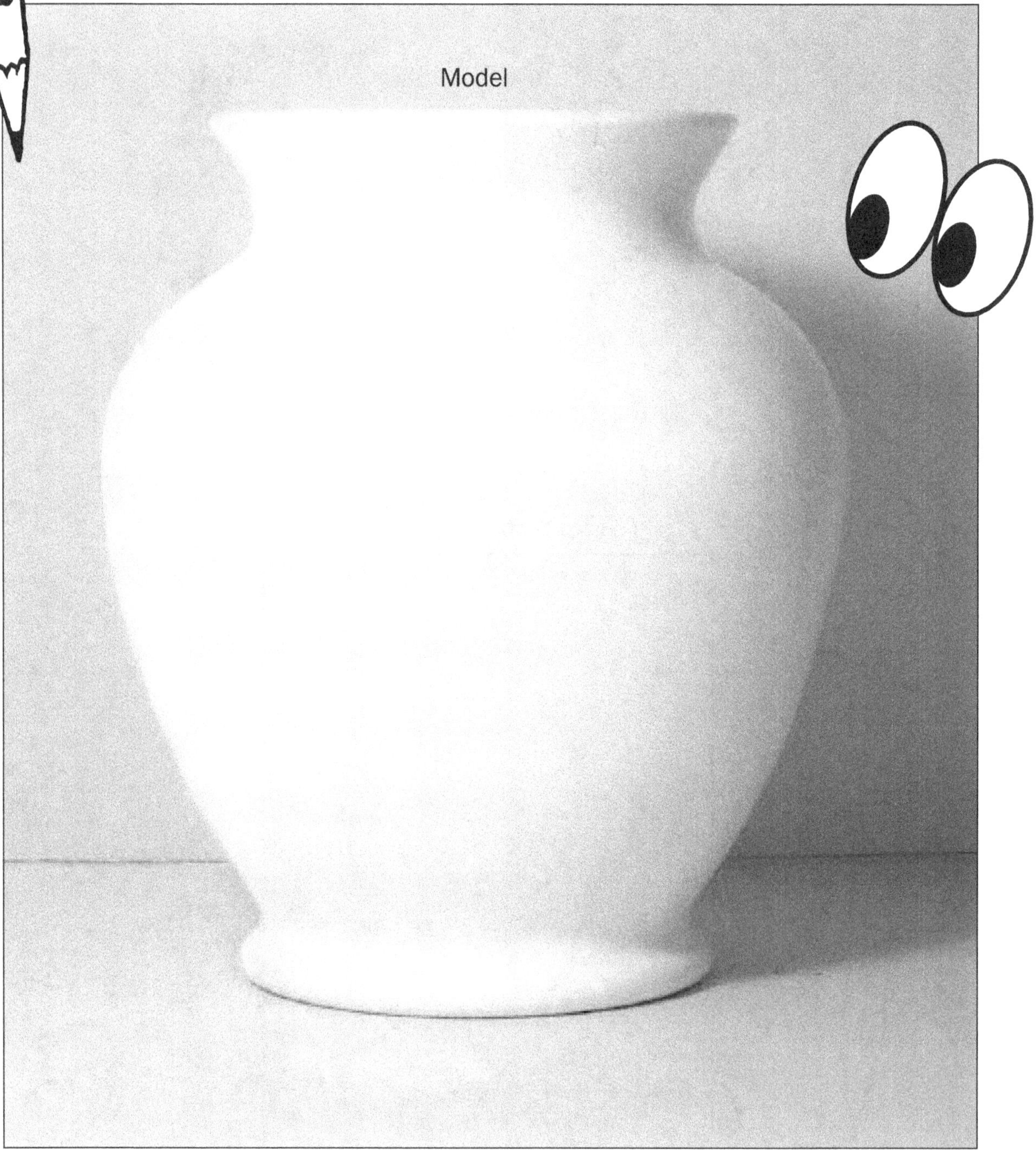

Model

Here's an example of a squiggle.

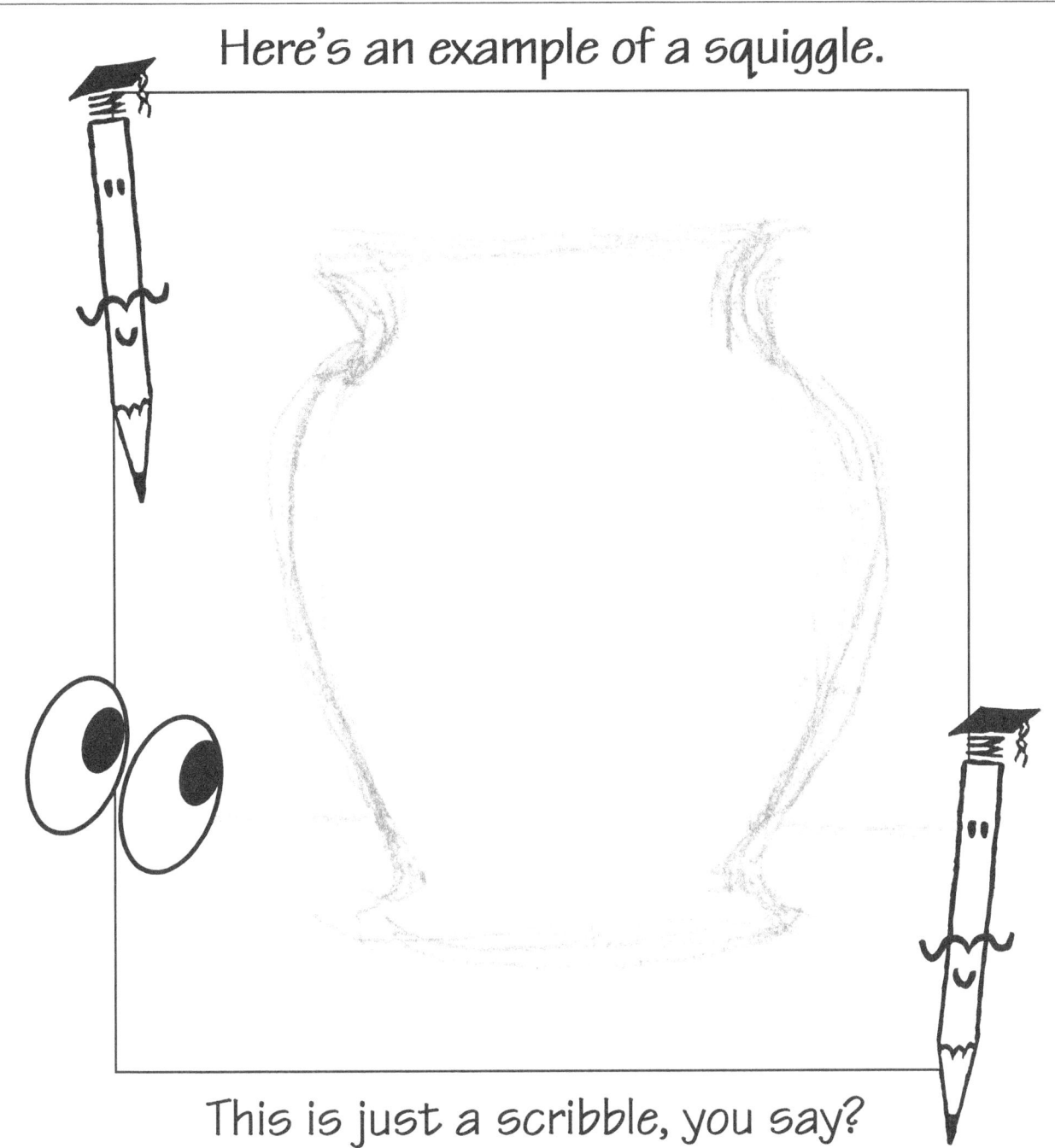

This is just a scribble, you say?

Yes, but it's a whole lot more. Squiggling is a form of doodling, generated by impulse. The mind is subordinate. Once the pencil touches the paper, it is seldom lifted until the job is done. As the eyes scan the model, the hand records the movements in synchronized succession. Before you know it, the image reveals itself seemingly by chance. Now you may be wondering, if squiggling is so haphazard, why not organize a layout with the structural method and be more certain of results. Or maybe you're thinking the random method is more appropriate. Although some control is sacrificed for speed, the process is far less of a gamble. Right on both counts. Squiggling definitely involves the most risk. But that's part of the fun. Outcomes are never predictable, yet they usually turn out awesome and spectacular. Personally, I find this squiggle already brimming with character and personality. It stands alone as a testament to the drawing experience. By the same token, like the structural and random approaches, a squiggle can also provide a foundation. After all, once something is down on paper, it's easier to spot the things that work and find those that don't. Keep reading to learn how this is achieved.

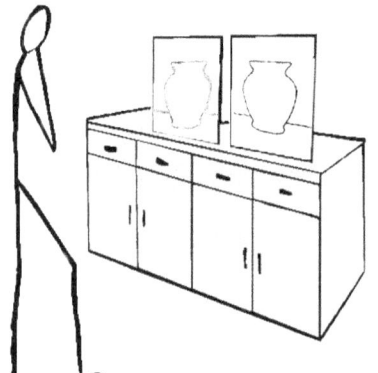

Side-by-side comparison and some minor adjustment does it.

Model

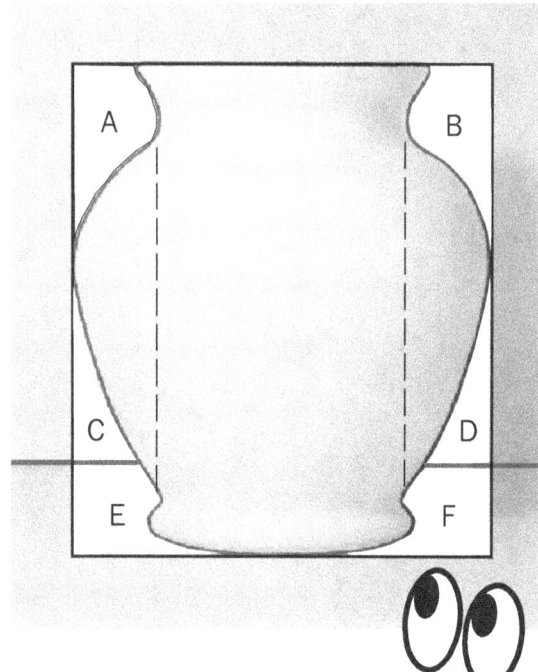

Watch how the squiggle from the previous page easily converts to a solitary outline. The method is similar to the way a structured drawing (p38-40) and a random sketch (p50-53) can be assessed and altered. The key is the TRUSTY 7 shaping components. As you will recall these are *reference points, alignments, straight lines, curves, angles, negative space and proportion.* For instance, compared to the model, the squiggle's overall *proportion* appears to be OK. *Alignment* wise, the *reference points* between the inside neck and base *curves* also confirm accuracy. As for *angles,* however, the top should not be tilted (1-51). Moreover, a survey for *negative space* shows B, D and F are a close match but, A, C and E are not (1-52). If the non matching negative spaces were extended and formed to more closely resemble the model, the figure's left side would improve as well. Diagram 1-53 illustrates.

1-51 Scale & Alignment OK

1-52 Left side negative spaces need extending and shaping

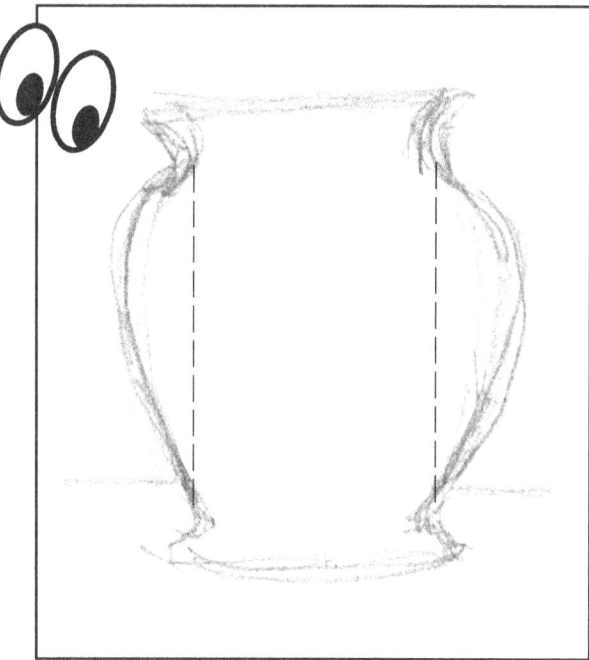

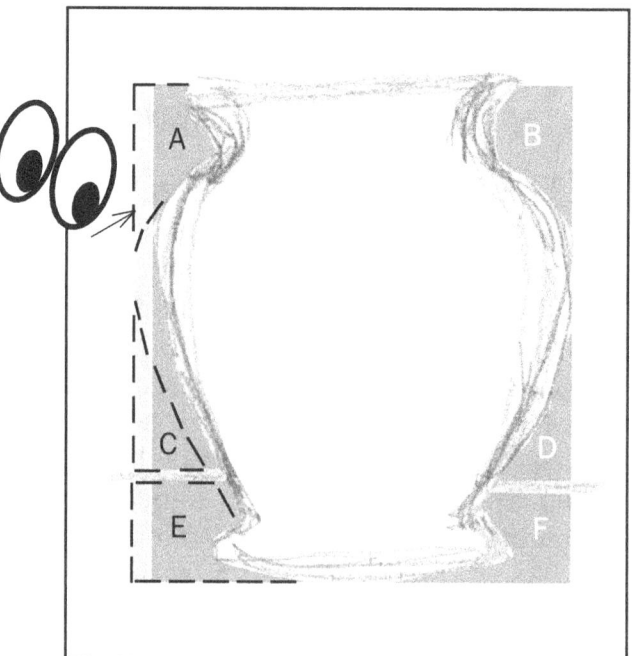

Examine former squiggle 1-52 and revised squiggle 1-53. Then study diagram 1-54 showing the potential (dark outline), if excess lines (light gray) are erased. Illustration 1-55 reveals the outcome. With additional fine tuning, the conversion is complete, (1-56). See how well a squiggle doubles as a foundation?

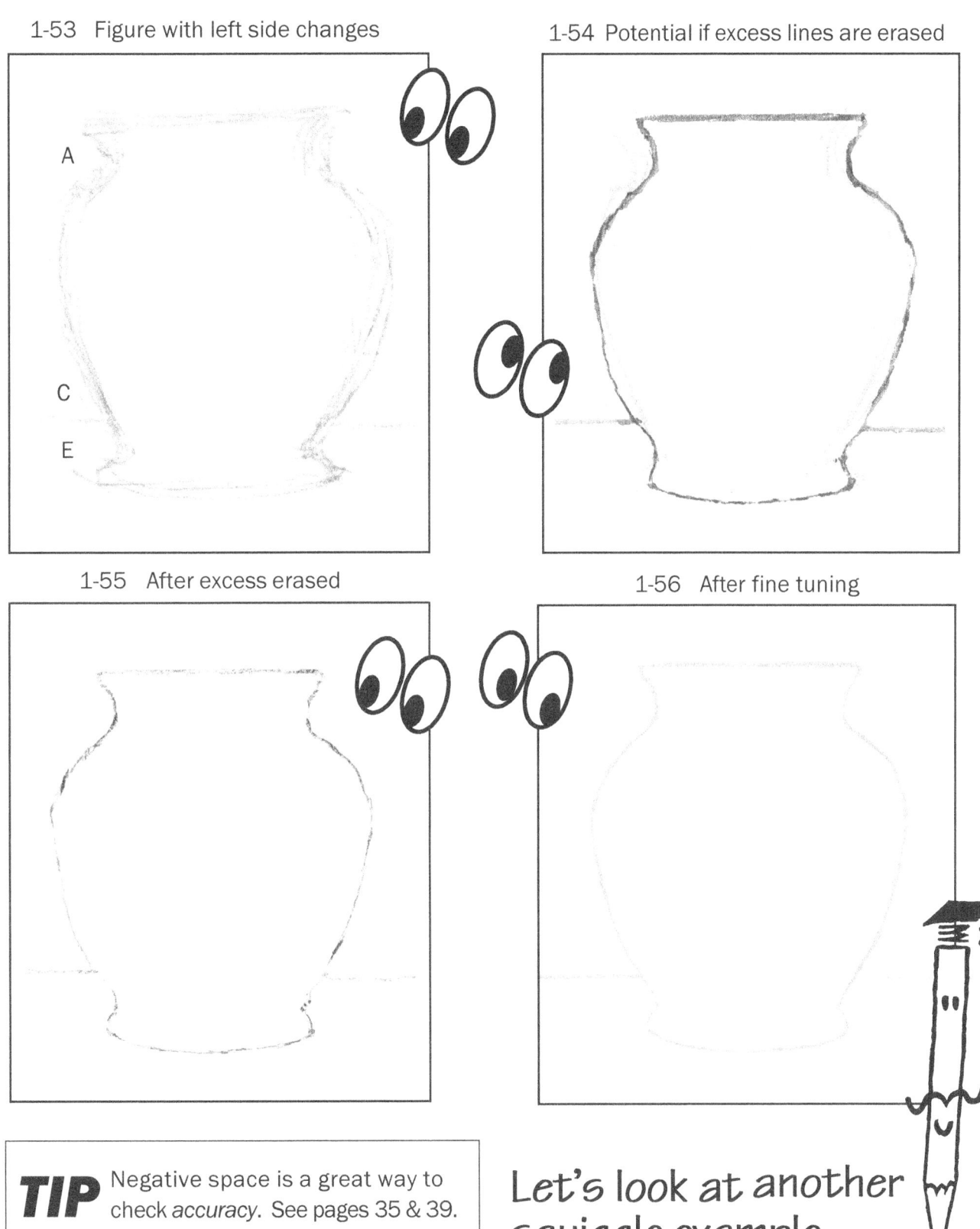

1-53   Figure with left side changes

1-54   Potential if excess lines are erased

1-55   After excess erased

1-56   After fine tuning

TIP Negative space is a great way to check *accuracy*. See pages 35 & 39.

Let's look at another squiggle example.

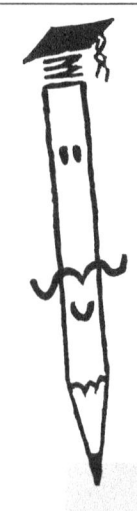

Observe the squiggle as it becomes an even closer version of the model.

As you can tell, squiggle 1-51 resembles the model rather well. By erasing the excess lines, the figure's edges can be clarified. The dark lines in diagram 1-52 indicate the prospect. Example 1-53 illustrates the erasure result. After a bit more adjustment, we see the metamorphosis (1-54). Compare the final outcome (1-54) to the original squiggle (1-51), with regard to the model.

Model

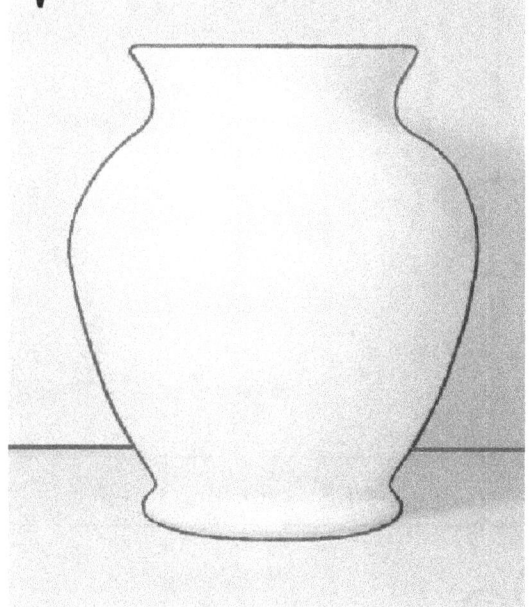

1-51 Squiggle

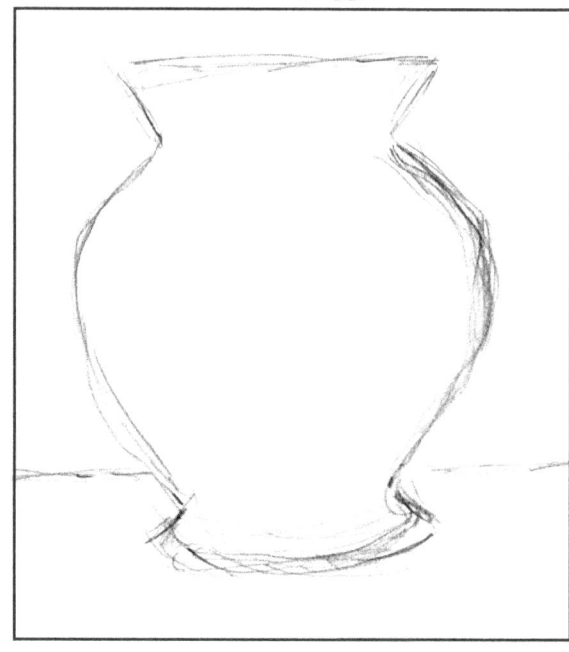

1-52 Potential if excess erased

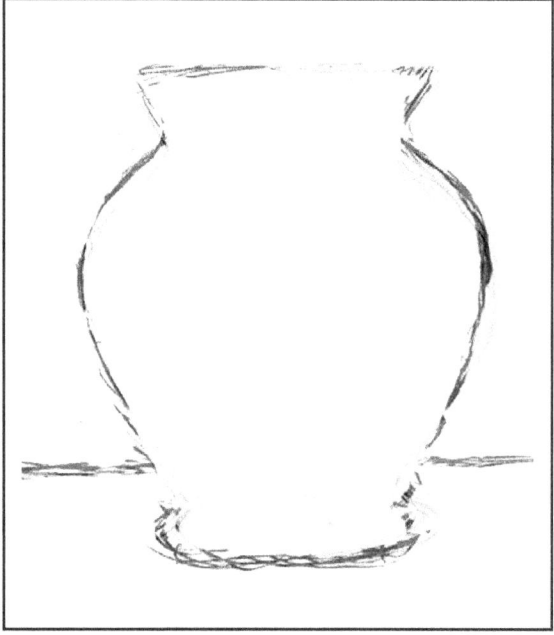

1-53 Figure after excess erased

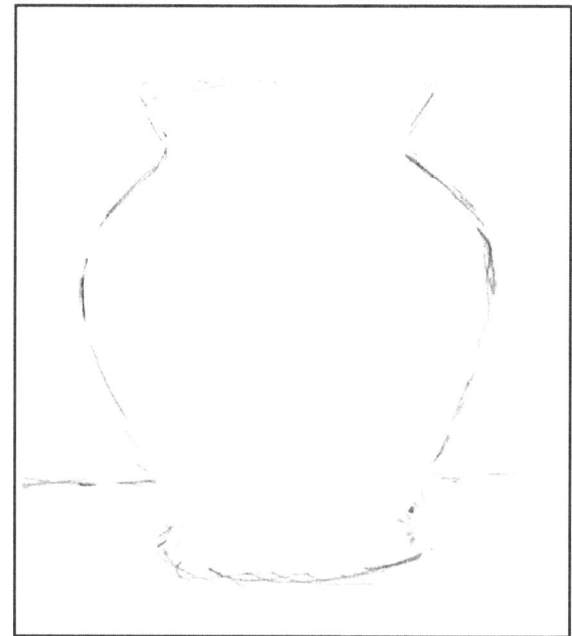

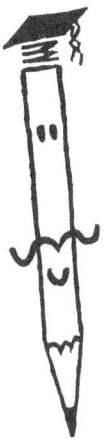

Now it's your turn. Get ready to squiggle.

INSTRUCTIONS

Turn to the photo on page 58. The moment you glimpse any portion of the figure, place your pencil on your paper and allow impulse to take over. As your eyes begin their sweep, record the movements with many quick, continuous lines or with one continuous line. Take your pick. Although your attention may jump from the figure's top left section to the bottom right, for instance, you need not lift your pencil and replace it during the skip, (unless compelled to do so). *Don't think about what you're doing. Just do it. Trust your instincts, your feelings and your reflexes to direct your hand.* Stop only when you sense you're done. Whatever happens, happens. Your strokes will probably look quite different than the examples. This goes without saying. Like your signature, squiggles convey your individual style. Don't be concerned if the procedure seems odd and your first attempt appears rigid. You were probably distracted, wondering how your picture can possibly succeed without a plan. Or perhaps you drifted off to thoughts about lunch or something else. Squiggling is like dancing. Soon you will feel the beat. "Lefties," try using your right hand and "right-handers," vice versa. This gives your untrained, subordinate hand an excuse to be less proficient, and *you* the opportunity to relax. With the pressure off, you can enjoy the ride. Loosen up. It's fun to let yourself go. Have a blast. Do many squiggles.

Conversion stage: Choose one of your squiggles to transform in to a fairly accurate outline. After making your selection, give it a thorough evaluation. Refer to the large example of the model on page 41 or turn to page 58 for comparison. Be sure to take advantage of the helpful suggestions on page 27 and page 40. As you convert your figure, you may feel uncertain about a possible change. Trace your drawing and test the revision on the tracing. Speaking of adjustments, you might find erasing and altering causes messiness, and/or your figure could wind up on your paper in an undesirable location. This is easy to remedy. You can transfer your drawing to a fresh sheet. The directions are on page 42. Of course you may choose to omit the transfer step, although it's convenient to have it in reserve, should the need arise.

After you squiggled and formed your outline, compare it to the one you did originally, without instruction. You will be surprised by your improvement. Be sure to also browse the student gallery on the next pages and remember to read the follow-up.

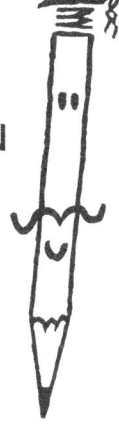

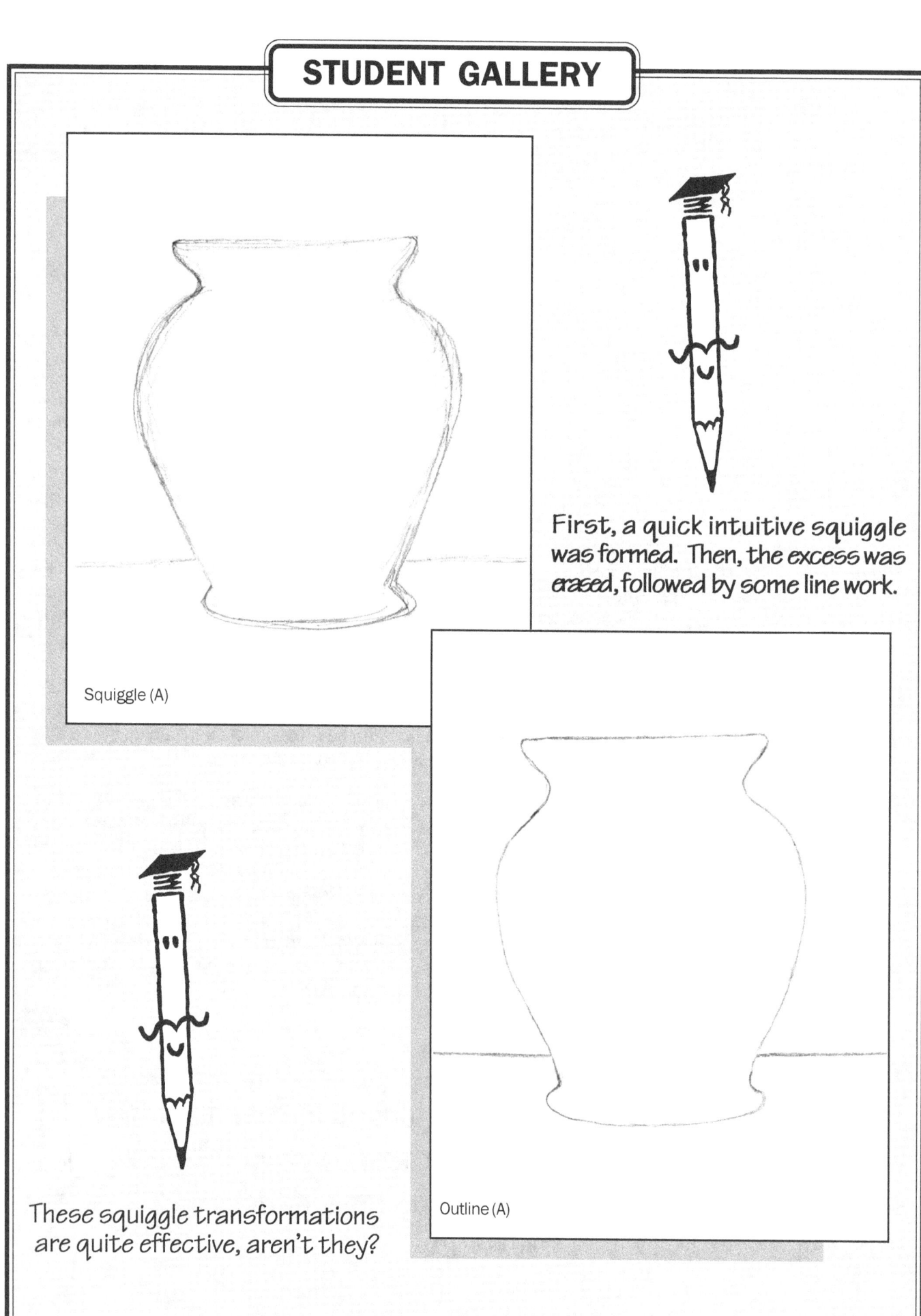

Squiggle (A)

First, a quick intuitive squiggle was formed. Then, the excess was erased, followed by some line work.

Outline (A)

These squiggle transformations are quite effective, aren't they?

Squiggle (B)

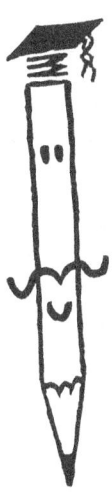

Isn't it interesting how the two styles vastly differ, yet they became similiar single outlines.

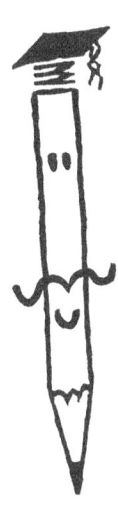

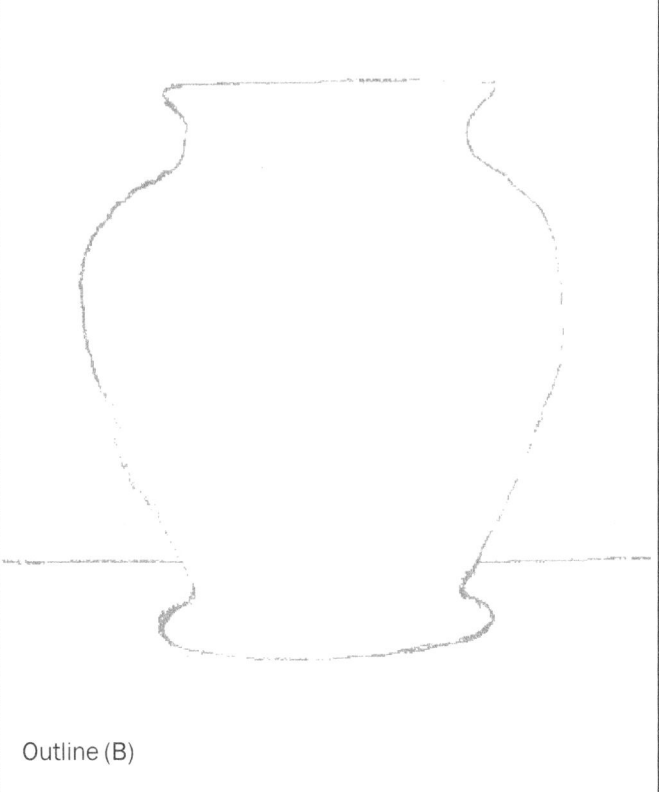

Outline (B)

The true measure of your achievement is not how well you think you did. It's what you learned that counts.

Chapter 1-B
FOLLOW-UP

When you stop to consider, you realize drawing skill is essentially achieved by three main factors. These are your vision, thoughts and actions. If they cooperate, great things happen. The irony is, usually they compete, by performing at separate speeds. Your brain is supersonic, your eyes are extremely quick and your hands are very slow. Yet for drawing it's important to make sure they work together. That's where squiggling takes center stage.

Contrary to the structure and random drawing methods, which require some degree of forethought, squiggling emanates from a mysterious place called your intuition. This region can be a little unnerving, but the trade off is a drawing thrill like no other. The instant you connect with your instinct and follow your hunches, your three abilities move in harmony. In turn, something wonderful emerges on the spur of the moment, manifested by your impulses. Undoubtedly, to the untrained observer, it's just trivial scrawl, or perhaps even silly scribbling. On the flip side, to those who understand, the same is perceived as spectacular engineering, worthy of respect and recognition.

Provocative and full of wonder, in my professional view, squiggling is an exceptionally valuable drawing tool. Besides helping you *unwind* and *stay tuned*, it *provides a base* as well. In other words, similar to the way the other two methods can work from a foundation, a squiggle may also be transformed with the aid of the TRUSTY 7 shaping components (p60).

Another boon is that squiggling not only helps improve your *eye-hand coordination*, but also tends to *enhance your creativity*. Doodles (synonymous with squiggles) are not meant to be detailed. Operating best when unplanned and unrestrained, they reflect your unique marks and your mood, caught in time.

Tap into your individual rhythm. Add squiggling to your repertoire and you will be amazed by what you are liable to discover.

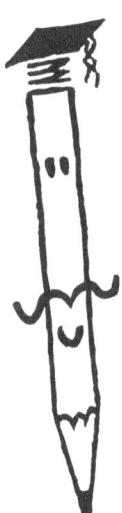

Now rest up. Another day, turn to Chapter 2.
Many other marvelous adventures are yet to come.

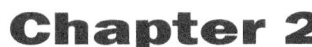

FROM SHAPING...

...TO SHADING

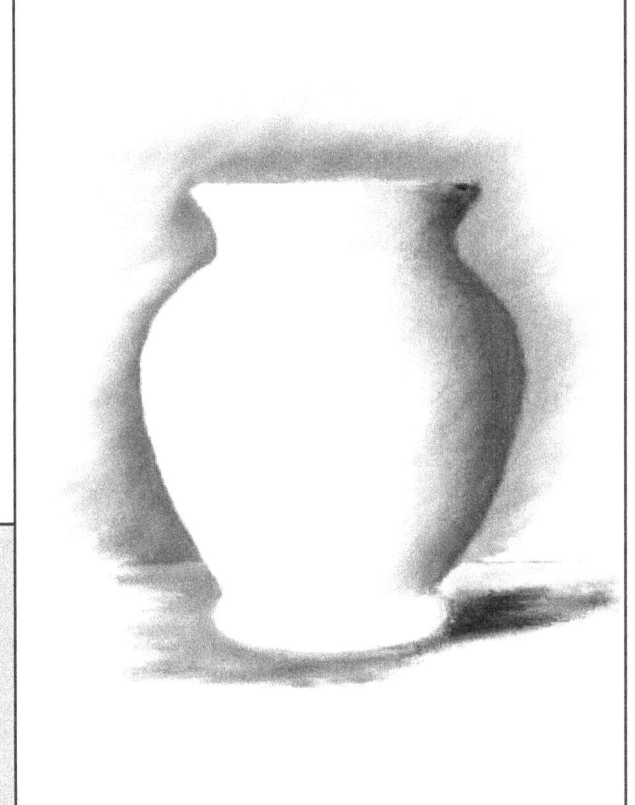

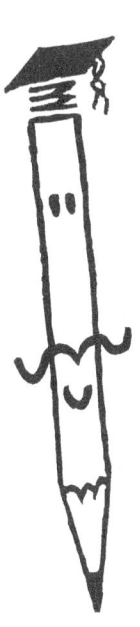

It's a cinch, when you know what to look for.

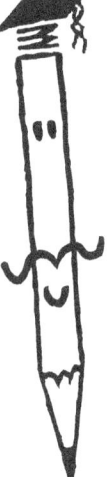

Observe what light reveals.

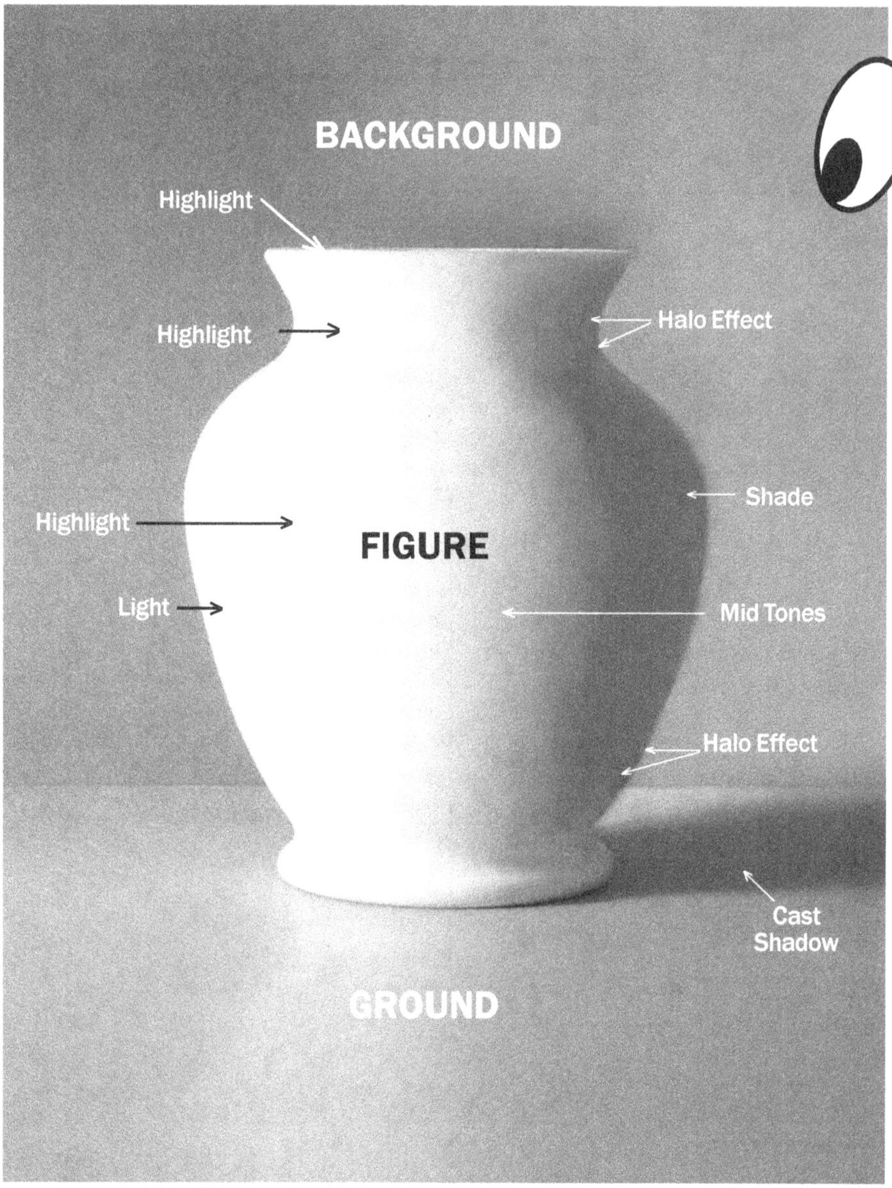

BACKGROUND

Highlight

Highlight

Halo Effect

Highlight

Shade

FIGURE

Light

Mid Tones

Halo Effect

Cast
Shadow

GROUND

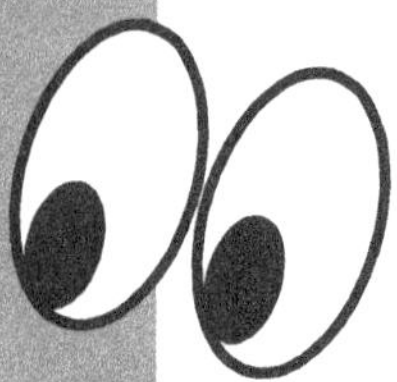

LIGHT shows many things. In this view, *light* is coming diagonally from the left. The most intense areas striking the FIGURE are called *highlights*. On the right side, where light can't reach, we find *shade*, or darkness, as evident also in the BACKGROUND. The GROUND (probably a table top), along with the figure's middle portion receive some light, producing medium grays, hence the name, *mid tones*. As for the *cast shadow* (on the opposite side from light), the appearance is dark, nearly black like the figure's shade side. With regard to the *gray* tones, overall they vary little so we can say they have moderate *CONTRAST*.

CONTRAST means *difference or visible change.* One way artists express this is with a wide range of light to dark *tones* called *VALUES*. For instance, a *light* gray value compared to a slightly *lighter* gray value registers very little CONTRAST. The same light gray value against a *dark* gray value shows a lot of contrast. Put another way, the more alike tonal values are to one another, the less the contrast and vice versa. Consequently, tones of great disparity such as white and black read as *high contrast*. Tones of *similar value* (all fairly dark or all very light) convey *low contrast*. Observe that the shade side of the figure's base is hardly visible beside the cast shadow due to the low contrast. Whereas, along the border between the figure's dark side and the medium value background, we see *stronger* contrast. In fact, the edge seems to be *optically* intensified. That's because where the boundary meets the figure and the background, the dark tone at the perimeter can look darker than it really is, and the light tone may appear to be lighter than it really is. I call this phenomena the *HALO EFFECT.*

-68-

Boundaries count.

2-1

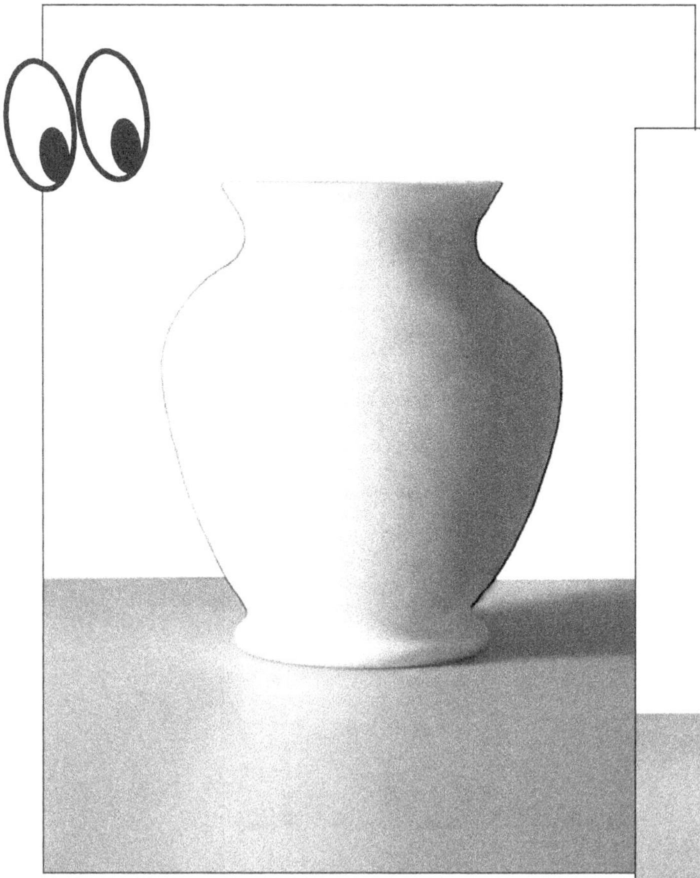

2-2

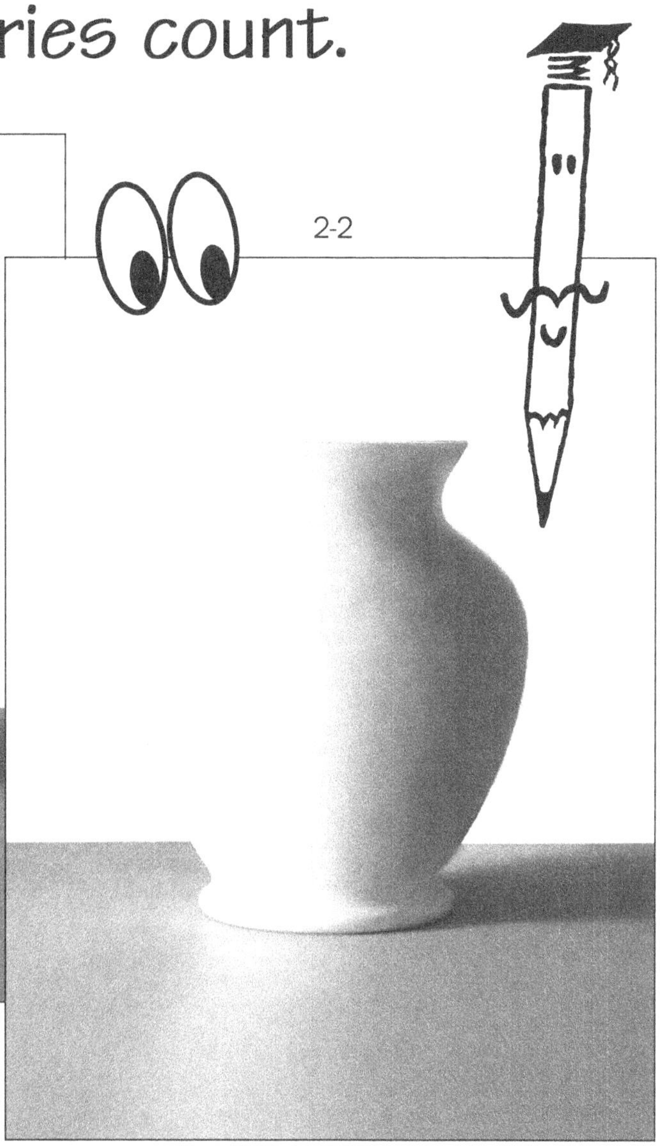

SOFT or HARD EDGE? In order to distinguish figure from background (form/space), the figure's light side needs a line, right? Not really. I'll let you in on a secret. A line is a man-made invention, used to separate boundaries. Here, it does little for the figure because the "hard edges" cause the sides to look as though they are flat. To create the impression that the form continues around and beyond our sight, a fading tone or "*SOFT EDGE*" is called for. Observe illustration 2-1 *without* soft edges compared to example 2-2 *with* soft edges.

Even the cast shadow has soft edges, due to the principles called *DIFFUSION* (spreading) and DIFFRACTION (deflection). When light passes along the edge of an opaque form, it *bounces off* and fans out. Where light is blocked by the figure, a cast shadow appears on the opposite side as a silhouette. The portion of cast shadow which is nearest to the figure looks darkest, gradually losing intensity further away (where light increasingly penetrates). When viewed up close, the edges of the cast shadow often resemble double images. From a distance, they appear blurry or "soft."

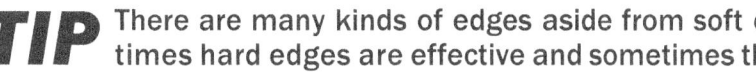

TIP There are many kinds of edges aside from soft or hard. At times hard edges are effective and sometimes they are not.

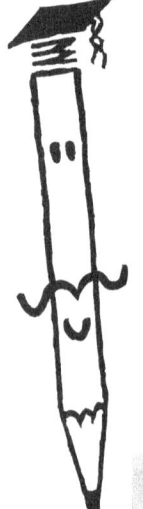

Planes are surfaces in the line of sight.
Contours indicate the planes.
Perspective signifies the viewer's position or point of view.

Surface direction is important.

PRINCIPLES of CONTOUR

2-3

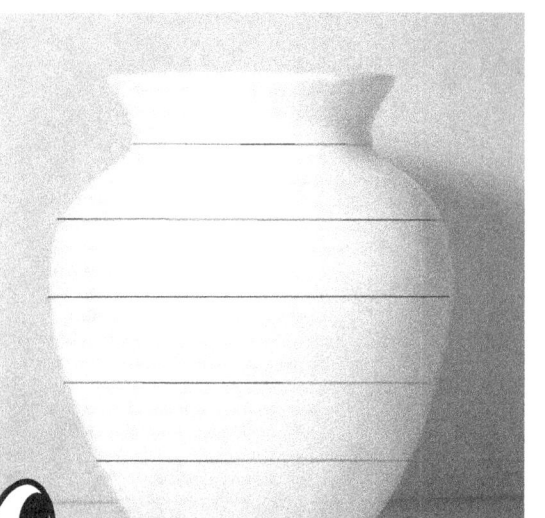

Straight, horizontal lines on this figure falsely convey a flat surface (2-3).

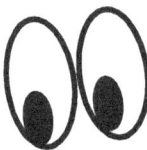

2-4

When the figure is depicted with lines BOWED, like string wrapped along the curved surface, the true form emerges (2-4). Interestingly, the bands appear more angular at the edges than in the middle, due to linear perspective. For the same reason, the top of the figure looks straight. That's because in this photo, it is directly at eye level. Below eye level, the bands arc, echoing the base.

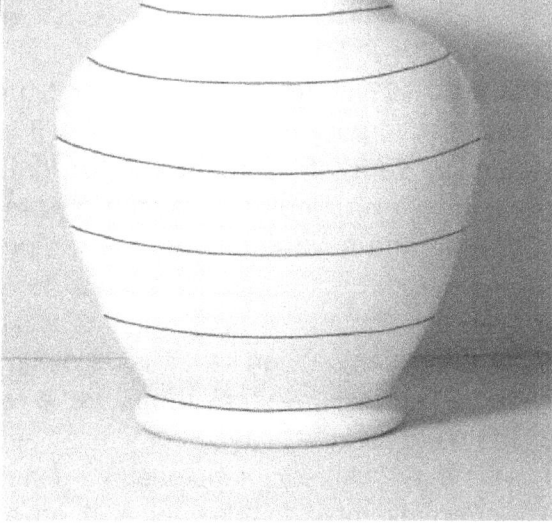

Straight, vertical lines also tend to flatten this figure's appearance (2-5).
Curved vertical lines that *follow the contour*, reveal the actual shape (2-6).

2-5   2-6

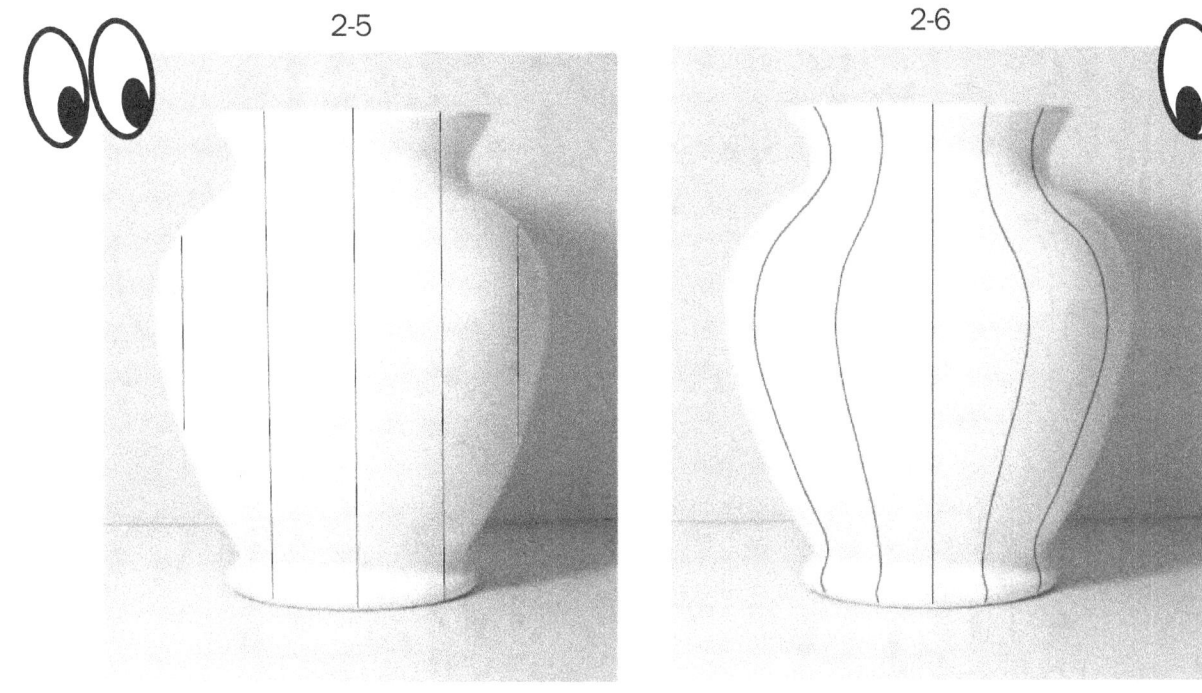

If TONES are applied *incorrectly*, they can distort form just as readily as inaccurate lines. Because *straight*, parallel, vertical increments of grays ranging from light to dark were used in example 2-7, once again the figure appears flat. When the tones conform to the *contour*, or surface planes, those same values express the bends, twists and turns, (2-8). So why is the *center* line *straight* in illustration 2-8, you may be wondering? Good question.   The answer is that in the middle of your view, you see neither one side nor the other side of the figure's wavy vertical plane.

2-7   2-8

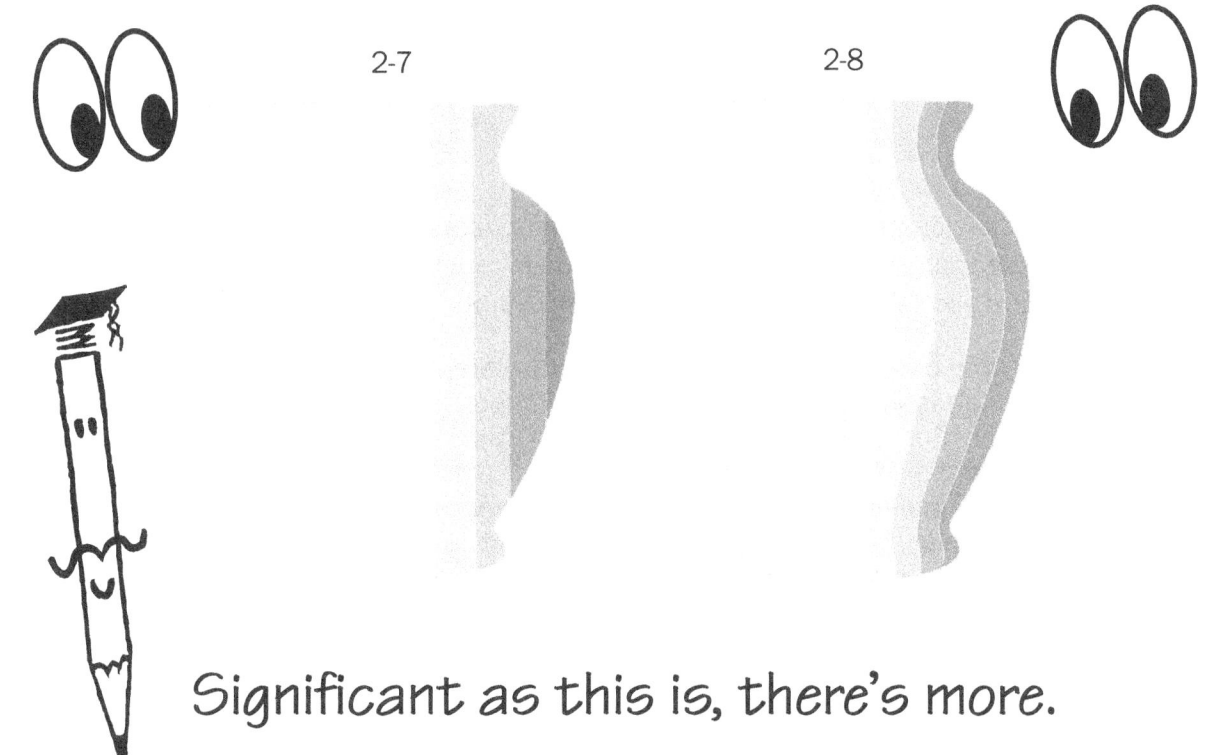

Significant as this is, there's more.

Look what we have here.

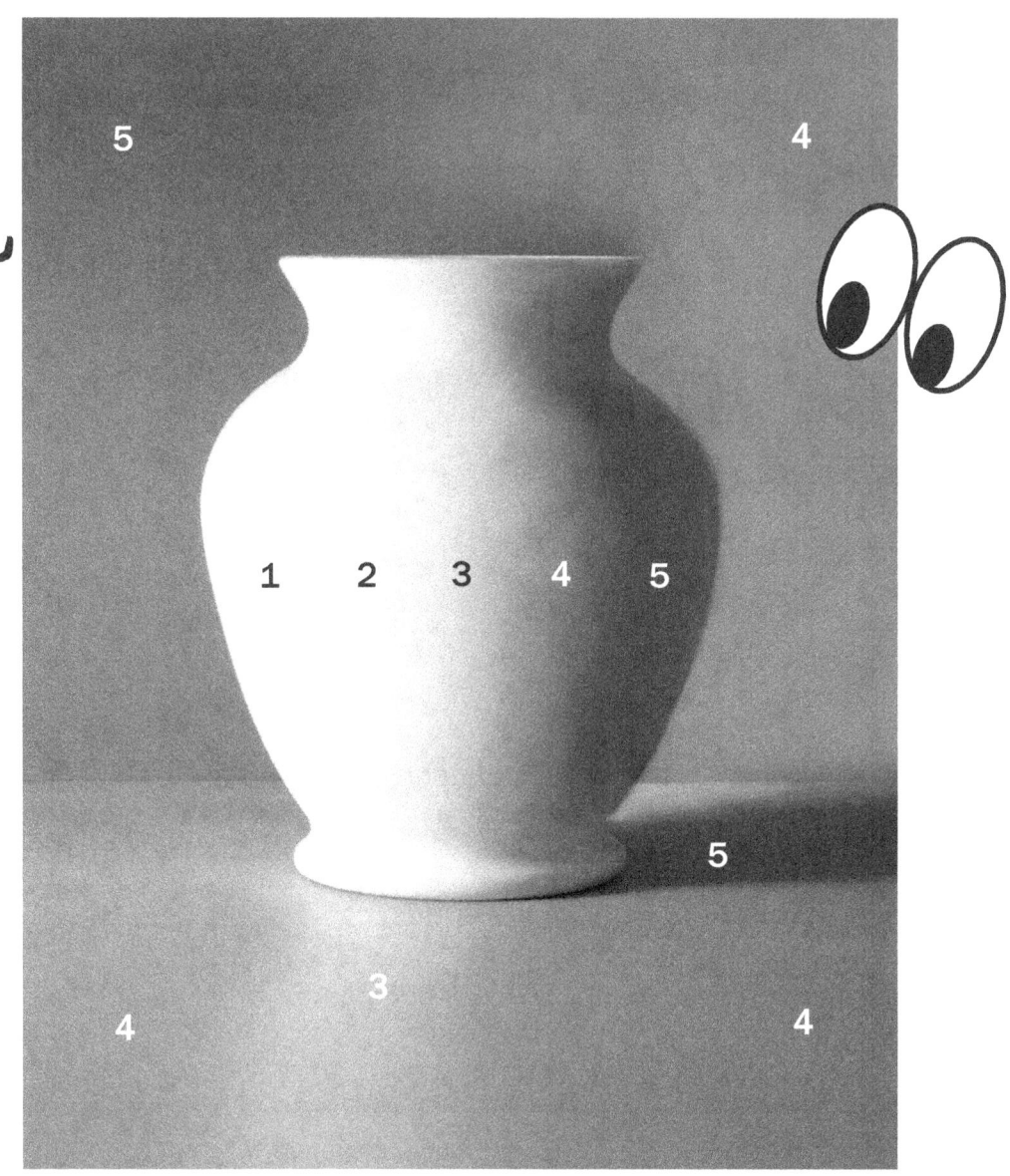

TONAL VALUES In this snapshot we see a vase which appears to be illuminated. To imitate the illusion (called *chiaroscuro*), at least five different tones ranging from light to dark are needed. The *value scale* here shows 1 is the light, 5 is the dark. Numbers 2, 3, and 4 indicate mid ranges.

INTERPRETATION You can copy the tonal values as they are, including those in the background and table top, to closely match the photo, but why? By exercising *creative freedom*, you have the opportunity to produce your own version or *interpretation*. The next page illustrates several options. For instance, compare the snapshot above to example A. The darkest values were changed to a moderate gray, thereby generating a more subtle appearance (low contrast). Continuing to take artistic liberties, in version B, I eliminated the background. The change was a bit tricky, due to edge consideration, not to mention that normally there are 3 basic factors to work with. These are the surfaces things are on, the area around them, and the objects themselves (figure-ground-background p68). Maybe this is why option (B) may seem incomplete. To remedy the situation, let's play "what-if." Suppose an *unevenly toned* table surface as well as an asymmetrically toned background are created as shown by version C. This is yet another option. The possibilities for interpretation are virtually endless, especially when you factor in style, technique and your individual preferences.

Version A

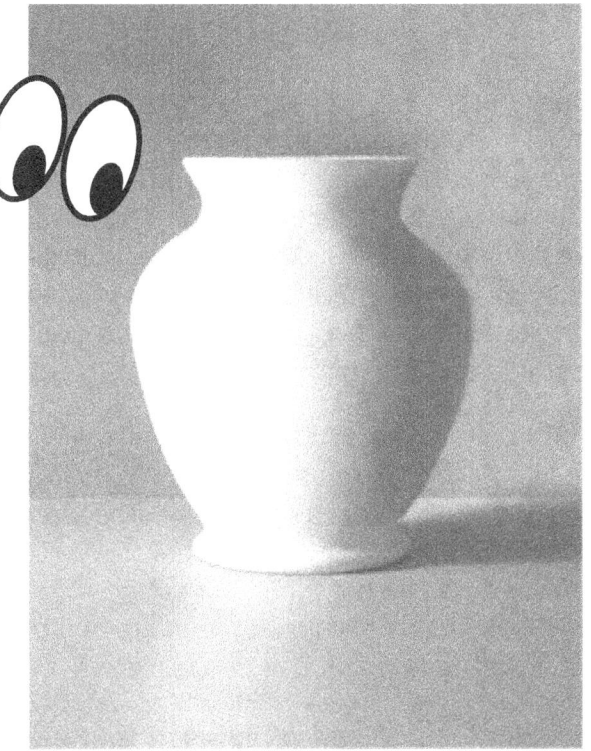

Version B

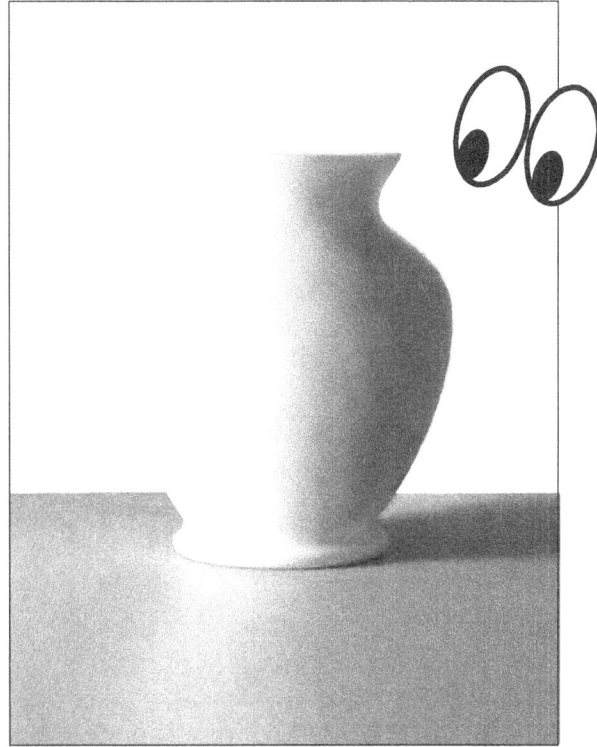

Version C

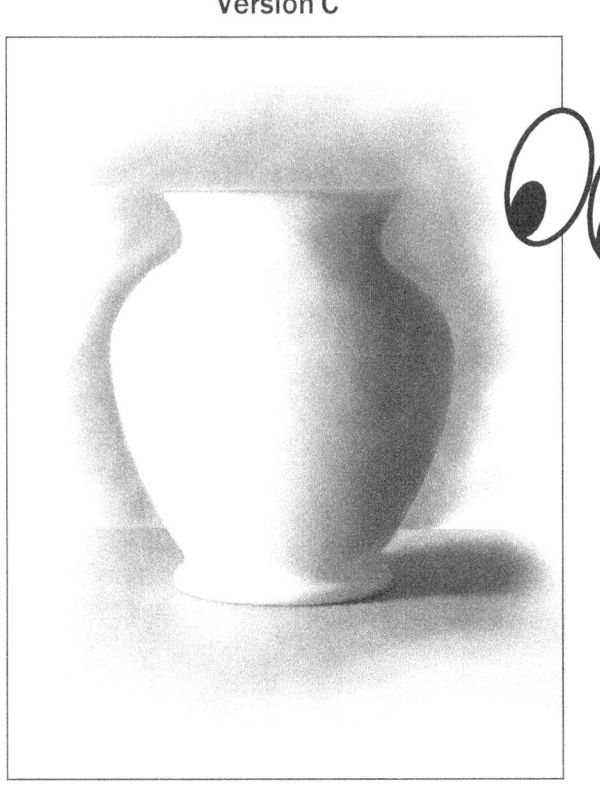

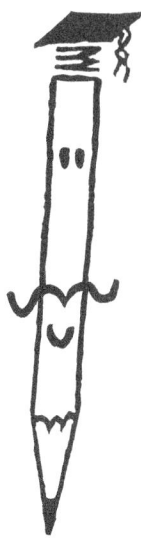

I opt for Version C.
Are you with me?
Good. Let's continue.

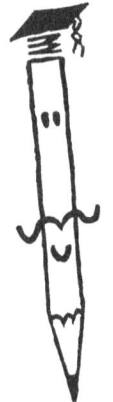

There are many ways to apply tones.

WHAT ARE TONES? With respect to the visual arts, tones can be an array of colors. They can also be just black and white. When only a mixture of black and white are involved, the outcome is practically an infinite variety of grays. Aside from that, tones can be independent, or fade into one another gradually from dark to light, and vice versa. If you will recall, this brings about a subtle transition known as CHIAROSCURO. Artists use the principle to help create the effect that a light source, such as the sun, a flame, or a lamp beam illuminates the form. On the previous pages we saw that a convincing impression requires five or more distinctly different values (highlight, light, shade and a minimum of two mid tones).

HOW ARE TONES ACHIEVED? Sliding your pencil lead against white paper is one method. Depending on the pressure, a certain amount of graphite will transfer from the pencil to the paper, leaving a mark. The harder the pressure, the more lead is applied, causing a darker appearance. If some space is left between strokes, the resulting tone is less dark. Why? The answer is OPTICAL MIXING or *visual assimilation*. How does it work? Your eyes see both the dark strokes and the white gaps of your paper and your brain mixes them, much like combining actual white and black paint. The outcome is that gray appears by either means, whether actual or perceptual.

MAKING TONES. Left or right handed, hold your pencil *underhanded*, between your thumb, index finger and middle finger. On a blank sheet of white paper, gently place your pencil point with the side of the lead nearly parallel to the surface. This enables you to PULL the pencil rather than push it for wider strokes. Begin by moving your pencil sideways, back and forth, descending as you progress. Try to keep your marks fairly uniform in length, while applying gentle, even pressure. Soon a light gray rectangle will emerge, resembling tone (A). If yours is darker, it means you were using a softer lead, or pressing more vigorously, and/or your lines were placed closer together. Should patches or large gaps appear, chances are your strokes were inconsistent. Occasionally, you may have pressed harder than other times. You may have switched between lifting and replacing

the pencil from the paper surface, unaware you were doing this. Practice and your control will improve. Vary the strokes left-to-right, then in the opposite direction, *at will*. Explore some with *sweeping* narrow arcs by pressing at the start and easing before the end of each stroke. Test several strokes with sharp and blunt points, tilting the lead at about a thirty degree angle to your paper, as well as nearly parallel. Alternate with strong pressure, followed by light pressure. Create sets of curved and slanted strokes. (B), (C), (D) and (E) exemplify. Also, stroke with your wrist rotated, so your thumb is sideways, (like the hand illustration shown in diagram 2-9 on the next page). Although certain positions may seem awkward initially, in time they will feel increasingly more natural, improve your dexterity, and amplify the quality of your marks.

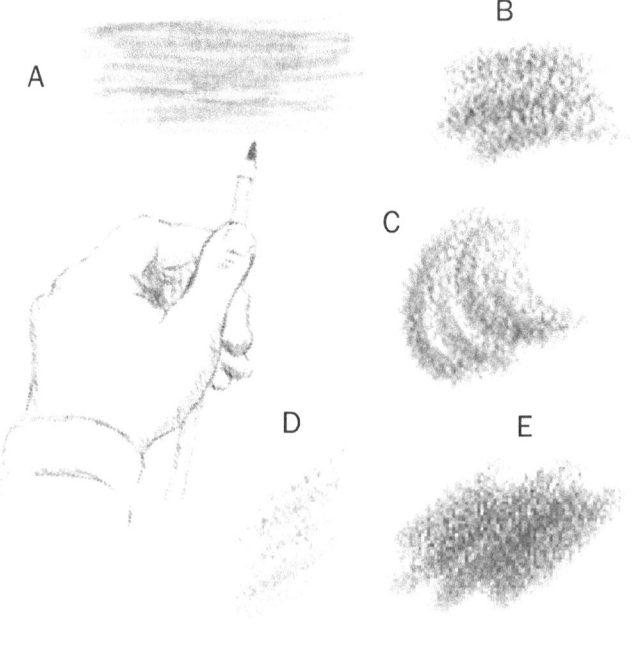

Having practiced your strokes, you're ready for "shading" (a.k.a. toning.)

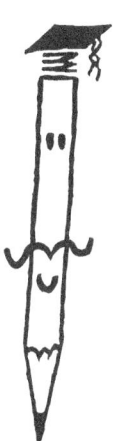

STEP 1 | **WHERE TO START TONING** On this occasion, the *background* is a sensible place to begin. If you toned your *figure* first, naturally your values would be based on the white of your paper. Initially your figure would look terrific but later it would likely appear too low in contrast against a toned background. Which brings me to a couple of other factors. 1. The background value should *NOT be any stronger than a medium gray*. The more intense value should be reserved for your *figure's* shade side. 2. Prior to toning, dab your lines with your eraser, otherwise you will find it difficult converting them to *soft edges.* In order to achieve an uneven background, you will need variable stroke lengths and sweeping motions. This method requires strong pressure close to the figure and less away from it. Start toning your background by positioning your pencil point above your figure, near the center. Using stroke style (E), shown on the previous page, stroke *upward, diagonally, left-to-right* advancing to the *left.* When you reach the side of your figure and make your way down, switch to a downward, *right-to-left angular* direction. It's OK if some over strokes invade your figure. They can be addressed later. Stop stroking upon reaching the horizontal line, representing the back of the table. At this stage, your work will resemble illustration (2-9.)

2-9

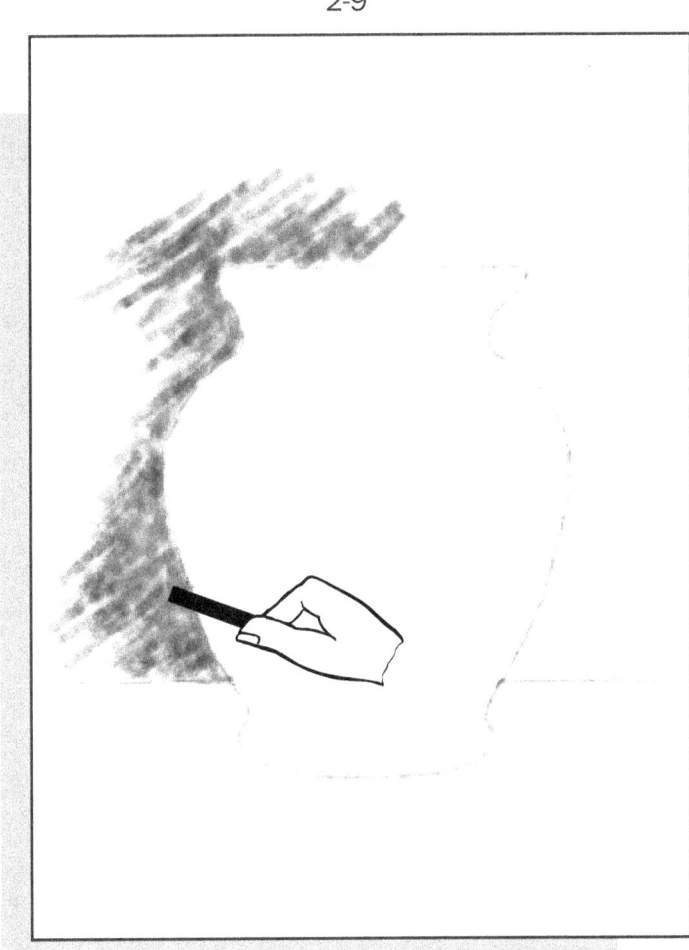

TIP Do not erase if any strokes go astray. Later steps will attend to them.

Tone the other half of your background up to the "table" line with *diagonal, left-to-right,* upward strokes only. This will minimize the number of unwanted marks that invade the figure. Start from the top center as before. This time, advance toward the right and down along the other side. Continue with uneven sweeping motions (stronger pressure close to the edge of your figure, and less pressure away form it).

TIP If your tones have a shine, you are over stroking and/or applying too much pressure. If absolutely necessary, dab shiny areas with your putty eraser. Blemishes, smears and strokes inside the figure can be remedied later.

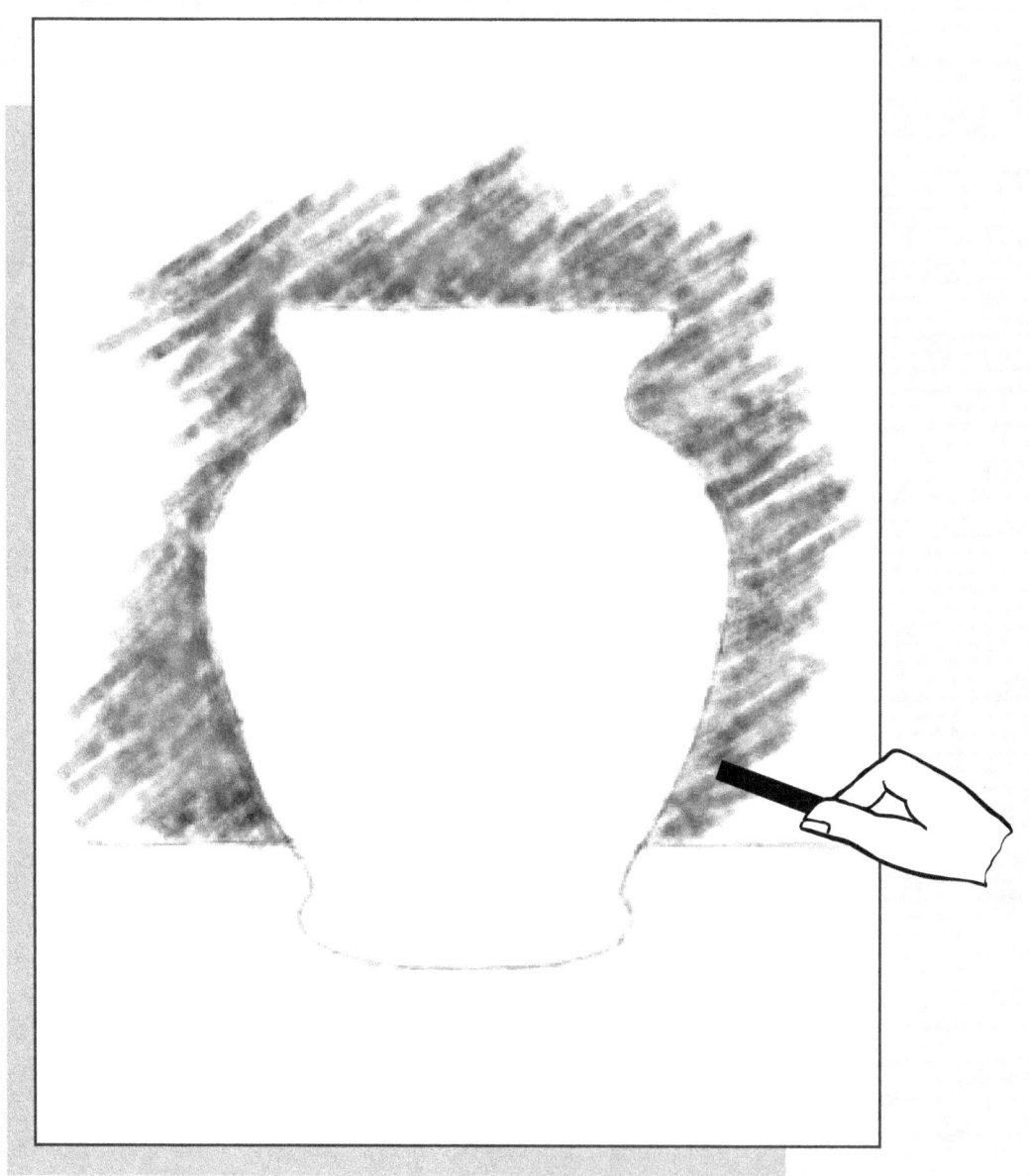

STEP 3 Tone the *ground* (table area) beside your figure on the left. Instead of angular motions however, switch to a *horizontal back and forth* direction to indicate the flat surface. Start from your line and advance downward (or forward) to mid-ground. For a more random appearance, try to keep your marks somewhat uneven. I prefer a minimum of ground area coverage to add more attention to the figure, but you should tone the amount that pleases you.

TIP Stroking underhanded has many advantages. Your hand doesn't block your view. In addition you gain greater range of motion and tonal variety.

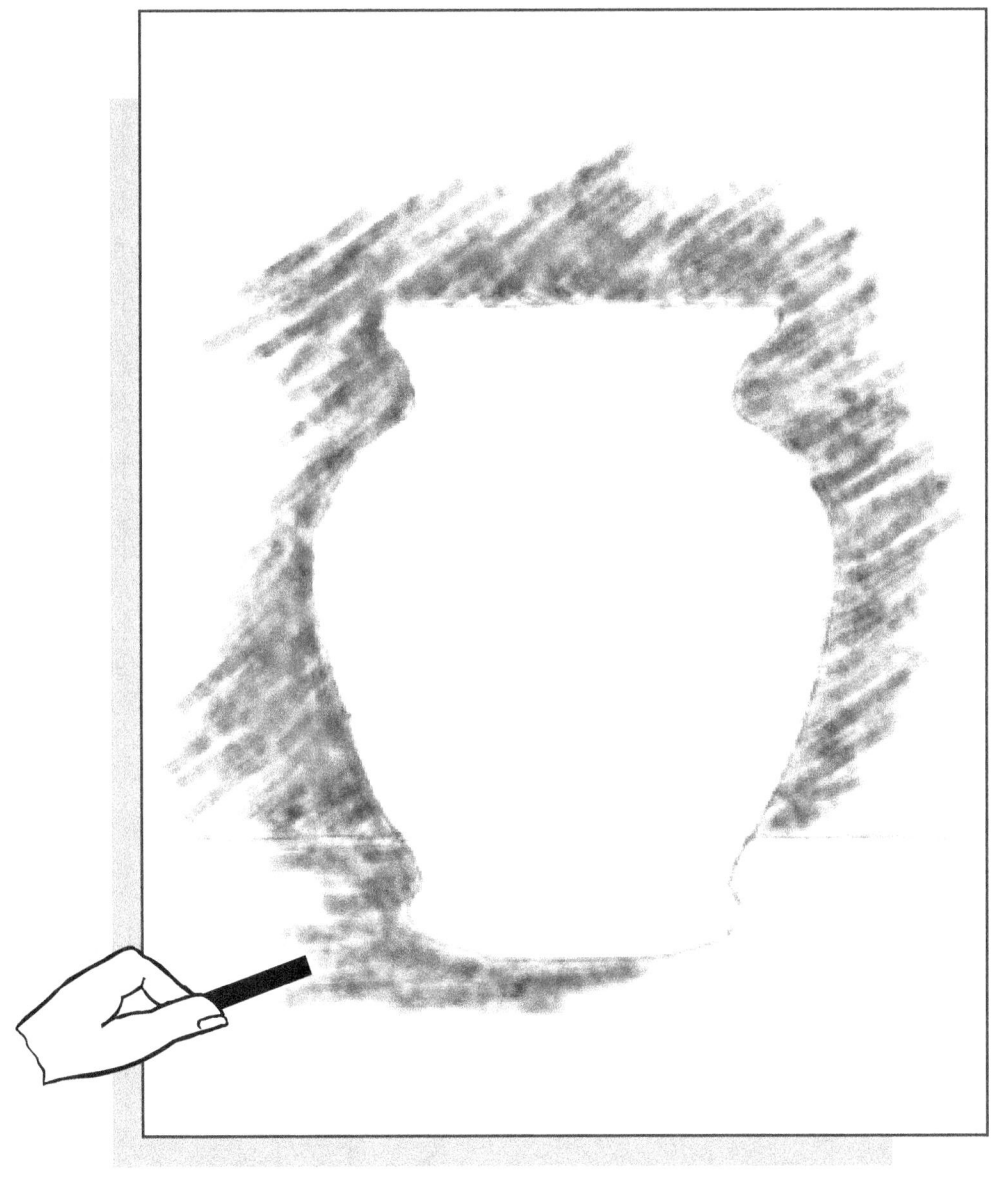

STEP 4 Tone the remainder of the *ground area* toward the right with lateral strokes. The cast shadow requires a slight upward slant to indicate that light is coming from the left (angling toward the back of the table). Light can't penetrate behind the figure but it reaches along the shadow edge. Therefore make the area where it's closest to the figure darker. Fade the cast shadow *gradually*, using decreasing left-to-right strokes. The back portion of the table (*ground past the cast shadow*) should also be a less intense dark value. Your extra care and attention to details of this nature will create a more convincing impression that the shadow is diffusing and light is diffracting. For a review of lighting effects, see page 68 and 69.

> **TIP** To help ensure your success, take your time. Handle each stroke carefully. Remember, the parts make the whole.

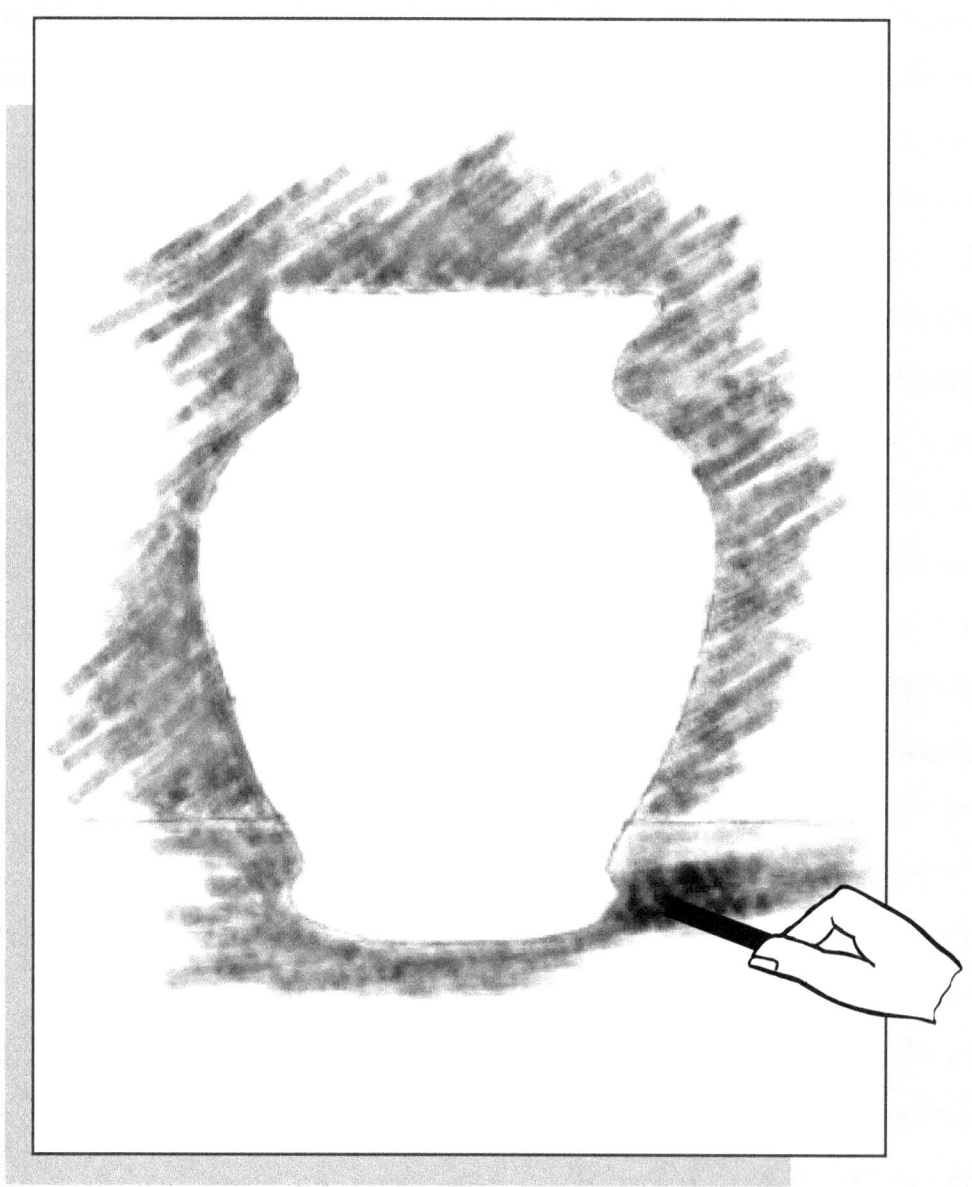

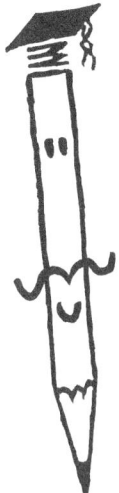

Prior to the next phase, explore blending.
If you do not have a blender, substitute
a cotton swab or rub with your finger.

Create angle strokes with your pencil as shown by sample (A). Blend by rubbing the area diagonally to achieve a soft appearance like example (B). Next, stroke another slanting tone by making half of it fairly dark and the other half less intense, (C). Blend your dual values at the *seam* for an effect resembling (D.) If you blend too much, your two tones will become *one* overall tone. Experiment by creating tones in a variety values and merge them several ways. For instance, blend a few with *sweeping strokes*. This means applying strong pressure at the start and gradually decrease to very little by the end, all in a continuous motion. Also implement slow, back and forth, as well as one direction, blending strokes. In addition, *feather* blend with a *very light* touch. Include up and down, plus circular experimentation, to learn other effective methods.

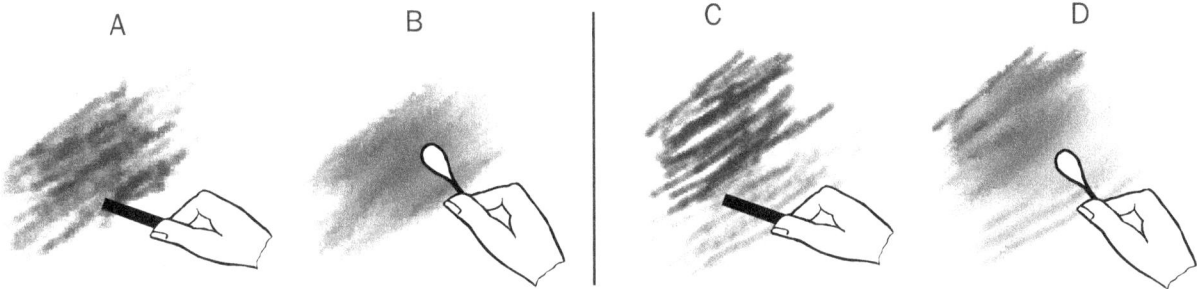

A   B   C   D

For yet another blending experience, form three vertical stripes of tone as indicated in example 1. Apply gentle pressure for the soft gray value (a). Place another stripe of tone with increased pressure to the right (b). Follow up with one more value using even stronger pressure (c). Of course, you could initiate with the dark and work backward. In phase 2, *blend the seam* between your darkest tone and the less dark beside it (d). Then merge the middle seam between your light and intermediate tone, like example 3e. Advance your toning and blending skill by making many values, occasionally starting with the dark on the left and lighter values moving to the right. Practice, practice, practice.

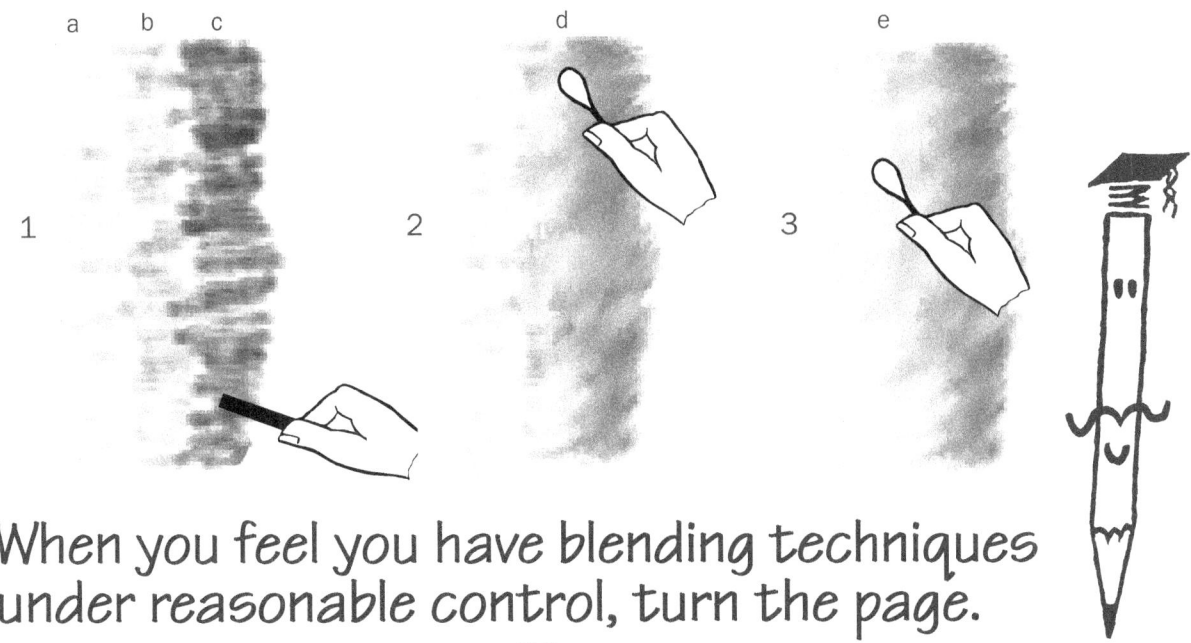

a   b   c   d   e

1   2   3

When you feel you have blending techniques
under reasonable control, turn the page.

STEP 1 Begin blending your background. Maintain the uneven look while fading the tones into one another, so the harsh marks mostly disappear. Go section by section. Start with the top left portion. Work your way down until you reach your boundary representing the back of the table .

TIP Graphite build up on your blender can cause darkening. To remove excess graphite from your blender, rub or twist it in your eraser. Blending tends to also make tones darker because the pores in the paper get filled in. It's practical to apply tone sparingly. You can always darken.

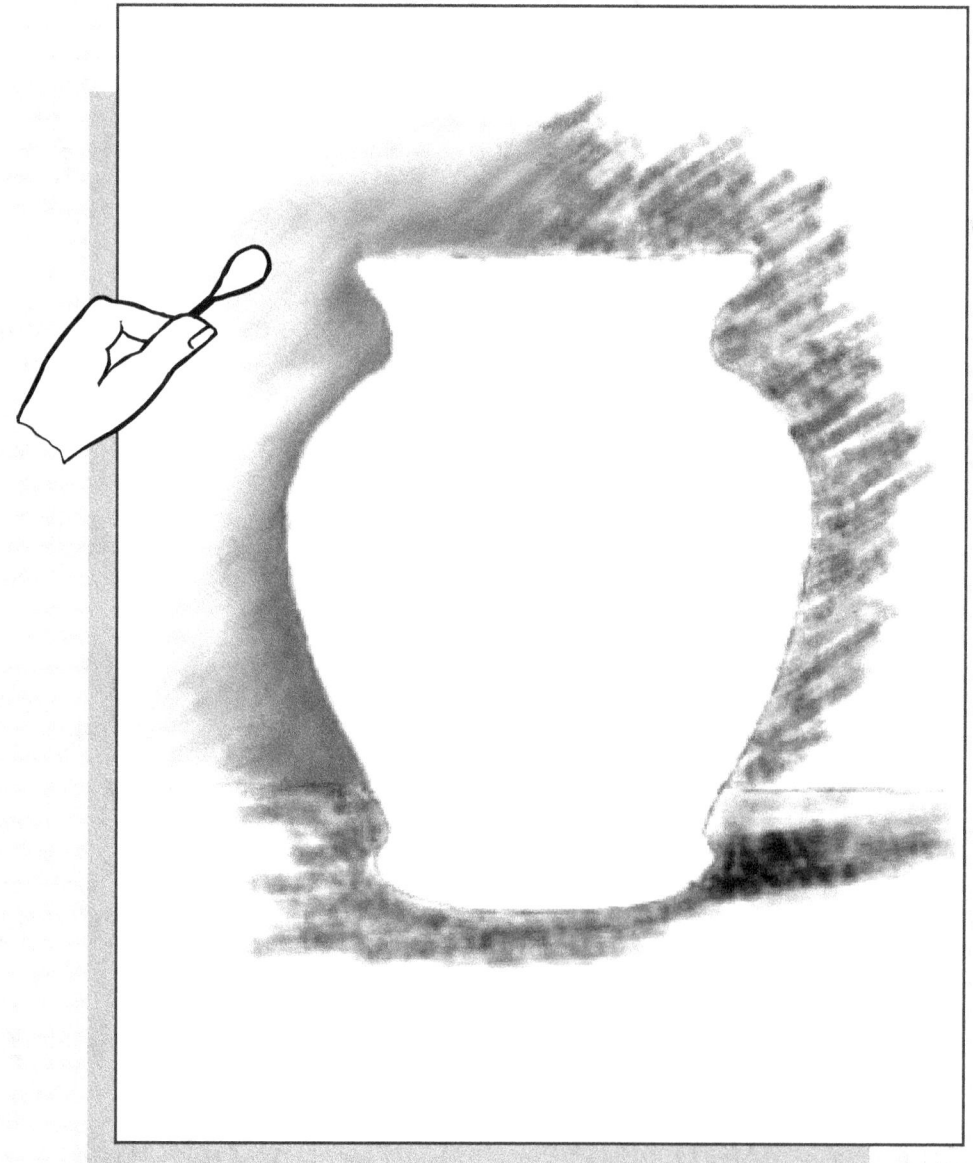

STEP 2 Fade the right half of your background, up to your horizontal line (or border). Don't fret if you accidentally rub some tone past your boundary line between your figure and background. The same goes should you accidentally leave some gaps. Spotting, smears and smudges can be addressed later, during the damage control phase.

TIP It's wise to do the background first. If you work the other way round, you would have a hard time melding the backgkround along your figure's edges.

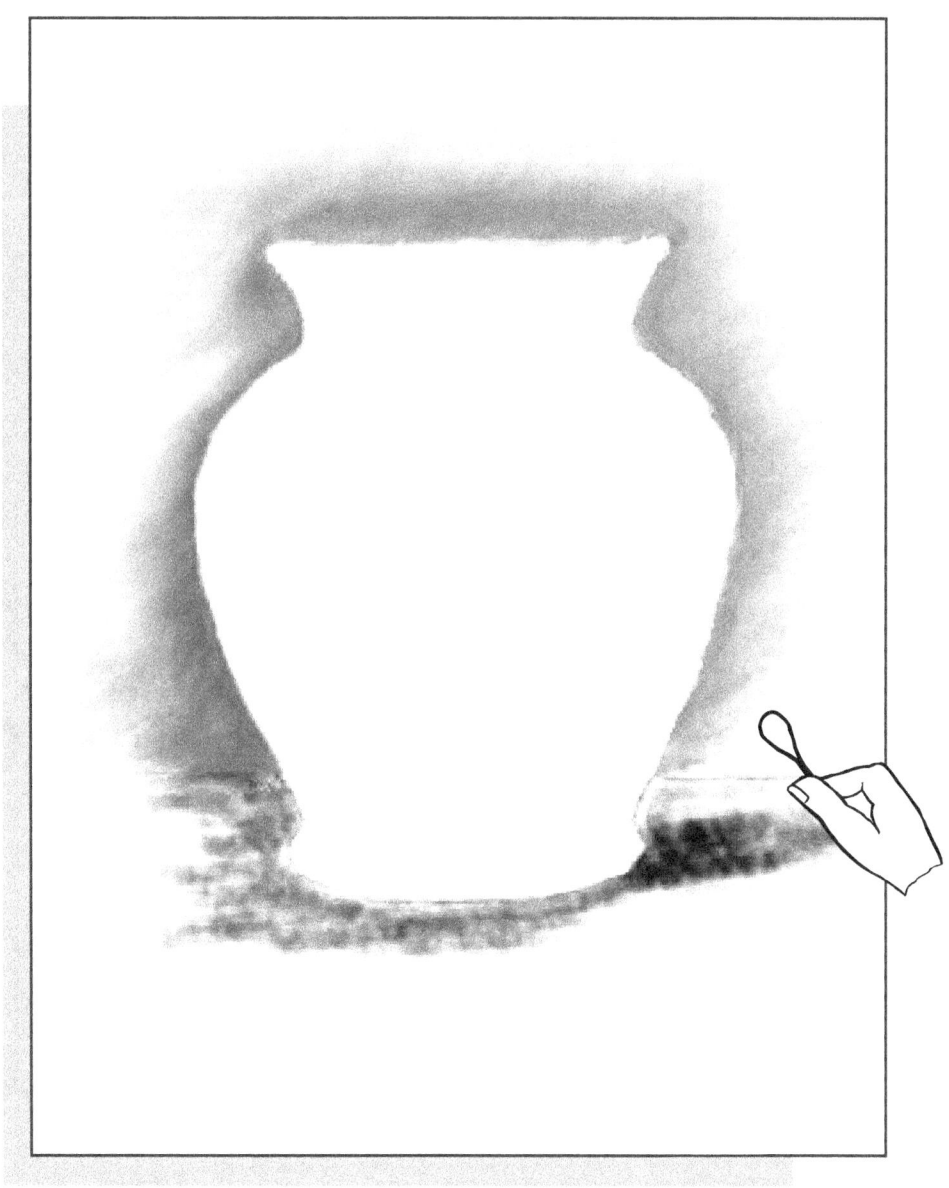

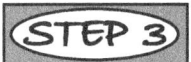 Soften your *background* tone by applying blending techniques (p.79). Switch to a sideways direction to maintain the horizontal appearance of the table (or *ground*).

TIP Work carefully. I know you are eager to tone the *figure*. But, remember the background and ground contribute to the scene. They deserve equal attention. Besides, you can use them to gauge the figure's values.

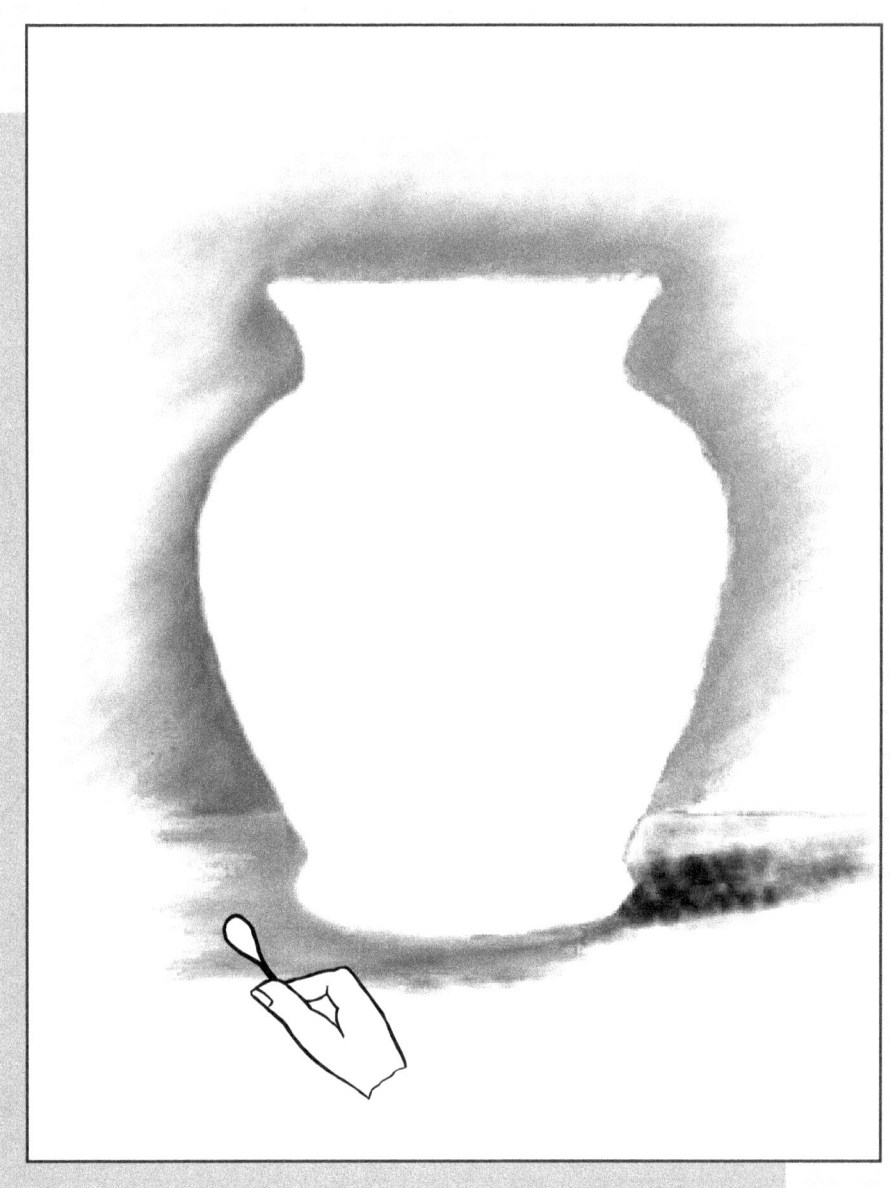

STEP 4   *Feather* (lightly sweep) the edges and the right end of your figure's cast shadow to indicate the illusion of diffusion and diffraction (p. 69). Having a very light tone near the right end of the cast shadow will not only be convincing, but also practical in composition. The viewer's eyes will not be led off the paper. As you blend, make certain the shadow does not extend above your table line, or the horizontal plane will be lost. In addition, be sure the cast shadow attaches even with the point where the bottom of the figure's base meets the surface, then slants upward. This will create the impression that light comes diagonally from the front left toward the right back.

> **TIP**   To avoid excessive attention to your cast shadow, do not make it the single darkest value in your picture. Make the other darkest areas the same value.

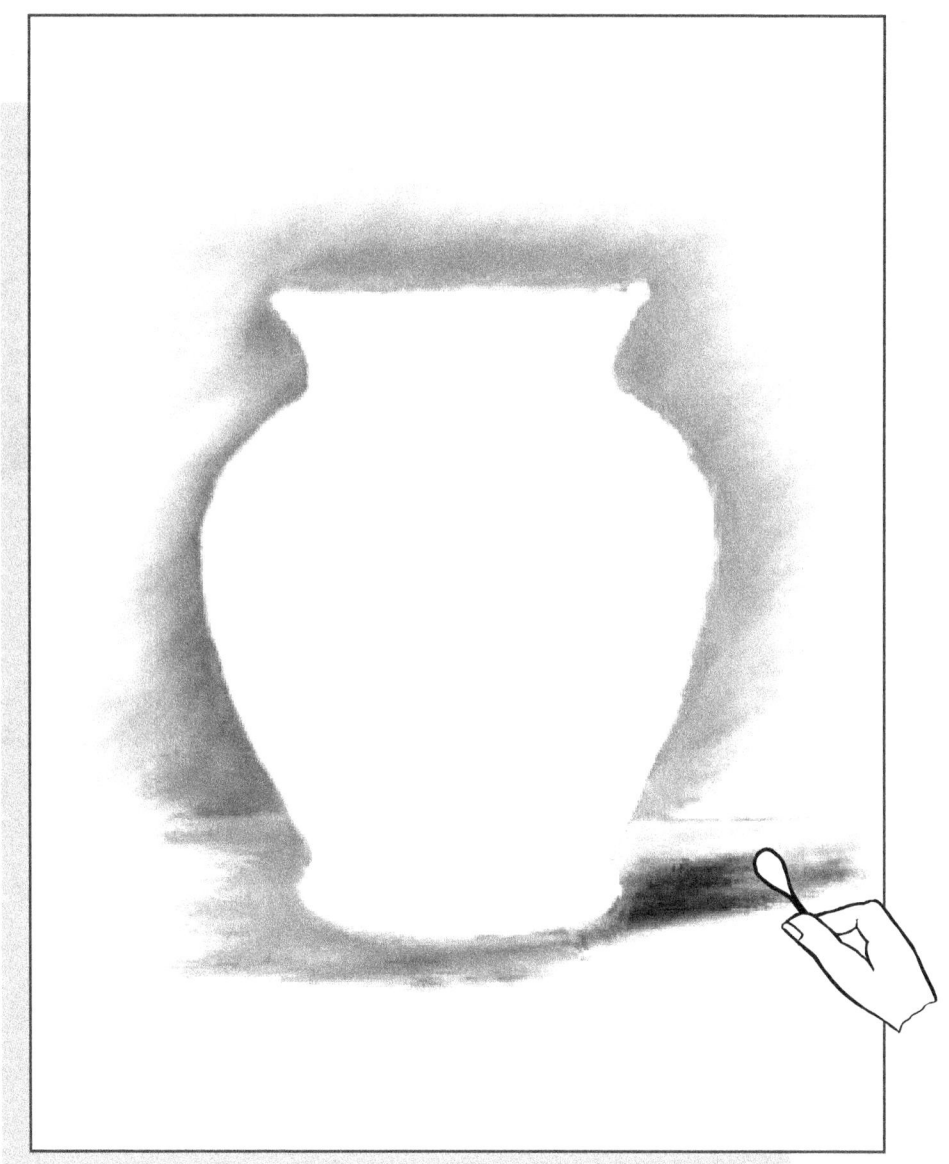

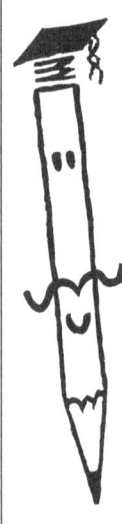

Prepare to tone your figure.
Here are two things to keep in mind.

1. On page 71 you learned that *five* distinctive tones can create the visual impression that the form is *illuminated*. To reproduce the effect, the *white* of your paper will represent *your* figure's *light side*. Three values, or mid tones, ranging from very soft gray to medium dark gray will recede toward the right, culminating with a very dark value for the shade. I used the word *recede* because dark tones appear to move away, while light tones seem to *advance*.

2. In order to properly tone the figure's shape, on page 70 you discovered they must convey the *contour*. The illustrations below remind us of the lesson. Specifically, we know that straight tones flatten this particular figure's appearance (A), whereas tones that reflect the surface planes truly show its bends and turns (B).

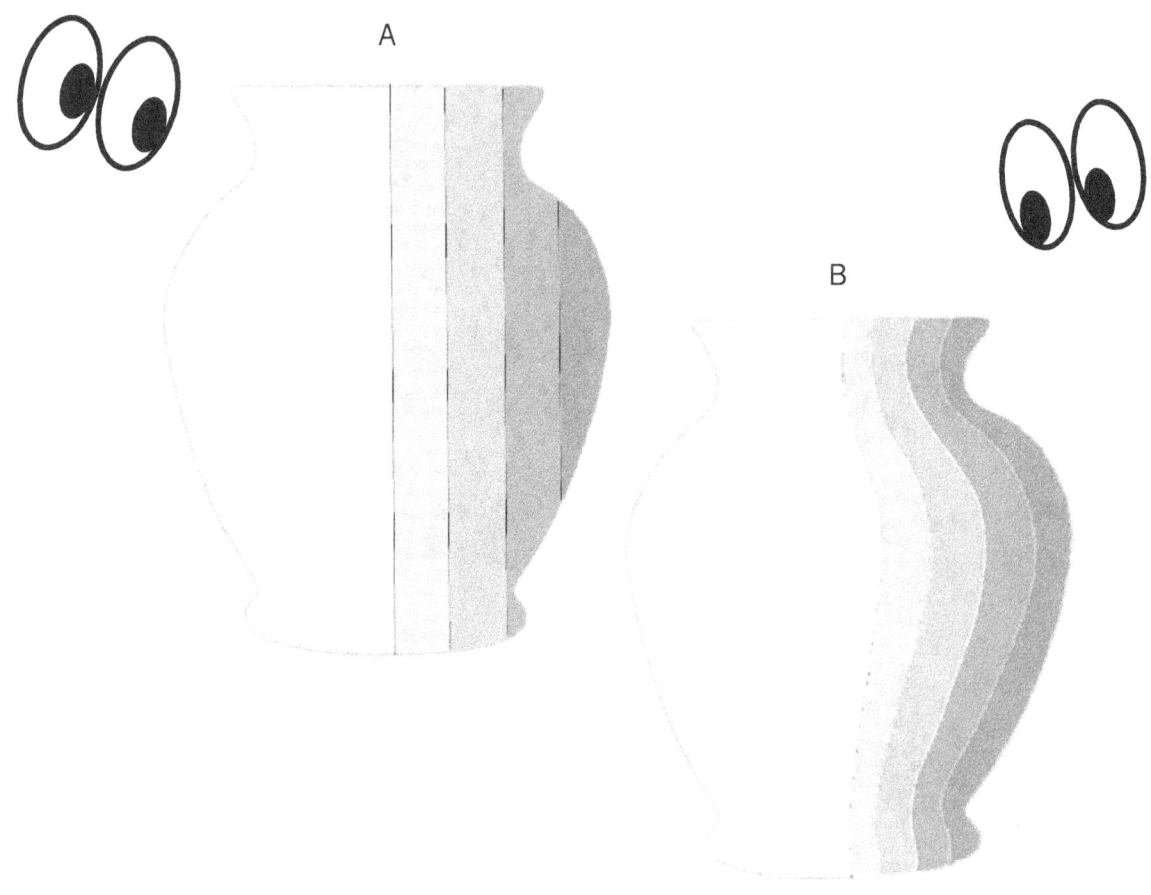

Since the tonal values need to follow the figure's *contour,* it's helpful to position some *barely visible* dots according to the bulbous shape. Apply them, row by row, *vertically.* When finished, you will have a guide for your tones to follow.

TIP Lines are more difficult to convert to tones than dots. Be sure to do yours LIGHTLY.

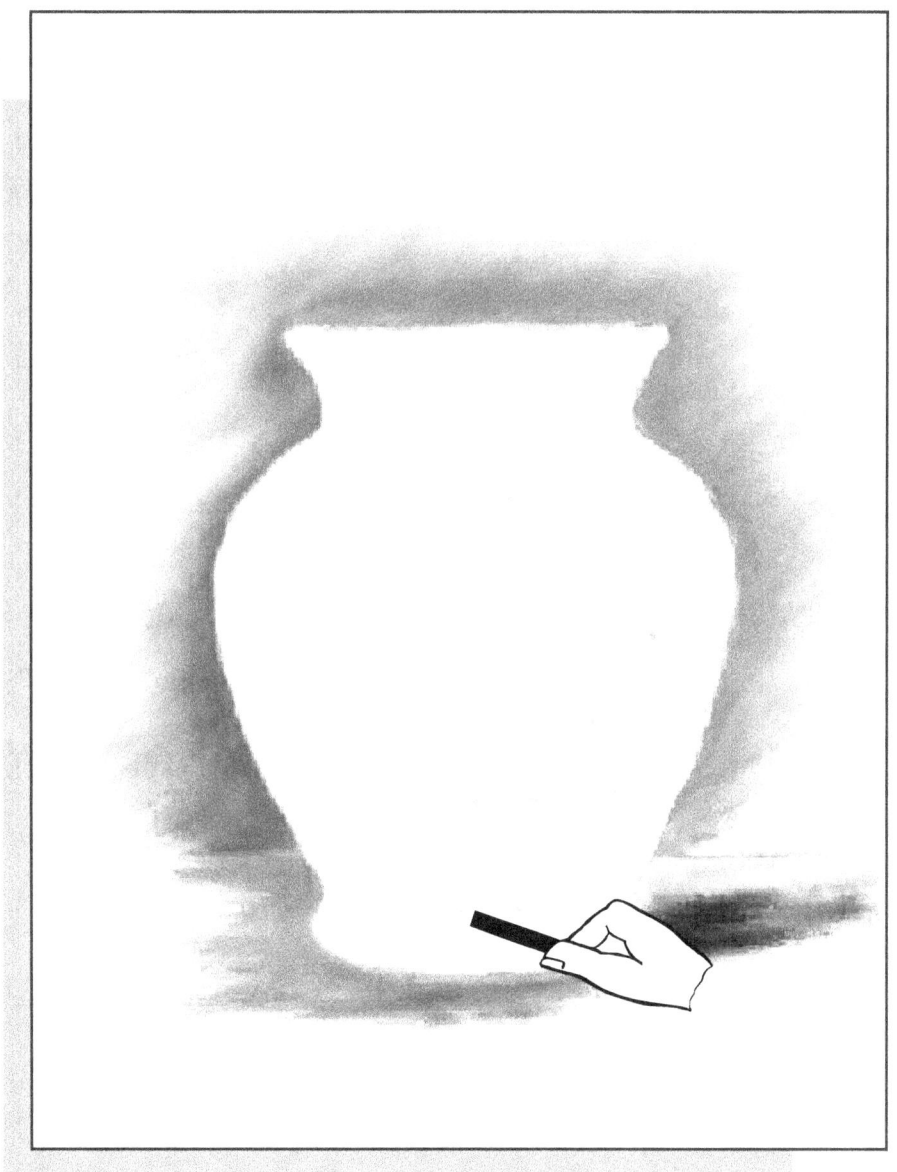

STEP 2 Tone your figure by initiating with its shade (dark) side. Be sure to stay within your dotted boundary and *angle* your strokes in order to convey the *contour* of the curved bulbous surface. Press harder for a darker value than the background, but *reserve the darkest intensity* for later steps. Start stroking at the top of your figure's neck. Use a horizontal *right-to-left* direction. When you arrive at the area between the neck and upper body, your marks should gradually tilt downward. Upon reaching midway, they should level out and little by little, they should slant upward as they approach the base. For a review on *contour,* see page 70 & 71.

TIP As you tilt your strokes, you may be tempted to rotate your paper. This is not a good practice because it tends to form a habit which prevents you from improving your manual dexterity.

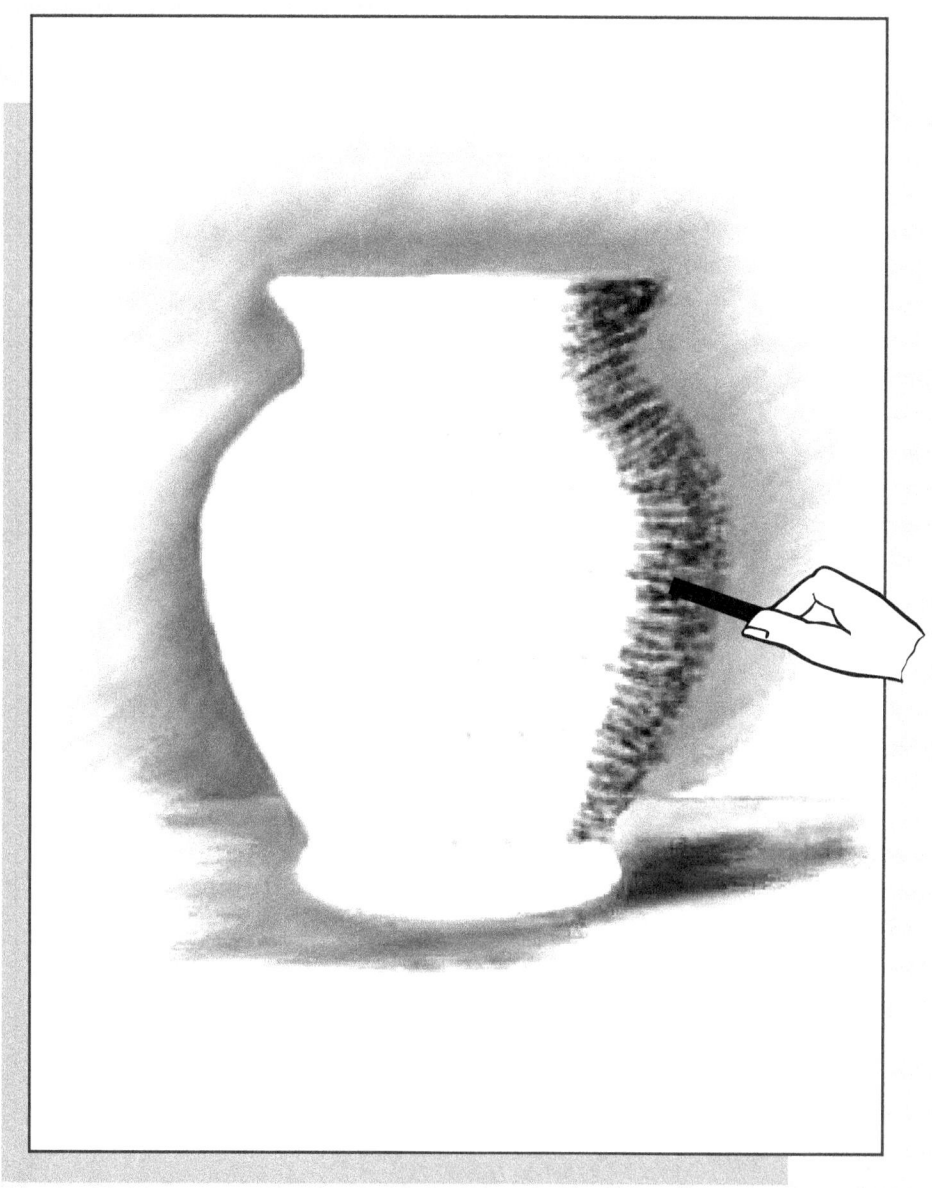

STEP 3 Add a row of tone adjacent to the left of your shade tone. Use a bit less pressure in order to convey the slightly less dark *mid-tone* range. For effective contour, be sure to follow the boundary indicated by your dots. Once again, stroke *level* at the top, like you did in the previous step, Upon reaching the upper part of the body, *tilt* your strokes downward. *Level out midway* and approaching the base, *gradually tilt upward*

TIP Having the background tone for reference enables you to gauge your figure's tone value. The dots help form the contour. Together, the combination makes your task more manageable.

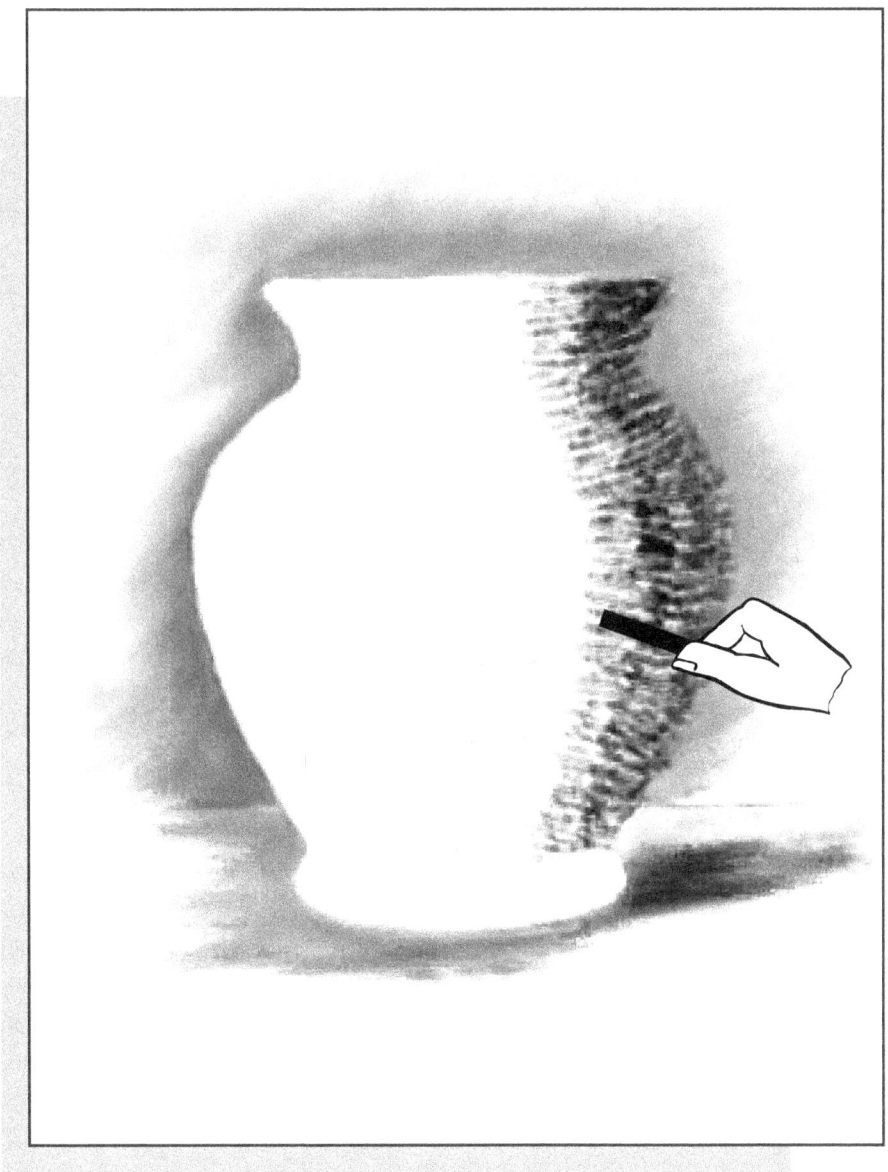

STEP 4 Create another row of mid tone toward the left. This region is nearly in the middle of your figure, almost reaching the light side. Still stroking right-to-left, now use mainly a *horizontal* direction, *without tilt* . Naturally, the value you create should be less dark than the tone to the right of it. To achieve this, apply gentle pressure.

TIP If your tones appear shiny, it's a sure sign you pushed your pencil's graphite beyond its limit. Accidental *overstrokes* that overlapped into the background can be addressed later, during the clean-up stage.

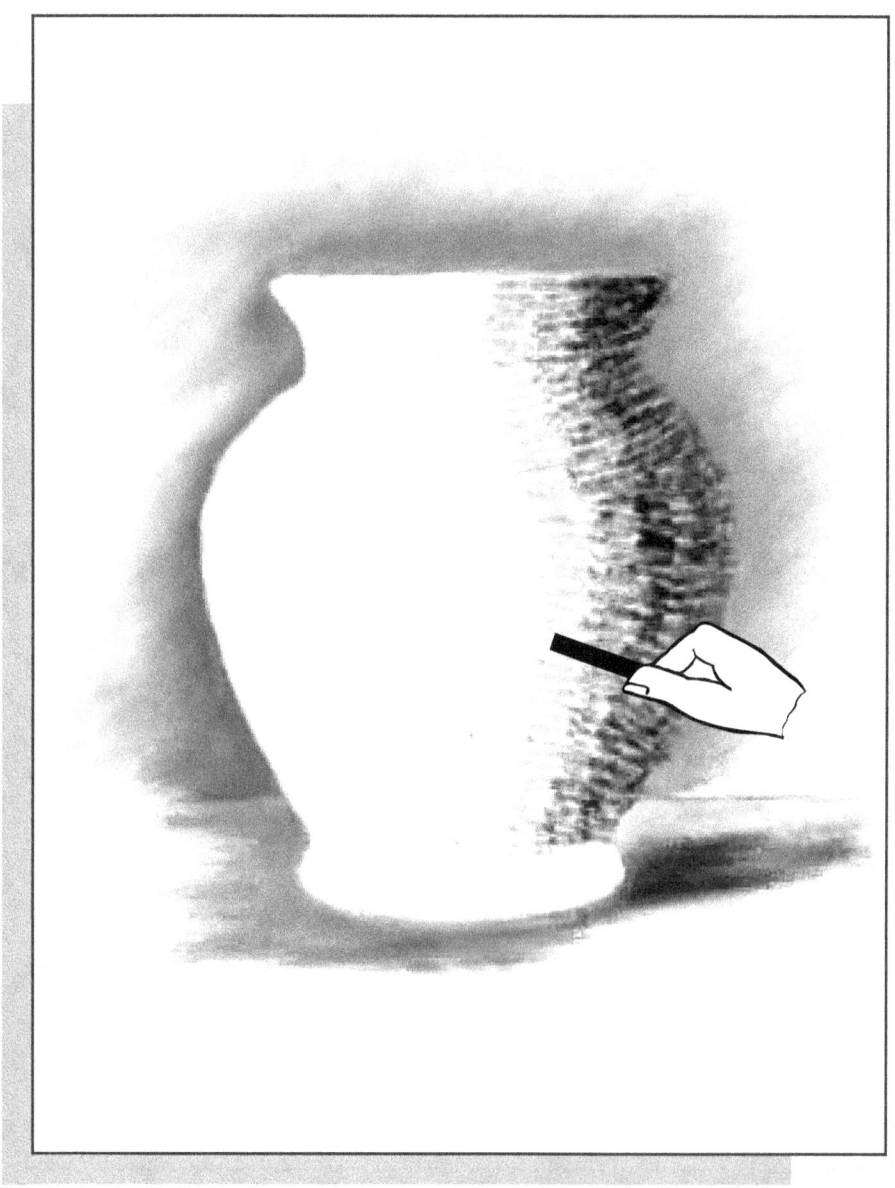

STEP 5 Form one more row of tone. Since this area represents the portion which is closest to the figure's light side, do your best to keep your strokes just slightly darker than the white of your paper. For best results, barely graze the surface with your pencil, stroking only right-to-left, *without slant*.

TIP There is no need to rush. Drawing takes patience, practice and perseverance: the 3 P's.

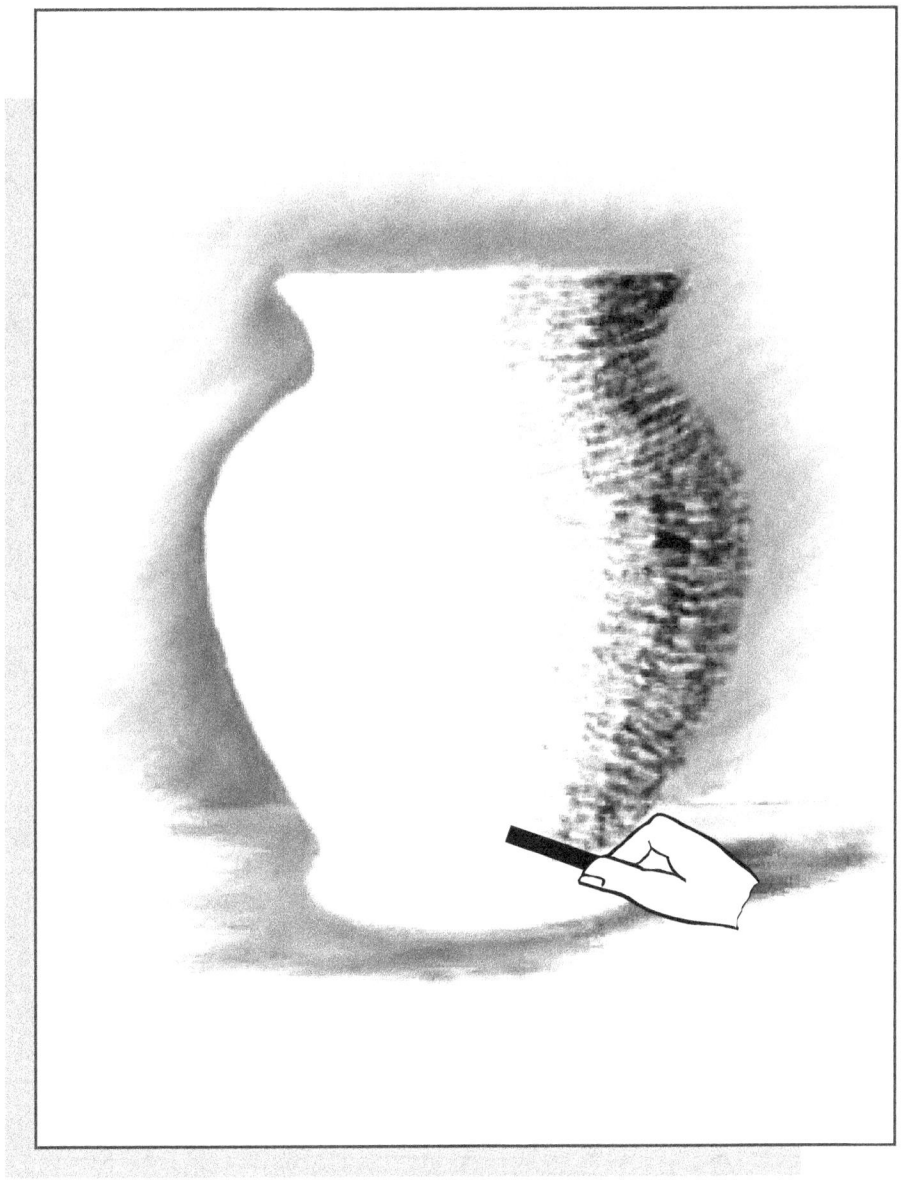

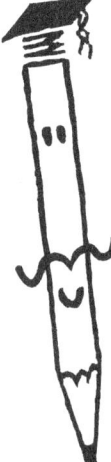

Your figure is ready for blending.

STEP 1 Having toned your figure, now *soften* or *fade* the *seams* between values. Start with the shade side. Use a blender, a cotton swab, or your finger to meld the *seam* separating your shade tone and the first mid-tone to the left. Press firmly with right-to-left *sweeping* motions, by gradually reducing pressure prior to the end of each sideways motion. To maintain the *contour*, vary the angles the way you did when the tones were originally applied. Stop blending at the boundary between your figure's body and the base .

TIP Vigorous circular blending motions will even out most rough, patchy strokes. Blend too much and your two tonal values will become one.

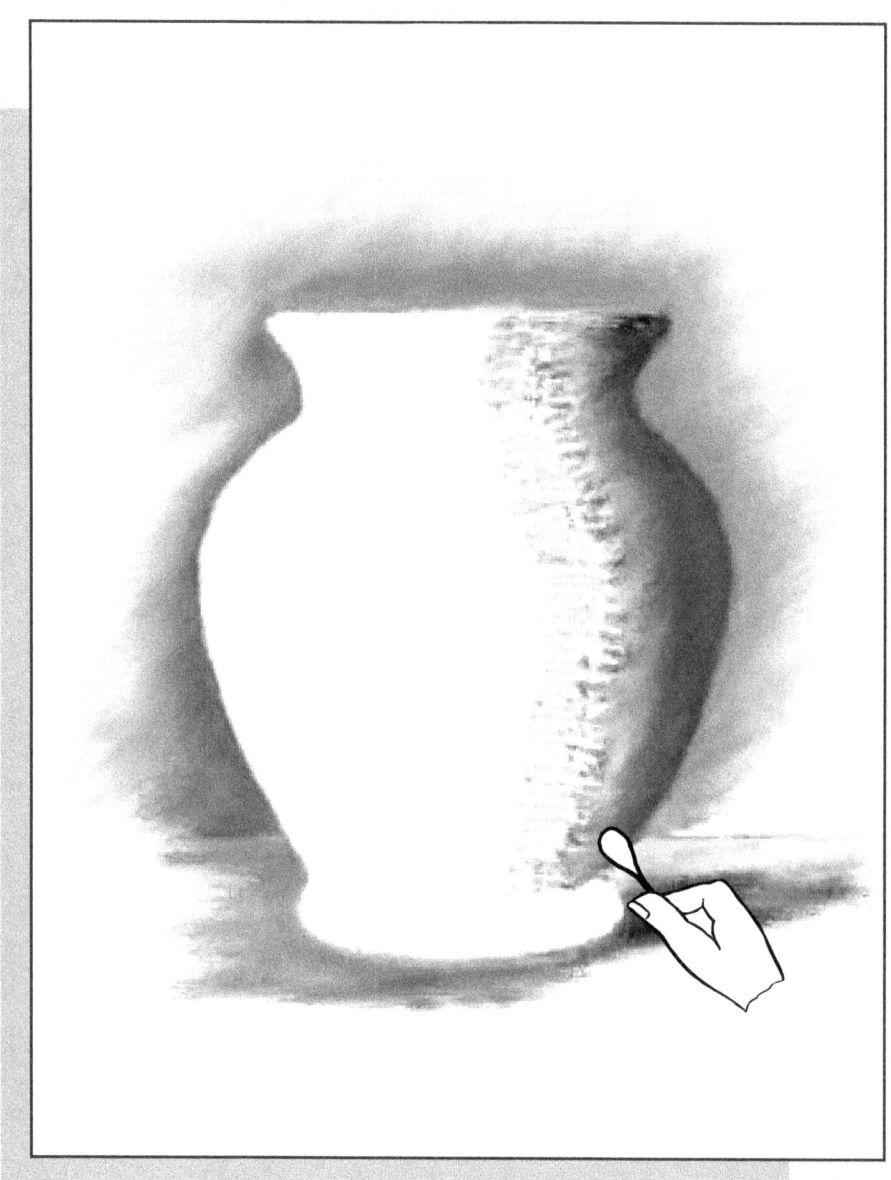

STEP 2 Fade your figure's seam between the dark mid-tone and the next slightly lighter tone on the left. Apply the same methods as in step 1. Next, take advantage of graphite build up on your blender and *also include a few backward "C" motions in the figure's BASE, (on the right).* This will convey shade with a slightly lighter value to contrast beside the cast shadow.

TIP If spotting occurs while blending, add more tone with your pencil in light areas and dab excessively dark sections with your putty eraser. Then, blend again as needed. To avoid smearing as you progress, use a white paper or wax paper covering. For detail work, refer to the photo on page 72.

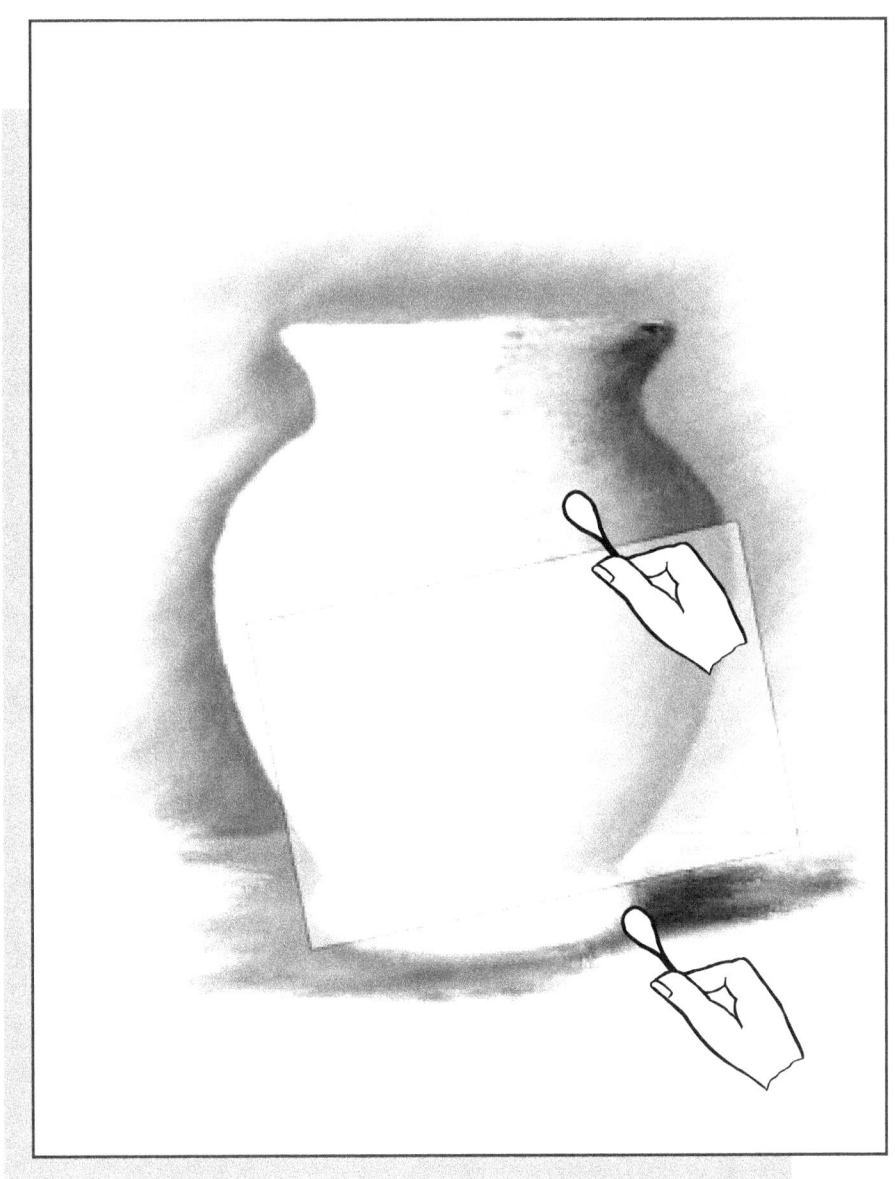

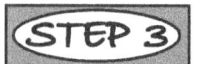 Continue softening your figure's mid-tones by gently fading the seam between the second and third tone toward the left. For optimum results, apply *sweeping* motions. These are stronger blending strokes at the start and gradually ease to a faint touch by the end. If spotting begins to develop, switch to circular motions to help even out the patches. Should the blotches persist, they can be addressed later.

TIP Graphite buildup on your blender can accidentally tranfer from a darker area to a lighter area in your picture. Inconsistent pressure can create similar blemishing. Do not rub spots with your eraser as smearing will occur, making things worse. Unwanted blotches and smudging is part of damage repair. It should be postponed until most of the toning and blending has been completed.

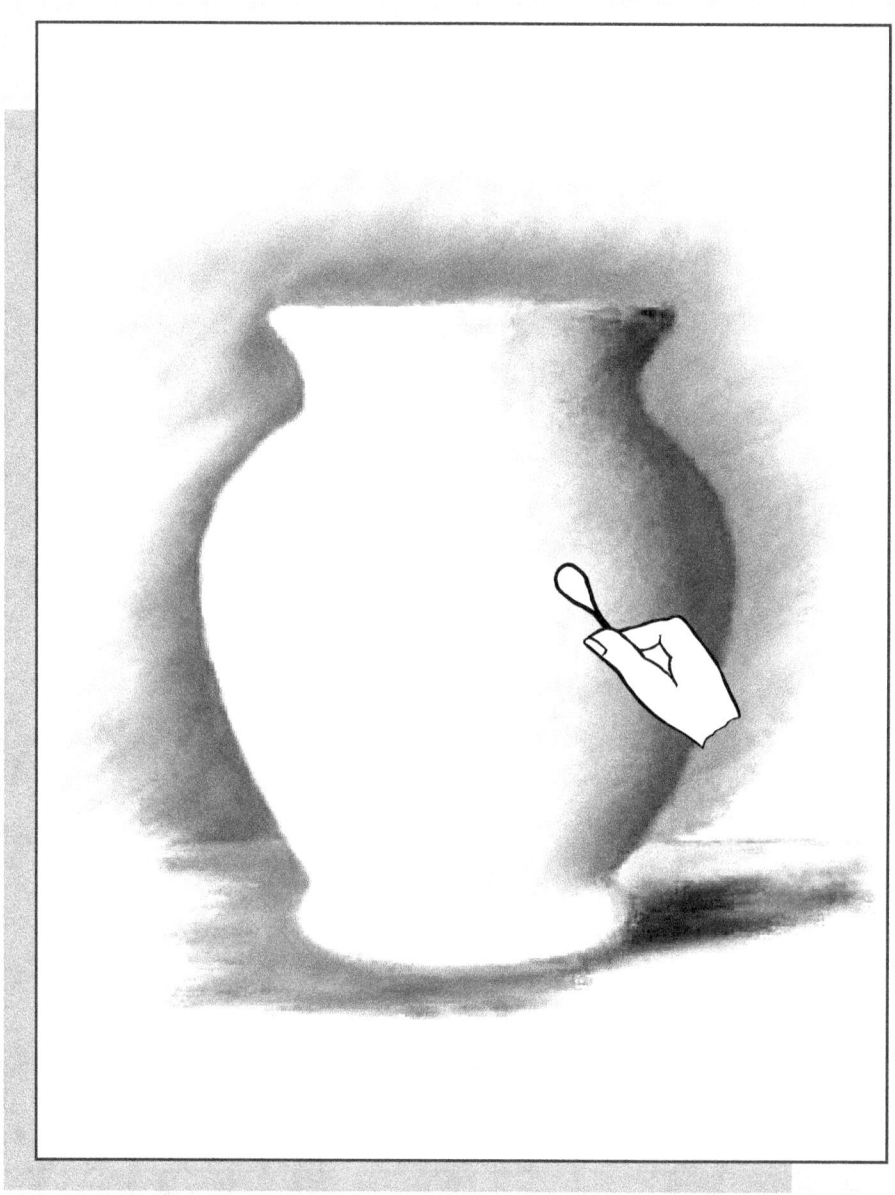

STEP 4 Merge (or fade) the *seam* by softening it between your mid tone and the lighter tone directly to the left . Apply *sweeping* motions to make the harsh strokes disappear. Then feather the edge of your light tone with circular motions. Fade it into the white of your paper until it is difficult to see where they meet. If graphite builds up on your blender and causes too much darkening, use a blotting motion to dab the seam with your putty eraser as many times as needed .

TIP If too much graphite builds up on your blender, causing more darkening than you want, twist it in your putty eraser to remove the excess.

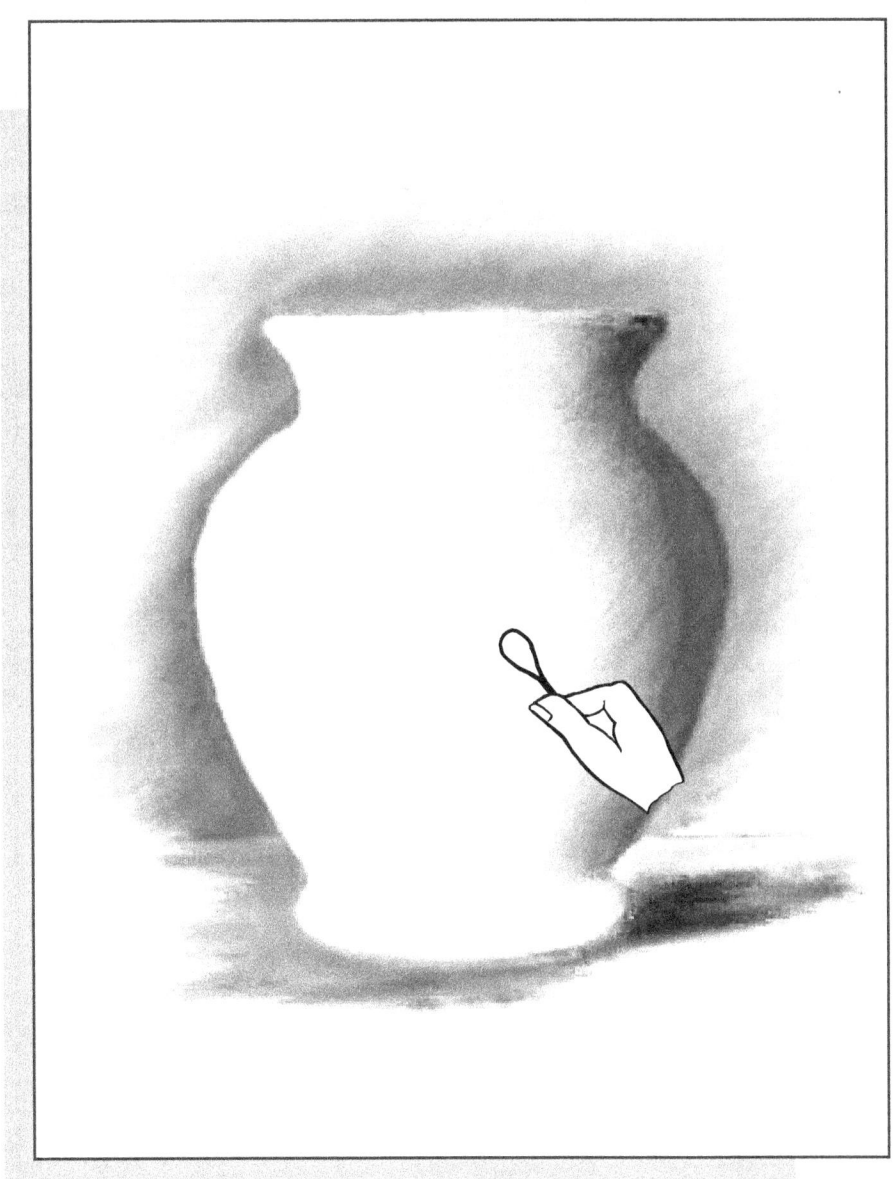

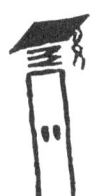

Toning and blending is bound to cause smudges, patches and overstrokes. A status check is wise.

These close-ups show rough spots. (1) The midtones in the figure appear uneven as though pitted. (2) The boundary along the shade side seems to have a rough, rather than a fairly smooth edge. (3) The background is too light in places and smudges are present in the figure's light side. For spotting, several remedies are available (see illustration Ⓐ below). To make the light tone as dark as the darker value, simply add tone with gentle pencil strokes or apply graphite to your *blender* tip with your pencil. Either way, stroke the light area *without adding tone to the already existing dark portion.* The outcome is an *overall darker* tone, Ⓑ. In order to achieve a consistent *light tone,* shape your *putty eraser* in to a point and dab until the dark tone becomes much lighter. Then gently blend for an even tone Ⓒ. *If you have unwanted dark and light blotches in the same vicinity,* tap the dark ones with your eraser. Fill in the light parts carefully with your pencil or blender, until your tone value is uniform. Sure, you may accidentally erase too much and add too much when refilling. That's common. Delicate procedures just need plenty of practice,

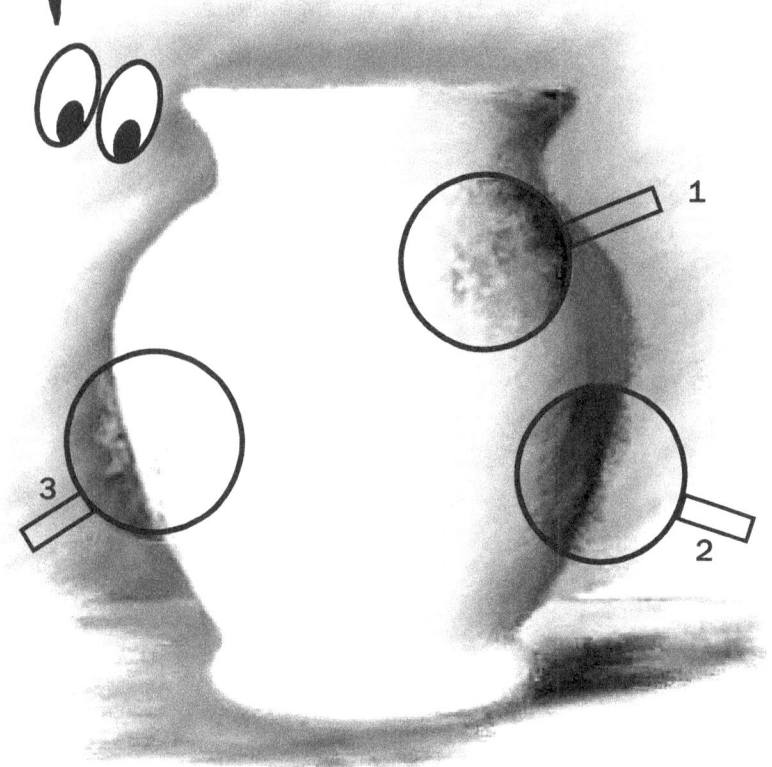

patience and perseverance (3P's). With experience, you will improve. Remember, you are learning. *Adjusting and readjusting, and working and reworking, are all part of the drawing routine; including damage repair.*

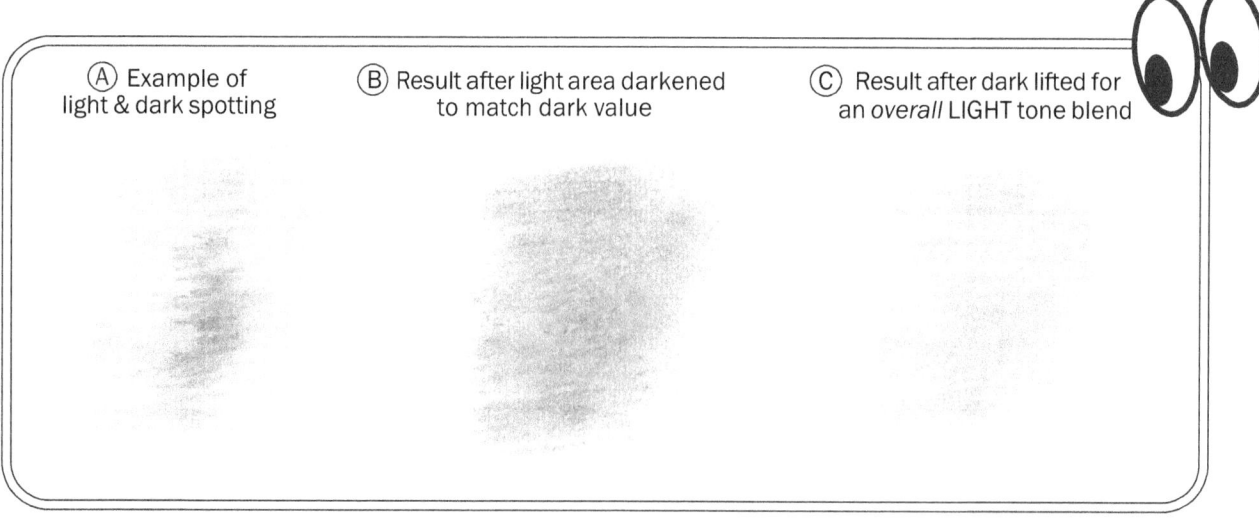

Ⓐ Example of light & dark spotting

Ⓑ Result after light area darkened to match dark value

Ⓒ Result after dark lifted for an *overall* LIGHT tone blend

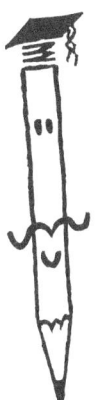

Toning and blending tend to form vague edges.

The methods explained on the previous page solved the patches and smudges (1 & 3). But what about the *overstrokes* that caused the rough, obscure edges (2)? Would line work be the answer? Not necessarily. Recall on page 69 we saw that lines with *hard edges* created an undesirable flattening effect. Compare the following two drawings. In example (A), an *outline* hides the ragged borders, but the image appears flat at the periphery. In example (B), the fuzzy edges are also absent. Yet *figure, ground* and *background* are unmistakably evident, along with a sense that the vase continues around and beyond our view. How was this accomplished? Areas that were too dark on both sides of the figure's perimeter received dabs with the eraser. Parts that were too light were carefully touched up with gentle pencil strokes. The process went on, back and forth until *form* and *space* became visually clear.

A   B

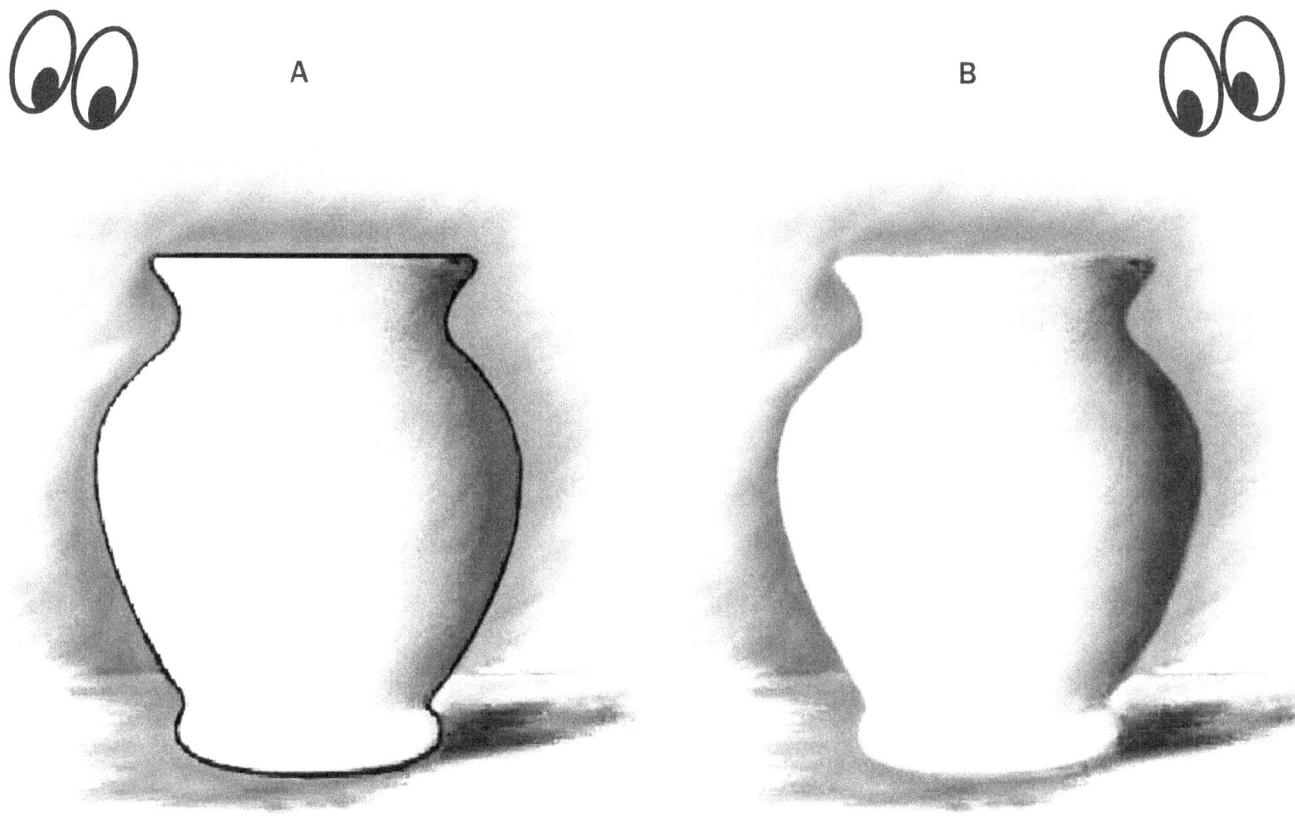

TIP Putty erasers have many advantages. You can shape them. They do not leave residue. You can lift tone to lighten by dabbing and still keep your existing marks. The putty eraser can be cleaned by tearing and restoring. You can even remove excess graphite from your *blender* by twisting it in your putty eraser.

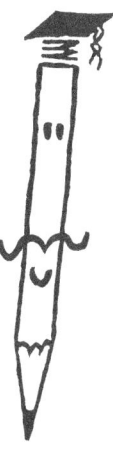

For more on "shading," keep going.

Look carefully. A quick glance is not enough.

A thorough scan of this student drawing reveals three concerns.

(1) The figure's *left side* appears flat, near and including the base because of the sharp *line*.

(2) The figure's midtone surface appears striped and patchy.

(3) The cast shadow on the *horizontal* table plane overlaps the *vertical* background plane.

BEFORE

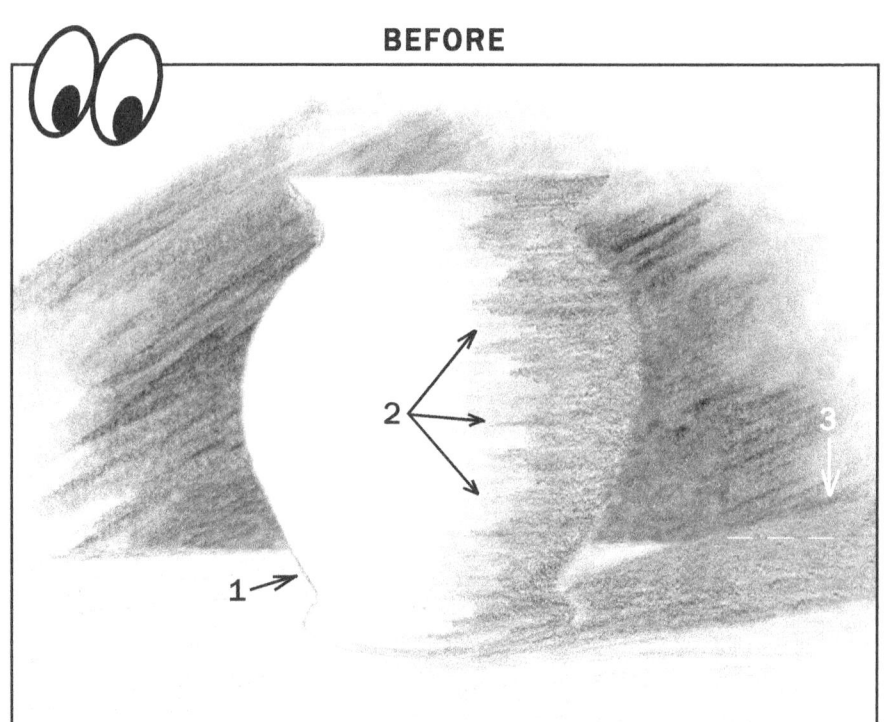

To resolve the issues...

(1) A *tone* matching the dark line value was feathered to eliminate the hard edge.

(2) The patchy look was remedied by blending the midtones in the figure until they merged more evenly.

(3) To restore the horizontal plane, the cast shadow was reduced to the boundary representing the back of the table.

AFTER

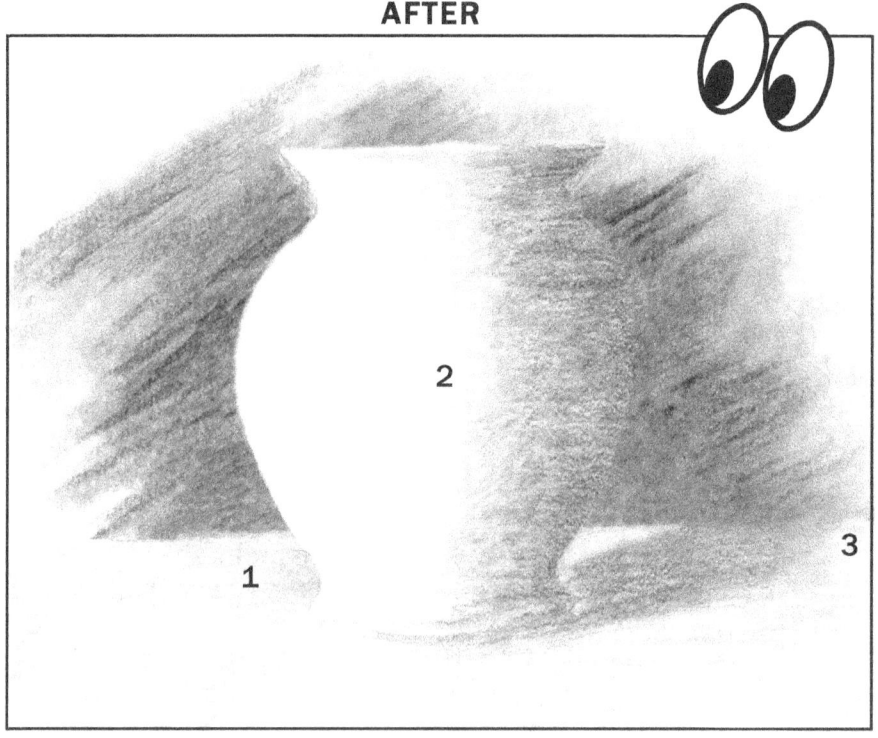

TIP Up close, we usually notice sections. Backing away, we see the whole. Things become more apparent. This makes it easier to spot needed adjustment. Each modification by itself may not seem like much. Combined, they can do a lot for the quality of your picture. Pay attention to every segment. They all contribute.

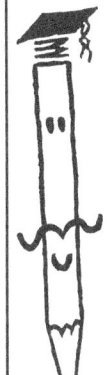

It's your turn. Survey YOUR work by comparing it to the model and do some refinements, as needed.

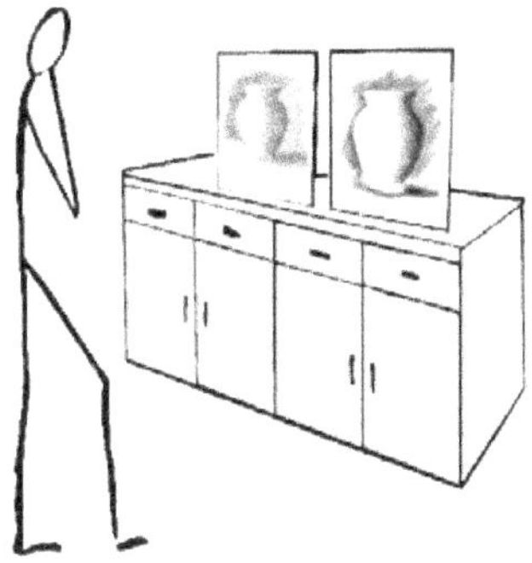

RECOMMENDATIONS:

1. Your drawing should be an interpretation, not an exact match.
2. Pretend someone else did the work. It's easier to be objective.
3. **Check SHAPING** (TRUSTY 7). Boundaries may have gone astray.
   a. See whether overall and sub *proportions* are OK.
   b. Are *reference points* and *alignments* still properly in place?
   c. Look for parts with too much *curvature*, or not enough, including *negative spaces*.
   d. Verify *straight lines* and *angles* for undesirable tilting.
4. **Check SHADING**. Blemishes become more visible from a distance due to *optical mixing*.
   a. How are the edges?   Are some boundaries too vague, others too sharp?
   b. Does your figure have values that softly fade into one another?
   c. Were unwanted smudges and patches mostly eliminated?
   d. Is the cast shadow too light, too dark, too crisp, or in the wrong place?
       Strategically, the figure should usually be more prominent than the cast shadow.

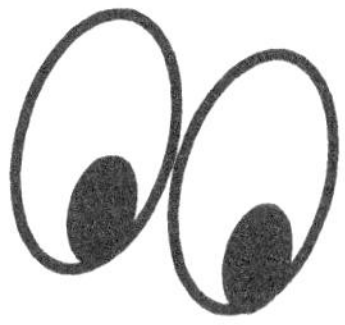

Model

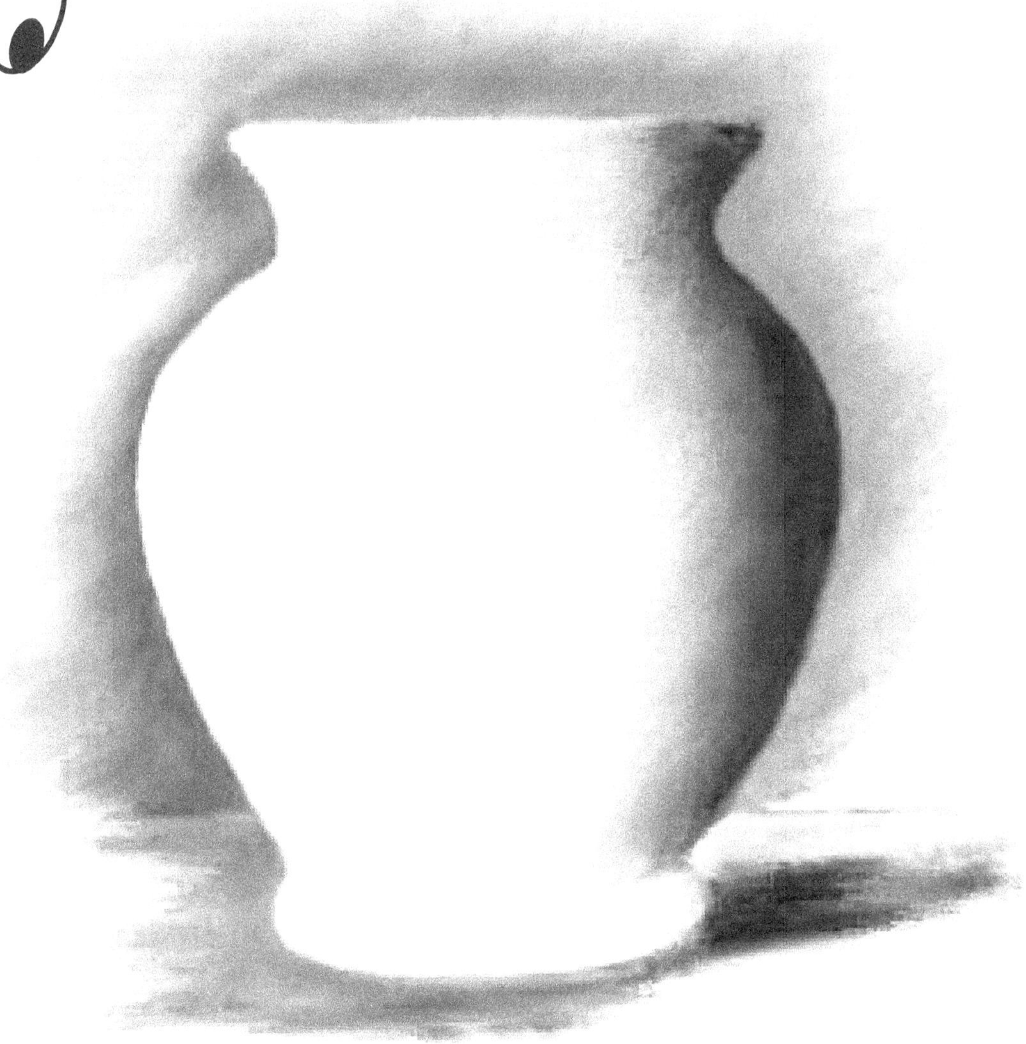

Assuming you made refinements, the BIG question is: how can you tell when your drawing is FINISHED?

It's common to feel uneasy at the start of a picture and again when approaching the completion. That anxious moment is close at hand: time to see whether your creation turned out as well and maybe better than you anticipated, or not. Wow, what a daunting thought, but it doesn't have to be. Nobody is perfect, so face your fears. Discard the blinders. You don't need them to protect your ego. The only way you can improve your work is to evaluate what you did, and be willing to do more, within reason of course. Your expectations should not exceed your present ability. With this in mind, don't declare your drawing done, just yet. From beginning to this point, it has undergone quite a metamorphosis. Your perception could be clouded by mid cycle memories. Strange as this sounds, it's very possible. For a *fresh perspective*, ask a family member or friend to place your drawing beside the model in an unexpected location, *without disclosure*. Later, when you run across the hiding place and catch a glimpse of your rendering, you will get that all important first impression. You can also launch a more objective evaluation by viewing a *backward comparison* reflected in a mirror. Or you can place both the model and your drawing *sideways*. Post studies of this nature could expose areas you may not have noticed before. Embrace the opportunity to explore and discover. Reference both the illustration on the previous page and the photo on page 72. Compare your work once more, by playing hide and seek. The answers are easy to find, if you take the time to look.

Scan for similarities and dissimilarities, but remember that your drawing is *your* version. Your unique strokes stem from your individual rhythm which manifests your special style. It's far more desirable than a close copy of the snapshot, or a replica of the commercial illustration. Strive to maintain the *aesthetic appeal* as you deem fit (see page 72 *"interpretation"*) and welcome *pleasant surprises*. Sift for features you would rather leave as you depicted them. Seek details you may have overlooked and would like to add. Cover all your bases by including a game of chance, I call *"what if's."* Take the refined drawing copied here from page 96, for example. Arrows indicate three compelling prospects. In area (1), suppose the uneven tone along the *left* side of the figure's neck was darkened to further define the edge. In area (2), imagine the shade side feathered with more dark for *contrast* between the background and the figure. This could create a stronger *push-pull effect* between form and space. In area (3), visualize the patchy light gray spot *darkened* beside the base in the cast shadow (where it *should* be darkest). Would these last modifications enhance the picture? See for yourself on the next page.

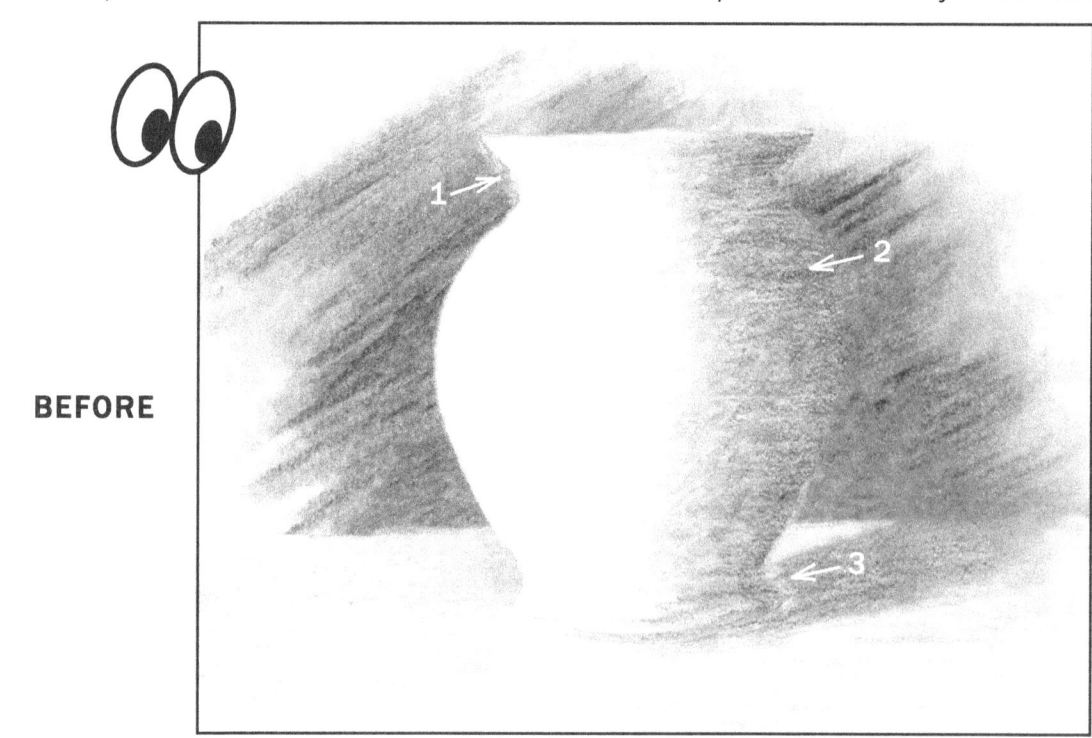

BEFORE

FINAL TOUCHES

Essentially, final touches are things you do when you think there is nothing more to be done. As the saying goes: "You never really finish a rendering. You abandon it." Whether you regard my post recommendations (shown here), as favorable or unfavorable, the choice is subjective. Preferences vary from person to person. Whenever you've nearly run the gamut, or feel uncertain about ideas *you* would like to try, I suggest you computer scan your drawing, or take photocopies. Test your revisions on them. You will see the effects almost instantaneously. The method works great by eliminating guesswork, while providing *painless experimentation* and extensive learning rewards.

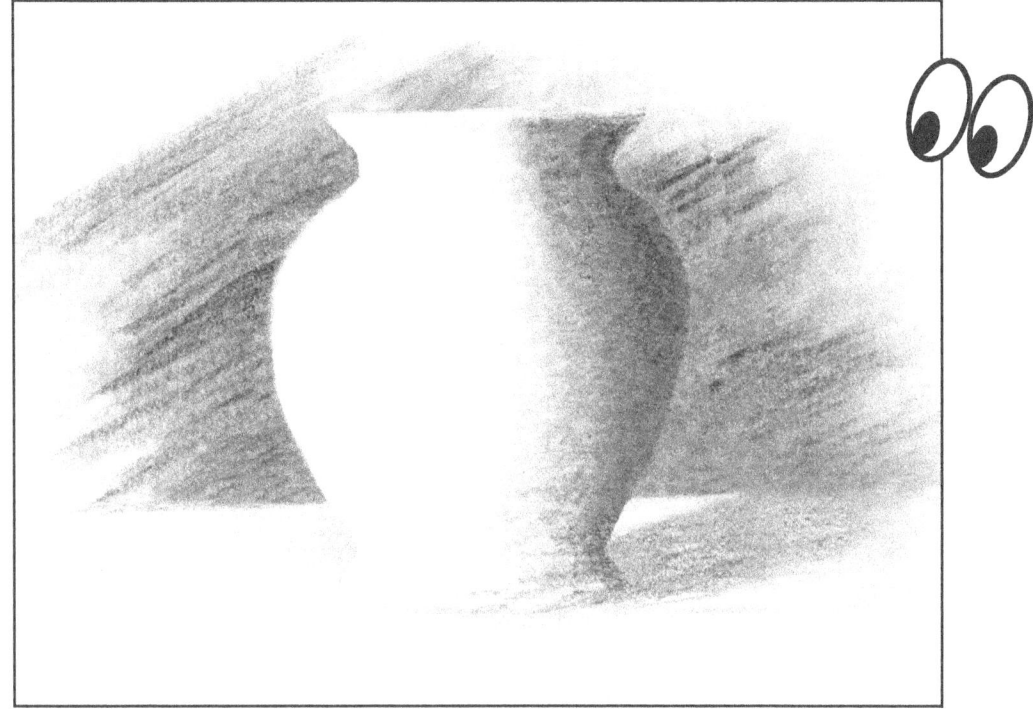

AFTER

TIP To intensify the value on your figure's shade side, don't just add dark tone along the edge. *Feather* to fade it into the lighter mid-tone on the left. Use gradually decreasing pressure and sweeping motions. If your pencil can't darken the value any further, you probably stretched your #2 pencil or HB equivalent past the limit. Do not continue applying graphite 'til it shines. Switch to a softer lead, such as a 4B or 6B rating. The B's are the soft leads. The higher the number, the softer the lead and the darker the value it provides with minimal pressure. Some people opt for many pencil strengths, but the constant switching can be impractical. I advise keeping a small assortment of pencils and train your hand to be increasingly obedient to your touch. In the long run, you will find this is more effective, versatile and skillful.

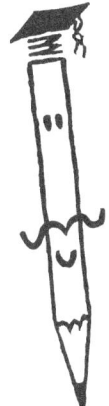

Slight and subtle changes that may not seem important can make all the difference. Review your picture for finishing touches. Then turn the page and study the examples proudly displayed in the student gallery.

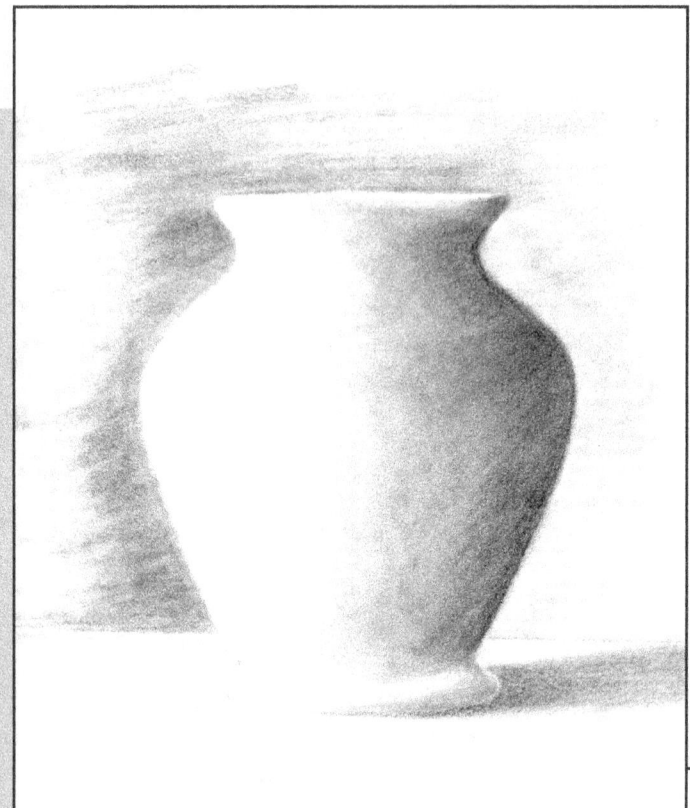

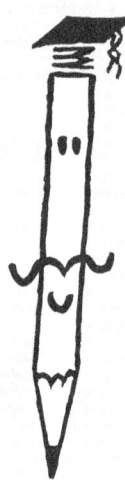

Remember: The objective was to create a unique interpretation based on the book example.

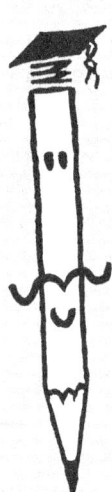

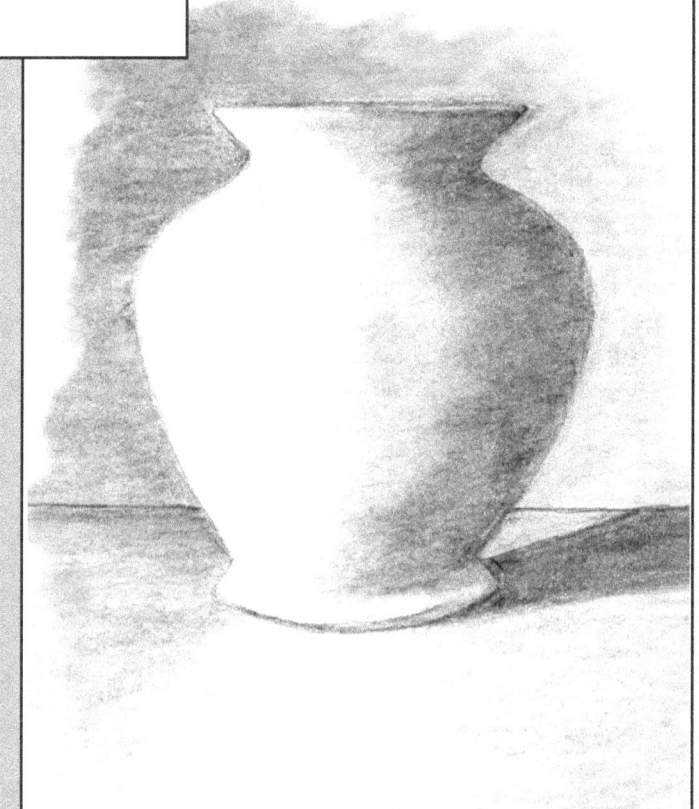

You can learn much by studying the work of others.

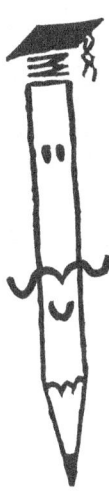

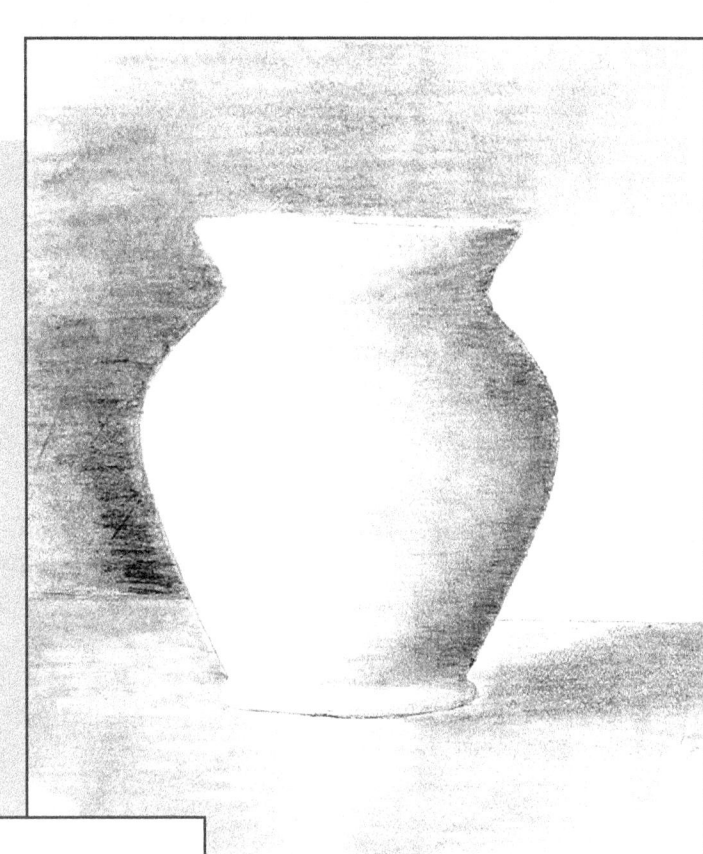

Wow! Each piece is a one of a kind rendition conveying individual quality and style.

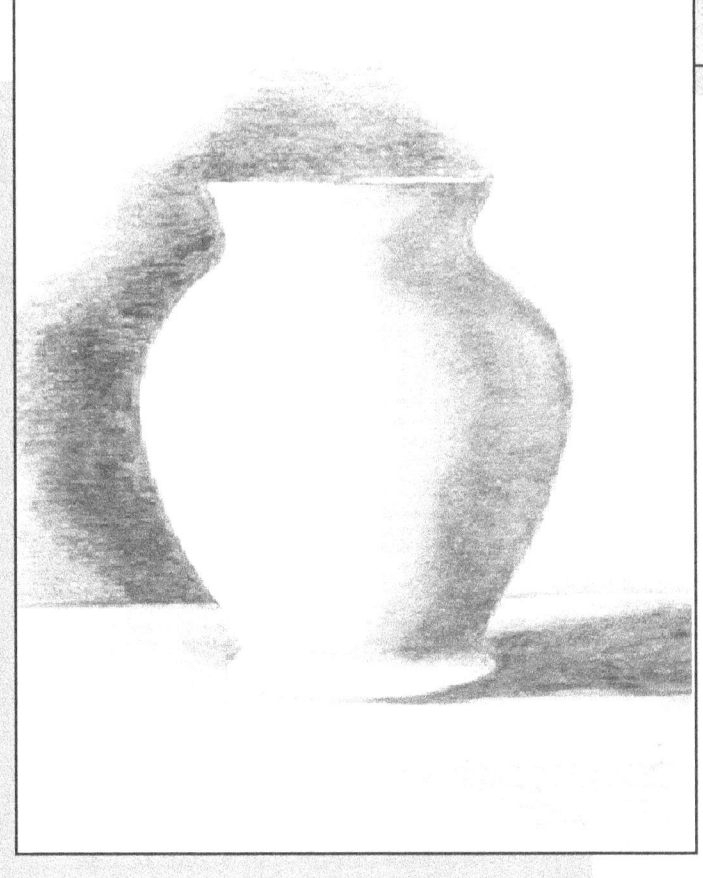

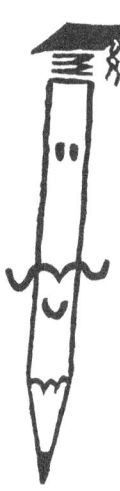

Take pride in your success. The reward is in the doing.

Chapter 2
FOLLOW-UP

Shaping is nifty, although toning is also quite exciting, wouldn't you agree? With variations of gray, your picture can take on another dimension. Plus, "shading" is fun, isn't it? Before your very eyes, you watched the figure's appearance change from flat and hollow to an impression that it's solid and illuminated. Such a remarkable transition from one state to another is one reason why students often tend to hurry past the *formative* phase and start toning *too soon*.

What am I implying? I'll tell you. Having ventured into a marvelous realm also termed *modelling* and *chiaroscuro*, from here on you may be tempted to neglect certain basics. Surely, your tones will hide the "flubs," right?

Not necessarily. If you accept this notion, odds are you will be disappointed. *SHAPING* and *SHADING go hand in hand.* They depend on each other, similar to the way construction works. For instance, a house with reliable footing and sturdy framing develops well, as other parts are added. Yet put them on ineffective supports and things topple. Maybe this is why art teachers often advise you to "construct your form," or they say "build it."

I submit, of course, that even poorly handled tones may dress up an *accurate* outline drawing. On the other hand, the most lavish attempts on a *weak foundation* can do *little* to improve the situation. Generally, you will merely produce *fancy* distortion. Catch my drift? For quality, you should strive to master *both* disciplines.

And now, it's my pleasure to present the official announcement.

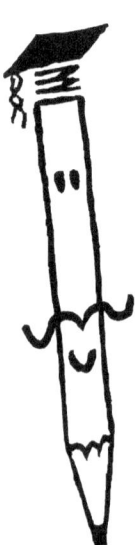

Congratulations!

You've graduated
Anyone Can...Arts
ANYONE CAN DRAW

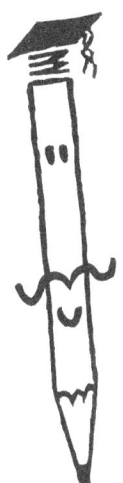

This isn't the end.
It's a beginning.

Having completed the course and considering the amount of effort that went into it, you may be wondering just how much you really accomplished. Quite a lot, I'd say. The skills you acquired in order to render the still life, work for *anything*. How is this possible? Visually speaking, everything is essentially shapes and tones. In this light, revel in the knowledge that *what you learned is the real treasure.*

Your odyssey has begun, filled with wondrous sights to behold. Look forward to more delightful ways you can advance your skills with Anyone Can...Arts, DRAWING MAGIC Guidebooks 1 and 2, and keep exploring that special artist in you.

ARTIST'S GLOSSARY

Terms and Phrases
as defined by Professor Pencil

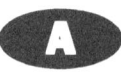

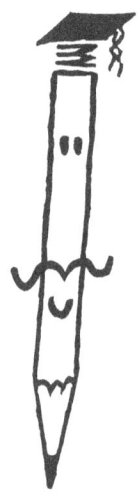

ACCURATE - reasonable likeness, not a perfect or exact match

ADJACENT - next to or beside something

AESTHETIC - visually pleasing

AFFIX - attach

ALIGNMENT - line up

ALTER - change

ALTERNATIVE - replacement

AMISS - not in proper order or accurate appearance

ANGLE - any direction other than plumb or level (*slope, incline, diagonal, slant, tilt*)

ANTICIPATE - expect or foresee

APPARENT - visible to the naked eye or obvious

APPREHENSIVE - feel nervous, anxious, uneasy

APPROXIMATE - almost or nearly accurate

ARC - a curve; or to bend, as in a curve

ASCEND - move upward in a straight direction, or at a slant

ASCERTAIN - find out

ASPECT - visible characteristic or appearance

ASSESS - survey, examine, evaluate, study

ASSIMILATION - process of merging tones optically or manually

ASTRAY - moved away from

ASYMMETRICAL - irregular, uneven, not precise in shape

AWE - impressive sight

AWKWARD - odd, poorly fitted together

B

BACKGROUND - visible scenery behind and through an opening in something

BASELINE - shortest line between two ends of a curve

BISECT - divide in half

BLEND - combine or mix together

BLOT - dab or pat (tap lightly)

BLOTCH - patches or spots of tone values

BOON - benefit

BOUNDARY - a limitation showing where something starts, or ends (*border, perimeter, edge*)

BOW - bend, or flex in a curve

BULBOUS - bulb like

C

CAST SHADOW - dark silhouette on the surface opposite from which something is illuminated

CHARACTER - distinguishable features

CHIAROSCURO - variation of tones to help give the impression that something is illuminated

COMPONENT - part or portion

COMPELLING - demanding, urgent

CONCAVE - curve that bends inward

CONCEDE - say as true, admit

CONCEPT - thought, idea, principle, approach, procedure or method

CONFIRM - make sure something is accurate

CONICAL - cone like

CONSECUTIVE - follow one after the other without any gaps

CONSISTENT - regular, not varying or changing

CONTINUOUS LINE - a line that starts at one point and moves nonstop until finished

CONTOUR - boundary between planes

CONTRARY - opposite

CONTRAST - visible difference between 2 or more things (for example - black and white)

CONVERT - change

CONVEX - curve that bends outward

CREST - maximum, or furthest extent of bend in a curve

CRITIQUE - objective, productive evaluation

CURVE - bowed line

DAB - tap lightly

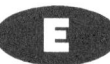

DAUNTING - alarming, scary

DEPICT - create a likeness

DESIGNATE - specify, point out, identify by name

DEXTERITY - skill

DIFFRACTION - visual effect of double edges due to illuminated light deflection (bounce off)

DIFFUSION - visual effect of soft edge due to illuminated light spreading

DILIGENCE - careful attention, perseverance

DISPARITY - difference

DISREGARD - ignore

DISSIMILAR - not alike, different

DISTINCT - stand out, different, or easily visible

DISTINGUISH - make visible or stand out

DISTORTION - deformity or misshaping

DIVERGE - branch off, like a fork or dove tail

DOODLE - spontaneous, unplanned drawing

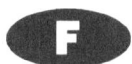

EDGE - where one shape stops and another begins

EFFECTIVE - able to achieve accurate or desired result

EGO - personal feelings

EIDETIC IMAGERY - detailed memory of visual images

EMANATE - come from

ESTIMATE - opinion or judgment based on observation (best guess)

EVALUATE - examine accuracy

EXACT - reasonably accurate

EXEMPLIFY - show by example

EXPANSE - distance, or span between two reference points

EYE-HAND COORDINATION - what you see you draw

EXTENUATING - understandable, excusable

FACSIMILE - close likeness or similarity to something else

FADE - gently or gradually change a tone from dark to light, or from light to dark

FAINT - barely visible

FARE - occur, result

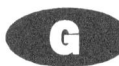

FEASIBLE - likely to work well or be useful

FEATHERING - sweeping blending strokes in one direction, with gradually reduced pressure

FIGURE - a shape; also the ability to think through, calculate, or estimate

FINAL TOUCHES - last things done to a picture before it is deemed finished

FLAW - not accurate, defective, undesired

FLEX - to bend a curve; or amount of bend or "bow" in a curve

FLUB - goof, botch, bungle, flaw, inaccurate, undesirable result

FLUX - variable, changing rate

FORETHOUGHT - think ahead

FORM - a solid shape or the procedure which makes it (*fashion, devise, draw, produce*)

FREEHAND - draw without a straight edge, ruler, or any other artificial or mechanical device

FRESH VIEW - observe from a different position

FUNDAMENTAL - basic

FUSS - overwork, or overdo

FUTILE - not useful

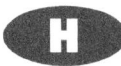

GAMUT - entire range of something

GAUGE - strength, intensity, or amount of something; or to observe, survey, figure out, judge

GLANCE - look quickly

GLIMPSE - quick look or observation

GLITCH - problem or malfunction

GRAPHITE - soft carbon used for lead pencils

GROUND - visible area that something is on

GUIDE LINES - temporary lines that help draw a shape

H

HALO EFFECT - where two contrasting tones meet, the tone between them appears to intensify

HARD EDGE - sharp, crisp boundary

HIGH CONTRAST - strong visible difference between two or more things (such as tones or textures)

HIGHLIGHT - point where light intensity is strongest

HONE - sharpen (skill)

HORIZONTAL - sideways

HYPOTHETICAL - playing "what if," or imagining how things would turn out if they happened

IDENTICAL - visibly alike

ILLUSION - a visual effect or amazing prank played on the eyes

IMPACT - effect or result

IMPLEMENT - tool or put into action

IMPLY - communicate indirectly, suggest

IMPRESSION - feeling

IMPROVISE - figure out or find solutions by applying resourceful thinking

IMPULSE - urge or whim

INADVERTENT - not intentional, accidental

INCONSISTENT - varying, changing, or irregular

INCREDIBLE - wonderful, terrific

INCREMENT - division, or section of distance, equal to the one before it

INDENT - move a certain amount of distance

INDIRECT DRAWING - form the space a figure displaces to reveal the figure

INDISTINCT - not easy to see

INEXORABLE - absolute, definite, unyielding

INFINITE - limitless

INITIAL - first, or original

INITIATE - start, or make a choice/decision and act on it

INSIGHT - understanding

INSTINCT - natural behavior

INTEGRAL - member of the whole

INTENSITY - strength, stress, pressure, force, rate, measure, or amount of something

INTERIM - span of time

INTERPRET (ation) - translate, change, convert, depict, or replicate

INTERSECT - cut across or through

INTUITION - an impulse or hunch based on feeling rather than thought

IRONY - opposite of what is expected or what may should be

INVERT (INVERSE) - position upside down, reverse, backward, or in the opposite direction

LATERAL - sideways position or direction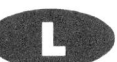

LAX - not careful

LAYOUT - a written or illustrated plan

LIGHT - illuminating source such as the sun, a flame or an electric bulb

LINEAR PERSPECTIVE- things in the distance appear smaller than they really are

LOW CONTRAST - little visible difference between two or more things (such as tones or textures)

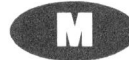

MANIFEST - indicate, make evident

MANUALLY - by hand

MARVEL - appreciate or admire

MELD - combine, mix, diffuse, blend, fade, or merge

METAMORPHOSIS - change

MID TONES - values of tone between light and dark

MINIMIZE - reduce to the least strength or amount

MODEL - subject or picture of a subject you intend to replicate

MODIFY - change

NEGATIVE SPACE - area that borders the edge of a shape

NEW PERSPECTIVE - observe from a different position

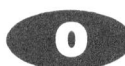

OBJECTIVE - goal/purpose, or judge by facts rather than by personal feelings

OBSERVE - look carefully

OBVIOUS - easy to see, stands out

ODD - different or unusual

ODYSSEY - an adventure in learning and experiencing new things

OMIT - take away

OPT - choose

OPTICAL MIXING - visual effect of merging tones

OPTION(al) - choice

OUTLINE - the surrounding shape of something revealed by a line

OVERALL PROPORTION - comparison of entire length to entire width

PARALLEL - things or reference points that are the same distance from each other at both ends

PERCEPTION - understanding based on observing and thinking

PERIMETER - boundary of a shape

PERPETUAL - continuous

PERSPECTIVE - point of view or way to depict three dimensional forms on a two dimensional surface

PHENOMENON - unusual event or occurrence that can be observed

PINPOINT - locate or place accurately

PLANE - surface as it appears in line of sight (front, top, side, bottom)

POST - after

POSTPONE - delay, set aside for another time

PRECAUTION - action to prevent unwanted result

PRECISE - exact

PRELIMINARY - first or starting point

PREVIOUS - before

PRINCIPLE - a basic truth, rule, or a way to do things

PROCESS - a method or an ability to figure out and understand

PROFICIENT - skillful

PROMINENT - stands out

PROPORTION - a comparison of length to width or a size comparison of one thing to another

PROSPECT - anticipated outcome, possibility

PROVOCATIVE - cause excitement

PROXIMITY - nearby or close

PUSH-PULL EFFECT - use of contrast to cause a figure to appear more prominent (stand out) and to cause the background to recede (appear to be further away)

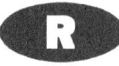

RAGGED EDGES - rough boundaries

RANDOM - action by choice or preference rather than logical sequence

REFERENCE POINT - a location or position

REFINE - improve

REFLECTED LIGHT - light that reaches a surface and bounces back, striking another surface

REITERATE - repeat

RELY - trust

R

RENDER - create, such as by drawing

RENDERING - finished drawing

RENDITION - a creation that resembles something but is not an exact match

REPERTOIRE - collection of skills

REPLENISH - put back or supply again

REPLICATE - create a reasonably accurate likeness

RESIDUE - remainder of something

RESTRICTIVE - hold back

REVERSE SPACE - adjacent area at the edge of a shape (a.k.a. *negative/opposite/indirect space*)

REVISION - adjustment or change

ROTATE - turn, pivot, twirl

ROTUND - big, fat, or round

ROUGH DRAFT - unfinished writing or drawing

S

SCALE - comparison of size

SCENARIO - anticipated chain of events

SCRUTINIZE - examine carefully

SECTION - part or portion of the whole

SEGMENT - division or section

SEQUENCE - a particular order or procedure arranged one after the other

SHADING - toning by creating variations of gray

SHAPE - visible boundary of something

SIGNIFICANT - meaningful, important, useful

SIGNIFY - indicate or show

SIMPLIFY - streamline; reducing forms to very basic shapes with straight lines

SIMULTANEOUS - at the same time

SKETCH LINE - a freehand line made with overlapping strokes

SMEAR - blur or spread by rubbing

SMUDGE - blur or spread by rubbing

SOFT EDGE - blurry or vague boundary

SOLUTION - way to remedy or solve a problems

S

SPACE - shape or area that borders a figure

SPAN - distance (or expanse) between two reference points

SPHERICAL - ball or sphere like

SPONTANEOUS - unplanned or to act without much forethought

SQUIGGLE - draw impulsively by following your whims, feelings, or mood

SQUINT - observe with your eyes partly closed

STATUS - current situation

STILL LIFE - scene consisting of nonliving or non-moving objects

STRAIGHT (freehand) LINE - line made straight as possible without use of ruler or other device

STRIVE - apply genuine effort

STRUCTURAL (method) a way to construct a shape

SUBDIVIDE - divide into smaller parts

SUBJECT - item/model to be replicated, or a topic

SUBJECTIVE - personal opinion

SUBORDINATE - secondary, or not as important as something else

SUB-PROPORTION - size comparison of one span to another in a shape or form

SUBTLE - barely detectable, delicate

SUCCESSION - something that occurs after something else

SURFACE - exterior or top layer of something

SURVEY - examine, study, observe

SYNCHRONIZE - work together

SYNONYMOUS - likewise, same meaning-different name

SWEEPING METHOD - harder stroke at the start, then ease up in one continuous motion

T

TALLY - examine, evaluate, assess, count up, total

TECHNIQUE - method or procedure

THREE P's - perseverance, practice, patience

TONE - range of light to dark color or gray

TRANSFORM - change from one appearance to another

TRANSPIRE - occur, reveal

TRANSITION - the in-between stages during which something changes from one appearance to another, or a switch from one procedure to another

TRUSTY SEVEN - basic structural components used to help draw shapes (reference points, alignments, proportions, straight lines, curves, angles, reverse space)

ULTIMATE - last or final

UNIQUE - different, unusual, extraordinary

UTILIZE - use

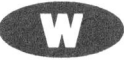

VAGUE - not clear, indistinct

VALIDATE - make or show to be correct

VALUE - visible difference in the intensity of tones

VARIATION - slightly different, not an exact match

VARY - differ or change

VERIFY - check to be sure

VERNACULAR - commonly used term

VERSATILE - able to apply skills in many ways

VERSION - translation, or interpretation

VERSUS - compared to, in contrast to

VERTICAL - upright

VIA - with or by way of

VIABLE - likely to work

VICE VERSA - other way round, reverse sequence

VIRTUALLY - mostly accepted or believed, seemingly real

VISIBLE - able to be seen

VISION - eyesight or understanding based on observation and thinking

VISUAL - relating to eyesight, such as estimating sizes or proportions by eye

VISUALIZE - picture in your mind, imagine, pretend, or make believe

VIVID - very bright, intense

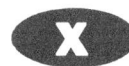

WHIM - act with little or no forethought

WITHIN RANGE - near the desired size or area

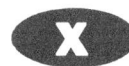

"X" RAY VISION - see through objects

"Drawing isn't just for some, it's for everyone."

"Just as there are methods by which to learn how to read and write, there are methods by which to learn how to draw."

Peter Kraus

ABOUT THE AUTHOR

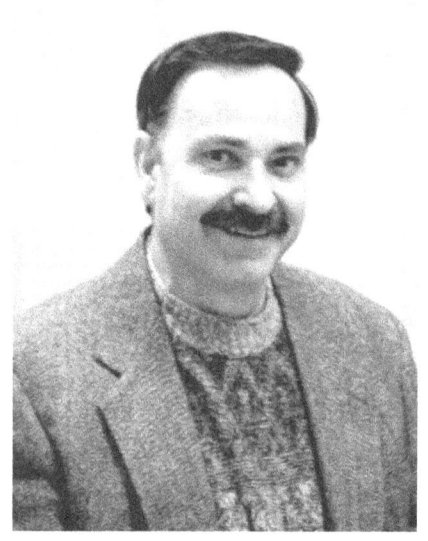

Accomplished fine artist, speaker, graphic designer, and instructor with over thirty-five years of excellent teaching experience, Peter Kraus is the founder of the ANYONE CAN...ARTS SCHOOL and the author of the *Drawing Magic* series of books. Born in Hungary, Peter emigrated to the United States as a child in 1956. Following graduation from high school, he opened his studio and gallery where he created commissioned pieces and fine custom frames. Studying psychology and art education, he earned his degree from California State University, Northridge. In addition to his dedication to *Anyone Can...Arts*, Peter Kraus is also an eminent instructor in a Los Angeles Community College. Highly proficient with multi medias and styles, Peter's aim is to bring out the expressive quality of each student. His unique approach to teaching is remarkably successful with not only the artistically inclined, but also with the artistically challenged, special needs children and adults, senior citizens and at-risk-youth. Proven correct time and again, his conviction that drawing skill CAN be learned is the heart of his ANYONE CAN...ARTS philosophy. "When we are growing up, we are taught that a very small percentage of people have the ability to draw well, but I'm convinced the opposite is true," confides Peter. While he was busy studying psychology, he questioned why some people have the talent to draw well and others don't. Was it in their DNA, did they have an extra gene? Something inside told him it was more than talent and his investigations led him to conclude that people were not only not getting the right encouragement, but that they were also getting instruction based on faulty premises. Schools teach that art comes from "intuition" and it simply flows from us. If a child isn't showing any artistic instincts from the get go, he never will. Peter doesn't deny the existence of artistically gifted individuals, but he believes drawing should be taught analytically as a skill. Instead of using the historically great artists as absolute models, our learning should start from the basics and evolve step-by-step at one's individual pace. This method gives the student a fair chance to discover he or she can actually draw well and do something with the skill. In fact, Peter prefers to look at drawing as "functional and we can use it any way we want."